Music City Melbourne

Music City Melbourne

Urban Culture, History and Policy

Shane Homan, Seamus O'Hanlon,
Catherine Strong and John Tebbutt

BLOOMSBURY ACADEMIC
NEW YORK • LONDON • OXFORD • NEW DELHI • SYDNEY

BLOOMSBURY ACADEMIC
Bloomsbury Publishing Inc
1385 Broadway, New York, NY 10018, USA
50 Bedford Square, London, WC1B 3DP, UK
29 Earlsfort Terrace, Dublin 2, Ireland

BLOOMSBURY, BLOOMSBURY ACADEMIC and the Diana logo
are trademarks of Bloomsbury Publishing Plc

First published in the United States of America 2022
This paperback edition published 2023

Copyright © Shane Homan, Seamus O'Hanlon, Catherine Strong and John Tebbutt, 2022

For legal purposes the Acknowledgements on p. viii constitute an extension
of this copyright page.

Cover design: Louise Dugdale
Cover image © The Tote hotel, Collingwood, Melbourne, 2016. Source: Zo Damage Collection.

All rights reserved. No part of this publication may be reproduced or transmitted in any form or
by any means, electronic or mechanical, including photocopying, recording, or any information
storage or retrieval system, without prior permission in writing from the publishers.

Bloomsbury Publishing Inc does not have any control over, or responsibility for,
any third-party websites referred to or in this book. All internet addresses given
in this book were correct at the time of going to press. The author and publisher
regret any inconvenience caused if addresses have changed or sites have
ceased to exist, but can accept no responsibility for any such changes.

Library of Congress Cataloging-in-Publication Data
Names: Homan, Shane, author. | O'Hanlon, Seamus, author. | Strong,
Catherine, author. | Tebbutt, John (John Anthony) author.
Title: Music City Melbourne: urban culture, history and policy / Shane Homan,
Seamus O'Hanlon, Catherine Strong, John Tebbutt.
Description: New York: Bloomsbury Academic, 2021. | Includes bibliographical
references and index.
Identifiers: LCCN 2021026055 (print) | LCCN 2021026056 (ebook) |
ISBN 9781501365706 (hardback) | ISBN 9781501369643 (paperback) |
ISBN 9781501365713 (epub) | ISBN 9781501365720 (pdf) | ISBN 9781501365737
Subjects: LCSH: Popular music–Australia–Melbourne (Vic.)–History and criticism. |
Popular music–Social aspects–Australia–Melbourne (Vic.)–History.
Classification: LCC ML3504.8.M45 M87 2021 (print) | LCC ML3504.8.M45 (ebook) |
DDC 781.6409945/1–dc23
LC record available at https://lccn.loc.gov/2021026055
LC ebook record available at https://lccn.loc.gov/2021026056

ISBN: HB: 978-1-5013-6570-6
PB: 978-1-5013-6964-3
ePDF: 978-1-5013-6572-0
eBook: 978-1-5013-6571-3

Typeset by Integra Software Services Pvt. Ltd.

To find out more about our authors and books visit www.bloomsbury.com
and sign up for our newsletters.

Contents

List of figures   vi
List of contributors   vii
Acknowledgements   viii

1   Introduction   1
2   The transformed city   17
3   The live music city   39
4   The media city   65
5   The recording city   89
6   The legendary city   113
7   The divided city   137
8   The branded city   159
9   Conclusion   181

Notes   189
References   193
Index   210

Figures

1. The Prince of Wales hotel, 30 March 1996. Source: Shellie Tonkin Collection/Performing Arts Collection/Arts Centre, Melbourne — 30
2. The Thumpin' Tum, 1 November 1965. Source: News Ltd/Newspix/Performing Arts Collection/Arts Centre, Melbourne — 44
3. Graham Geddes resigns his teaching role as criticism of the Catcher increased, *The Age*, 29 June 1967. Source: Fairfax/Nine — 47
4. Sergio G and the Flippers. Source: Sam Manuelle Collection — 51
5. Advertising a Flippers gig at the Copacabana, Brunswick, 1969. Source: Sam Manuelle Collection — 52
6. The Age comments on the licensing reforms. *The Age*, 25 April 1987. Source: Fairfax/Nine — 57
7. The Sports, 1987; venue unknown. Source: Ruth Maddison Collection — 61
8. Stan 'The Man' Rofe at the 3KZ studios (seated) with performers (left to right) Lonnie Lee, Johnny Devlin and Johnny O'Keefe Source: Laurie Richards Collection/Performing Arts Collection/Arts Centre, Melbourne/RSN — 75
9. Bakehouse Studios, Richmond. Source: Quincy McLean — 108
10. Amanda Palmer performing at Bakehouse Studios. Source: Quincy McLean — 109
11. The SLAM Rally, 23 February 2010. Source: Zo Damage Collection — 126
12. 'Please leave these premises quietly'. The Prince of Wales hotel, 30 March 1996. Source: Shellie Tonkin Collection/Performing Arts Collection/Arts Centre, Melbourne — 128
13. Toxic Shock, 1982. Source: Ruth Maddison Collection — 144
14. Wet Lips, 2016. Source: Zo Damage Collection — 148
15. Statue of Molly Meldrum looking on to the Corner hotel, Richmond and mural celebrating live music. Source: Catherine Strong — 178
16. You Am I's Russell Hopkinson and Tim Rogers at the Forum, 23 October 1999. Source: Shellie Tonkin Collection/Performing Arts Collection/Arts Centre, Melbourne — 187

Contributors

Shane Homan is Deputy Head of the School of Media, Film and Journalism at Monash University, Melbourne. He has written widely on the popular music industries, including commissioned reports for the City of Melbourne, Creative Victoria and the Australia Council. His most recent book (with Stephen Chen, Tracy Redhead and Richard Vella) is *The Music Export Business: Born Global* (Routledge, 2021). He is co-editor of the journal *Popular Music History*.

Seamus O'Hanlon teaches contemporary and urban history in the School of Philosophical, Historical and International Studies at Monash University, Melbourne. His research interests focus on economic, social and cultural change in the twentieth- and twenty-first-century city, with a particular focus on Melbourne. His most recent book is *City Life: The New Urban Australia* (New South 2018).

Catherine Strong is Senior Lecturer in the BA (Music Industry) program at RMIT University in Melbourne. Her work focuses on forms on inequality in music, particularly gender, and popular music as a form of collective memory and heritage. Recent publications include the edited collection *Towards Gender Equality in the Music Industry* (with Sarah Raine) and articles in *Gender, Work and Organisations, Cultural Sociology* and *Continuum*, along with an industry report on the effects of COVID-19 on Victorian music workers. She is co-editor of the journal *Popular Music History*.

John Tebbutt is Adjunct Associate Professor at RMIT University and the City University of Hong Kong. His research on media histories of the Australian Broadcasting Corporation, including the ABC in Southeast and East Asia and the Corporation's talk network Radio National, has been published in various journals. He is a managing editor for *Continuum: Journal of Media & Cultural Studies*.

Acknowledgements

We are very appreciative of the time and effort from our interviewees, many who travelled to Monash University at Caulfield and endured the technicalities of the filming process.

We would also like to thank our Research Assistants who assisted at various times with archival work: Sam Whiting, Alicia Cerreto and Abigail Belfrage. In particular, a huge thank you to Jen Rose, whose enthusiasm, expertise and sharp eye across a range of activities were invaluable.

Thanks also to key City of Melbourne staff. As Music Coordinator, Hannah Brooks provided valuable input, not the least in setting up a forum in which those working on history could engage. As Senior Curator at the Australian Music Vault, Carolyn Laffran advised on different components of the project, and her enthusiasm for Melbourne popular cultural histories is infectious. Thanks to Linda Bosidis and Ian James (Mushroom) and Paddy Donovan (Music Victoria) for providing interview contacts.

Thanks to Zo Damage and Ruth Maddison for access to their impressive collections for photographs in the book; and to Claudia Funder for stellar assistance in accessing the Performing Arts Collection at the Arts Centre. Thanks also to Brian and Jason Goldsmith for the use of Brian's 1960s images.

This project/book was funded by an Australian Research Council Discovery grant, and we are appreciative of the funding and time provided to investigate all things Melbourne.

1

Introduction

In 2005, the city of Melbourne was described by one music/culture writer as central to Australian creativity; 'its citizens, its suburbs and its climate pervade the lyrics of some of our best-known songs, and have inspired some of the most creative artists to fashion a soundtrack for several generations' (Kruger 2005a). Indeed, Melbourne was accorded more than a walk-on part in Australian creative life, centrally cast as a principal 'character' in which its 'moods' account for considerable influence in Australian popular music (ibid.). This might not be too far-fetched, given that Liverpool has sometimes been described as 'the fifth Beatle'; yet it does align with various narratives that place Melbourne at the centre of recreational and industrial life in relation to popular music. State governments (conservative or centre-left) are ever ready to announce other indexes that confirm Melbourne's place, especially The Economist Intelligence Unit annual rankings:

> ... we're proud to have consistently ranked as one of the world's top three most liveable cities since the index began in 2002 ... Melbourne's inner-city atmosphere is fuelled by a creative, culturally diverse community and is globally recognised as one of the most concentrated dining and fashion cultures in the world. Our city's interlocking laneways and the buzzing inner-city precinct reveal one-off boutiques, hidden cafes and world-class restaurants ... No matter what time of year you visit, Melbourne city pulses with a dynamic and cutting-edge arts and culture scene (Global Victoria 2020).

It is the particular intersections of space and place, embodied in the city's live music scenes, that the city is especially proud of, confirmed in various policy reports and annual census data (e.g. Newton and Coyle-Hayward 2018). Based on *per capita* accounting, government and industry sectors argue that Melbourne is *the* live music city in the world, 'beating out the urban super-powers of New York City and London' (Davino 2018). Adding to the city's 'buzzing inner city precincts' (Global Victoria 2020), it is the diversity of live venues that arguably remains at the centre of industrial activity as other Australian capital cities' live music sectors have withered.

Popular music (and other visible forms in the city, including music theatre and classical/art musics) has played its part in the historic rivalries between Australian capital cities. As with other cities (e.g. Manchester/Liverpool), Sydney and Melbourne have engaged in occasional battle in regard to industrial, cultural and political dominance. This 'urban beauty contest' (Morris and Verhoeven 2004: 30) has included interstate battles over sporting and cultural rights (who will host sports code Grand Finals; or which city is chosen to host lucrative theatre productions), with supposed consequences for cities not sustaining (and even enjoying) the rivalry. Yet it also says something about not just national competition for residents, tourists, capital, labour and city branding that also might induce healthy doses of myth-making; it also reveals such cities as part of the wider 'world city' club, thought to be of sufficient size to compete globally on cultural and other terms (e.g. King 1990).

Beginning in the 1950s, this book attempts to chronicle how Melbourne earned its place as one of the world's 'music cities'. The arrival of rock and roll in Melbourne in 1956–7 is a useful (and obvious) dividing line to begin mapping the development of popular music life, and the concurrent shifts from 'variety', cabaret and other forms before rock and roll; and subsequent changes also afforded by the arrival in television in 1956. Focusing on pop and rock, this is the first book to provide an extensive historical lens of popular music within this specific urban cultural economy. We have sought to assess the increasingly complex relationships between government and music industry sectors, its successes and policy innovations and the problems and limitations of 'music city' policy. In relation, we are also interested in the ways that 'how did we get here?' histories can in turn provide insight into the contemporary nature and challenges of urban music activities, industries and policy, amidst the role of culture (and cultural policy) in contemporary city life in general. Drawing upon interviews with musicians, venue owners, artist managers, fans and policy-makers, documenting their ambitions and experiences in different periods, the book explores the development of different sectors of Melbourne's popular music ecosystem in parallel with broader population, urban planning and media industry changes in the city.

Themes

The book derives from an Australian Research Council project, *Interrogating the music city: the cultural economy of pop and rock in Melbourne*, conducted by Monash and RMIT universities from 2017 to 2019. The project's five research themes – gender, urban planning/policy, music-media, live music and recording infrastructure – were identified as key areas of activity that combine industrial and government sectors. Firstly, we were interested in how the practices and understandings of gender and ethnicity were apparent in different periods of the city's popular music development, not the least in how women musicians and related workers (such as artist managers) have become visible in a set of industries that has been historically and trenchantly dominated by men. The book continues earlier work in exhibitions and writing (e.g. Melbourne Arts Centre's *Rock Chicks* exhibition in 2010) seeking to capture the often invisible contributions of women and girls as artists and fans within wider narratives of the Australian music industries. Reflecting events and constructions elsewhere, the Australian music industries were founded, shaped and dominated by men (Young 2004) in circumstances that only recently have warranted sustained empirical investigation (e.g. Music Victoria 2015; Victorian Women's Trust 2016; Strong and Cannizzo 2017) about the consequences for viable careers for women.

Equally, we are interested in the influence of different ethnic sounds, circuits and genres that have influenced Melbourne popular music. In addition to the Indigenous voices that have struggled to be heard but have always been present since before colonization, the city has certainly been shaped by the successive waves of migrant populations, benefiting from cross-border flows of people, ideas and cultures since the Second World War. Here we seek to understand Australian culture from an urban, multicultural and globally focused context; the book's starting point is that of Melbourne as a post-industrial, internationally oriented music city that looks outwards for both exchange and inspiration. This emphasis is also an important corrective to Anglo-Saxon accounts, given the predominance of US and British influences since the 1950s and 1960s. In relation to our other major themes, we provide snapshots of instances where migrants established opportunities and related thriving music scenes that flirted with mainstream sensibilities.

The second theme of the book is urban planning and policy. The book explores the mixture of governance and regulations that shape popular music activity, and the preoccupations of local and State governments in different periods. As we shall see, State governments held particular sway in providing the blueprints for sometimes radical planning changes configuring streetscapes and related ideas about public/private land use. Yet it was often local council policies driving change, either through specific, gradual commitments to music activity or providing innovation in their ideas about the uses of the CBD and surrounds. Unsurprisingly, given the related emphasis in the book on live music structures, liquor law histories are prominent in understanding the signal moments when State governments were determined to change drinking behaviour and the (often unintended) consequences for the city's venues.

This is, of course, part of wider shifts in seeing the importance of the night-time economy to cultural activity. According to another music city, the night-time economy 'describes the social, cultural and economic activities that take place between 6 pm and 6 am'; while this incorporates all the usual economy sectors (such as transport, manufacturing, health and many related services), '"nightlife" constitutes a significant part of this mix' (City of Toronto 2018). Popular music has been at the forefront of Melbourne governments' efforts to envisage a vibrant city-at-night, with accompanying payoffs in economic and cultural viability, through exciting offerings of drink, food, entertainment; and popular and 'high' culture offerings including live music, museums, art galleries, festivals, traditional theatre and music theatre. In turn, the different ideas of the '24 hour city' (Bianchini et al. 1988; Bianchini 1995) and the 'creative city', while conceptualized in very different ways and in different periods, are related in marrying unfettered access to leisure/pleasure to ensuring that there is a healthy set of creative industries able to provide it. Creativity should not be simply an outcome within these industries, but also a process for governments in reassessing the regulations and incentives regime and moving towards a more 'creative bureaucracy' (Landry 2008: xxi–xxii). The book traces particular moments when the state attempted to open up spaces and places to music through creative policy solutions, and those moments when it battled internal and external calls to reign in (music venue) behaviours thought to be 'anti-social'.

The third theme of the book, live music, is unsurprising, given the proud claims by industries and governments that Melbourne is the 'live music capital' of the world (displacing the claims of Austin, Texas to the title). A 2017 *Live Music Census* reported over 73,000 gigs in 533 music venues, with an estimated economic contribution to the State of $1.42b (Newton and Coyle-Hayward 2018). This per capita claim in connection to venues is often supported by related indicators of wider senses of community, through strong DIY aesthetics driving various local 'indie' scenes and quirky venues (Shaw 2009). While we do not dispute such claims, there is a danger in reverting to myth in explaining live music structures and activities. The book traces the changing venues of live performance from the 1950s, from town hall to concert stadium to local pub. Performance sites are rich terrain for a range of interconnecting themes and events: moral panics and accompanying fears about youth, music and alcohol; the financial and regulatory burdens upon venue owners in different periods; and precisely where particular musicians and audiences were 'allowed' to exist (or not) in the city based upon racial discourses. We provide snapshots of key venues and debates to represent wider shifts in behaviour and policy, including performers and venues situated outside the typical licensed rock venue circuits.

Fourthly, we look at the range of media involved in the promotion, dissemination and assessment of Melbourne popular music. We chart the development and influence of commercial radio in the 1960s amidst interstate rivalry. The emergence of an energetic and thoughtful music press, such as *Go-Set and Juke*, demonstrated a vibrant engagement with youth cultures and the city's music. The arrival of community radio in the mid-1970s was important in providing Melbourne with considerable firepower to maintain local scenes through broadcasters such as RRR, PBS and 3CR, eventually joined by indigenous broadcaster 3KND. The book provides snapshots of key television and radio programs that identified with Melbourne. Overall, we examine how forms of media innovation – accidental and opportunistic, as well deliberative and provocative – have contributed to sustaining music in Melbourne. In doing so the book contributes to understanding of media with regards to music city discourse more broadly. In putting the relationship between urban music and media into a long historical view, we suggest that media is more than a marketing adjunct to a music city. Media in its various forms at times is antagonistic to music and musicians, while it also provides important forums for reviving traditions as well as expanding knowledge of new music.

The final theme of the book (to a lesser extent) is the recording infrastructure of the city. A particular emphasis is on the city's dominance in the 1960s and 1970s in recording the nation's rock and pop stars, assessing the competition between recording studios (and Sydney and Melbourne) for technological innovation. Recording studios are obviously important in providing local artists with sites for presenting their material in the best light; yet they also have roles in wider scenes, connecting with venues, key figures and senses of place. The role of commercial and 'indie' recording companies is similarly important in documenting the opportunities afforded to Melbourne artists. While Sydney is regarded as the national headquarters, with its cluster of major international labels and larger studios, smaller labels and studios have been prominent, exemplified in recent historical treatments of the influence of Mushroom Records, and its growth from 'indie' label in 1972 to 'national major' in the 1980s (in 2013–14, RMIT University produced an exhibition, *Music, Melbourne and Me: 40 years of Mushroom and Melbourne's Popular Music Culture*). This book was completed at the time when Mushroom Records' founding owner, Michael Gudinski, died on 2 March 2021. The subsequent outpouring of grief in Melbourne and across the nation revealed the importance of Mushroom to Australian popular culture.

Across these five themes – gender and ethnicity, urban planning and policy, live music, media and recording – we were also interested in ideas and practices of cultural heritage. Speaking of an entity as large and diverse as a city, there are several means in which heritage comes to be defined through practices of 'critical acclaim, historical importance and cultural value' (Bennett 2009: 478). This involves assessing the accumulation of physical and built heritage (historical objects, buildings) and more intangible items such as memories of a concert or infamous dance party, and how together these form impressions/collections of histories that move between formal and informal spaces and uses. For example, heritage is invoked as both practice and status symbol in the City of Melbourne's argument that 'it's time for Melbourne to take its rightful place alongside some of the great music cities of the world including Austin, Berlin, Nashville and Toronto' (City of Melbourne 2014: 6). At various times, heritage is deployed as part of wider branding strategies, or at the very least, aspirations to be regarded as a music city that is something more than its contemporary scenes. It is also interesting to assess how contemporary moments and events are judged against the glow of past histories and memories (and we recognize that this book is in one sense an exercise in nostalgia, and itself a selective series of reconstructions). Calls to show visible reminders around the city of Melbourne's popular music history were increasing as we started the project, reinforcing the need for the assessment of an urban heritage as much as a music one, documenting the canonization of genres, venues, performers and scenes and institutions.

The music city

Since the 1980s, there has been steadily increasing interest across cultural geography, urban, cultural and popular music studies in the urban contexts of cultural activity. The ways in which cities find comparative advantages through specific cultural forms means that we can envisage, for example, the 'literature city' or the 'film city' (Hall 1998). Similarly, we can entertain how cities have been promoted through the specific prominence of music genres: Nashville (country), Liverpool (Merseybeat), Detroit (Motown and Soul) and Manchester (Rave) are useful examples of prior work in this vein (Haslem 2000; Du Noyer 2002).

What else is imagined or defined in the understanding of a 'music city'? Notions of the 'Sonic City' are not helpful, insofar as 'sonic' is not defined at the expense of an emphasis upon the urban as a series of settings for clusters of labour and capital, where cities 'contain the key elements for appropriating and commercializing ... musical creativity' (Florida and Jackson 2010: 312). Those possessing the hyper-advantages of specific clusters of creative industries at the centre of global capitalism can be regarded as 'global music cities' (Watson 2008; Bader and Scharenberg 2010). London is cited as an exemplar here in its ability to marshal considerable formal networking of expertise and firms that is boosted by informal networks and scenes (bars, restaurants and of course live music venues) that in turn 'facilitate learning and the sharing of knowledge across economic and cultural boundaries' (Watson 2008: 21). In contrast, as one industry executive explained, this has historically made it difficult for artists to emerge outside the larger 'supercities': 'You can't crack a band in Sunderland. Who gives a s**t if you crack a band in Sunderland?' (cited in Mean and Tims 2005: 6). In similar ways to Florida and Jackson's (2010) analysis, the emphasis upon geographical and locational structures does not sufficiently address the various combinations and relationships between the cultural and the economic.

There is, however, one further aspect of 'locationalism' to be assessed before moving on to other considerations. 'Cultural quarter' policies significantly informed later conceptions of the cultural or creative city,

> ... fusing it with tourism, "flagship projects" such as festivals and a more general concern with city planning in the name of "quality of life" (Landry & Bianchini 1995; Landry 2000). In some cases, an almost missionary zeal seems to have attached itself to these strategies for the remaking of cities in the name of culture and creativity.
>
> (Hesmondhalgh and Pratt 2005: 4)

The carving out of city and town spaces for creative/cultural uses has become a significant component of urban regeneration, at once linking local identity with cultural and economic development (Roodhouse 2010). The hot fever of 'cool cities' driven by cultural industries [specialization] raises important questions about measuring the real effects and economic benefits, the impacts and desires of different stakeholder involvement and the need for attendant inquiries into relevant policy areas such as planning (Markusen and Gadwa 2010: 388). Nonetheless, popular music has been at the forefront of regeneration strategies, from flagship rock/pop museum projects (such as the doomed National Centre for Popular Music Museum in Sheffield from 1999 to 2000) to embedding recording, live music and management businesses in particular zones of related creativity. In successive analyses of Liverpool's efforts to reconstruct itself after the economic and cultural troubles of the 1980s, Cohen (1991, 2007) has demonstrated how de-industrialization encouraged efforts to reclaim and mobilize popular music, leveraging its Beatles heritage and contemporary networks of venues and education for wider economic benefits.

An allied concern of the uses of popular music and other cultural forms in regeneration strategies are the processes and outcomes that can significantly alter cityscapes for the worse. Gentrification in cultural terms has come to mean 'suburbanization' of the inner city, with accompanying homogenization of retail and leisure activities, and the inability for artists and cultural consumers to reside or work in such areas where rents and housing prices require displacement to cheaper city areas (Holt and Wergin 2013: 9–10). The consequent fear is that 'conditions do not favor low-budget cultural production and lead to the migration of scenes into more peripheral microscenes. The implication is a separation of DIY and commercial cultural production between neighborhoods and therefore a weakening of the ecology that constitutes a scene and ultimately a vibrant neighborhood' (ibid.: 19). In Melbourne contexts, Shaw (2009, 2013, 2014) has explored the effects of rising rents, land use values and zoning changes upon the ability of cultural practitioners to both live and set up businesses in key parts of the city. Indirect policy settings have no doubt played a role in the broader historical shift Shaw (2013) identifies in the location of cultural enterprises from South Melbourne in the 1970s to its current strongholds in the inner north (see also *Now Sound: Melbourne's Listening* 2018). This book locates the story of popular music in Melbourne within broader debates around social and demographic change in the city in the 1960s and 1970s, and the role of culture and leisure as important drivers of the Melbourne economy in the post-industrial era since the 1980s (O'Hanlon 2005, 2010; Dingle and O'Hanlon 2009; O'Hanlon and Sharpe 2009).

Continuing debates about the 'cultural city' (including the traditional arts and older forms such as heritage) versus the 'creative city' (with its emphasis upon the bases of creativity and how they radiate out into other sectors, including new media) have revealed ongoing tensions between the economic uses, and the stubborn centrality of popular culture to make meaning in everyday life. It is interesting that in the Melbourne music industries' 2010 negotiations with the State government in regard to 'alcohol-fuelled violence' and accusations against venues (and subsequent licensing controls), United Nations discourses were invoked in citizens' broader rights to cultural enjoyment and expression. Often submerged amidst fierce protests about the mechanics of venue operations, the belief in the right to participate in city cultural life was at the core of the SLAM (Save Live Australian Music) rally and related city protests (see Homan 2010, 2016).

'Creative city' debates have provoked renewed interest in the role of cultural policy in not only the choices made about which cultural forms to support, but which forms of support have visible benefits (Rushton 2002; Grodach and Silver 2012; Markusen 2014). Yet how has the 'music city' descriptor been deployed and understood within uses by local councils, State, regional and national governments and public and commercial organizations? A 2005 *In Concert: Growing NewcastleGateshead as a Music City* report is indicative of many commissioned reports that avoid definitions, instead explicitly arguing for popular music to be part of an

> ... urban renaissance keen to embrace culture as an agent of urban renewal and social change, NewcastleGateshead encapsulates the experiences of a number of other cities in the country that are undergoing an upsurge in enthusiasm for music and an interest for developing music. For NewcastleGateshead we could easily read Cardiff, Sheffield, or Leeds (Mean and Tims 2005: 4).

As another example, Denver's *2018 Music Strategy* promises the transition 'From Music Scene to Music City', broadening existing strengths (venues, festivals) and incorporating them into much wider components of an ecosystem, for example, linking hip hop initiatives for youth education; redevelopment projects 'anchoring downtown landscapes' through music retail and music businesses that in turn build forms of community, the 'intangible benefits occurring when people are drawn together by music' (Denver Arts and Venues 2018: 2). The ecosystem as an organizing principle is forcefully argued in Sound Diplomacy's *This Must Be*

The Place report (2019), where 'music city' is again left undefined, but certainly regarded as part of a wider 'Future Cities' movement. In similar ways in which roads and energy are integrated into wider planning, governments must do a better job at integrating Governance; Education; Community Engagement and Media in respect to music activity, as part of a 'Future Cities' strategy (ibid.: 17).

Building on Florida's (2002, 2005) 'creative class' arguments, the United Nations recognized creative cities as key sources of employment, urban identity and heritage (United Nations 2008: 16–20) situated within a broader 'creative economy'. The UNESCO Creative Cities Network established in 2004 included the capacity to anoint City of Music status upon those with demonstrable track records in distinctive music activities and structures. In keeping with the types of music city reports cited above, it was noted that the award's more celebratory aspects had given way to 'a more economics-based interpretation of this requirement, shifting the focus from fine arts/tradition and its upgrading or adornment effect on the city to a more innovative ... and market-driven ... approach to the development of creative industries within the cityscape' (ibid.: 20). At last count, the UN had conferred Music City status upon thirty-five cities in 2020. Calls for Melbourne to apply for Music City status were misplaced: the city had already been granted City of Literature status in 2008, ruling out other claims to other industries, while the UN granting of Music City status to Adelaide in 2015 caused some disquiet in Melbourne circles. In 2014, advocacy body Music Victoria were recommending an application for UNESCO status (Music Victoria 2014), signalling the city's desire to be recognized beyond Australian contexts. Globally, the UNESCO exercise does accord with emerging understandings of the music city, where later fine-tuning of the criteria – the visible promotion of festivals, music education, genres and prevalence of the cities' music industries (UNESCO 2014) – emphasizes a joined-up approach of interconnecting excellence and reputation.

Melbourne has produced three strategy documents commissioned by its City Council. A 2010 report provided thirty recommendations based upon interconnecting themes of knowledge, networks and skills, highlighting the city's strengths in venues, labels and media, while emphasizing problems in planning and noise regulations; access to city spaces and community uses of popular music beyond the industrial (Homan and Newton 2010). Its subsequent *2014-2017 Strategy* emphasized six themes of a three-year plan (visibility; promotion and positioning, spaces and collaboration, funding and support, policy reform and advocacy; research and information) to be driven by a Music

Advisory Council (City of Melbourne 2014: 11). By the time of its *2018-21 Music Plan*, it had confirmed the city as a 'global music capital' that 'leads the world in helping emerging and established musicians to be creative and self-reliant. Outward looking and entrepreneurial, Melbourne knows how to showcase its rich musical offering … ' (City of Melbourne 2018: 9). It also indicated some shifts in emphasis, including 'innovation and technology', 'visitor economy and international profile' and 'regulation, urban growth and infrastructure' (ibid.: 8). This represented an emphasis as much on promotion and tourism as industrial growth. It also formed part of a wider policy ecology, with the State Government's 2015 release of its *Creative State Global City* TaskForce report. The following 2016 *Creative State* report emphasized the city's live music sector as part of an 'always-on approach to culture in the city' with new funding (across all creative industries) for talent development; 'strengthening the creative industries ecosystem'; economic and social impact; participation and access; and international engagement (Creative Victoria 2016).

Two different reports – one industry-based, the other composed by a consultancy firm – have provided the clearest sense of linking particular policy goals to music city ideas. In arguing for a processual emphasis, where 'music cities is a concept, not a definition', Sound Diplomacy's *The Music Cities Manual* is designed as a toolkit, providing examples of policy solutions and plotting interconnected components across research, health and well-being, heritage, infrastructure, tourism, entrepreneurship, the night-time economy and land uses (Sound Diplomacy 2019: 4, 11). Melbourne is offered as a case study in establishing its 'Agent of Change' policy in protecting venues from noise complaints (ibid.: 30).

The International Federation of Phonographic Industries (IFPI) and Music Canada's 2015 report, *The Mastering of a Music City*, states that a music city simply ' … describes communities of various sizes that have a vibrant music economy which they actively promote' (IFPI/Music Canada 2015: 10). Its essential elements contain 'Artists and musicians; a thriving music scene; access to spaces and places; a receptive and engaged audience; and record labels and other music-related businesses' (ibid.: 13). Of equal importance are the series of strategies and positions required to enable amenable governmental foundations: 'music-friendly and musician-friendly policies; a Music Office or Officer; a Music Advisory Board; engaging the broader music community to get their buy-in and support; access to spaces and places; and audience development' (ibid.: 13–15). The report reflected Music Canada CEO Amy Terrill's and others' work within Canadian contexts in stitching programs and ambitions together through local council, State and federal government levels in Canada; sites such as Toronto and Montreal represented more advanced policy wins than many other cities. Again, Melbourne is prominent through case studies of 'Agent of Change', and the SLAM (Save Live Australian Music) rally of 2010, with the city cited along with Austin as places where 'The outsized impact of music on both the lifestyle and economic fortunes of [these] places ... has become a beacon for other cities' (ibid.: 93). Again, Richard Florida's work is cited, with music acting as attractor of talent, a driver of creative clusters and stamp of city identity (ibid.: 27–8). The *Mastering* report was a well-written document that became an important primer for various music industries to place before various tiers of government, given its explicit calls for greater cooperation between industry and the state in delivering mutual (primarily economic) benefits. This has included Melbourne, with invitations from Music Victoria and the Victorian Government for Amy Terrill to be part of panels and presentations discussing future Melbourne policy directions (that included some of the authors of this book).

Framing Melbourne

From the (admittedly brief) survey of the idea and contexts of a 'music city' above, we can observe the interplay of different strands of cultural policy studies work upon industry thinking, and moments where industry and government shifts have influenced disciplinary work. The 'city policy' moment has continued, for example, through global discussions about the value of appointing 'Night Mayors' to govern night-time economies, although city ambitions were dialled down after the budgetary restrictions imposed by post-Global Financial Crisis landscapes.

Beginning in the 1950s, this book explores Melbourne popular music activity in eras well before the economic discourses of cultural or urban contexts were explicitly connected to more formal planning, branding and industrial exercises (although reputational ambitions were always evident in different guises). In this sense, we seek to chart both utilitarian and symbolic meaning-making properties of urban popular music where, in the absence of coordinated strategies, city structures were often simply technologies of pleasure. This fuses the social and the cultural with the gradual emergence of economic and place-making discourses. The project thus situates the Melbourne experience within a global story of the emergence and consolidation of the 'music economy' in the second half of the twentieth century and the first decades of the twenty-first. In this book we engage in making sense of the Lego-building work (venues, studios, media, etc.) that is crucial in the development of Melbourne's cultural life. Our five themes of investigation – gender and ethnicity, urban planning and policy, live music, media, recording – in part reflect the ecosystem approach that is now dominant within industrial, academic and governmental literature, in ascertaining the ways in which different components influence others (see, for example, Holden 2015). The breadth of the themes also counters the predominance of live music as the flagship sector that often receives the most media (and policy) attention.

Beyond the building blocks of music city infrastructure, we are also mindful of how particular events and attitudes informed decisions about which populations in the city could participate in music life, and those who were forced to construct alternative avenues of entertainment. Here we depart from recent works on the unique qualities of Melbourne-as-music-city. Horne (2019) provides an interesting account of the different periods in which live performance dominates, dating back to 1920s jazz. The historical span of genres and periods is impressive, although, amidst the many musicians' anecdotes, the promise on the cover – 'How Melbourne became the live capital of the world' – is amply demonstrated, but never really answered. Baker (2019) offers comparisons of Berlin, Austin and Melbourne as *Great Music Cities*, through combinations of policy, politics and branding histories. There is an emphasis here on attempts to expand Florida's indexing methods, producing 'algorithms' (in truth, simply categories) as a series of metrics for assessment (Baker 2019: 15–21).

Melbourne clearly possesses the essential and secondary (history, tourism, recognition as economic driver, strong community radio, distinct local sound or sounds (IFPI/Music Canada 2015: 17)) elements cited in reports such as *The Mastering of a Music City*. As authors we are not interested in providing a stocktaking exercise of Melbourne's existing qualities in music production and consumption. We are more interested in accounting for the quirks in local conditions, and the longer effects wrought by the accumulation of histories, policies and local behaviours. This involves the various ways in which localized policy differed from that of other Australian cities and States, producing distinctive Melbourne solutions. It has been acknowledged that 'In many respects Canada, Australia and New Zealand have developed more coherent approaches based not only on a recognition of the economic value of the cultural industries, but also of the importance of the construction and defence of a national culture' (Hesmondhalgh and Pratt 2005: 4). We cannot ignore Melbourne's role in the development of a broader Australian cultural policy, and in turn, how the city was influenced by both national (e.g. the federal construction of community radio licences and their very particular Melbournian adaptations) and international flows of capital, people and concepts.

As hinted at above, we are not interested in reinforcing simpler city narratives that argue that, for example, Nashville's music is 'magical' (*For the Love of Music: The Story of Nashville* 2014). Rather, this book seeks to make sense of the complex interplay of forces that reveal certain pathways as not inevitable or achieved by accidental design. We are, however, interested in the ways that mythologies contain the potential to provide closed feedback loops between agendas, outcomes and discourses. The 'music city' descriptor is both self-referential and self-enabling, encompassing a handy set of resources and discourses for its proponents to demand further resources and policies in its maintenance.

Methodology

As outlined above, this book takes the arrival of rock and roll in Melbourne as the starting point to map the development of pop and rock in the city, where we end investigations in the early 2000s. This involved tracing popular music in the 'usual' formal spaces, but also attempting to informally record histories, especially with musicians and fans.

Archival work was important to the project. This included investigating the State Library of Victoria collections which houses commercial journals and business records; promotional material of commercial pop radio broadcasters, and a series of photographs of iconic Melbourne music landmarks and music pub/bar photographs from the 1960s and 1970s. The State Library was also useful in locating documentaries, fan histories and a collection of music business material of key booking agencies and recording companies. Arts Centre Melbourne's collections of photographs, posters, magazines and related agency/industry material were particularly useful (and the Centre also contains many iconic performance costumes of performers ranging from Dame Edna Everage to Kylie Minogue). The National Film and Sound Archive (NFSA), and its collection of TV music and variety programs were of relevance, especially its

Oral History program that contains interviews of relevant musicians. In addition, the National Library of Australia also houses a collection of mainstream and alternative media (street press, magazines); business and fan club archives and the Women's Register, which includes material and interviews with important female performers.

Hearing from performers about different periods of Melbourne's development was also essential to our project. Over a four-year period, the authors interviewed fifty-two (thirty-one male; twenty-one female) people with experiences ranging from the 1950s to the early 2000s. This included artists, venue owners, artist managers, fans, promoters, recording studio owners, music journalists, policy activists and music historians. In addition, we thank Geoff King (RMIT) for access to interviews conducted with key Melbourne figures as part of his work with RRR and Lilith Lane for access to recording studio producers and engineers interviewed for her Masters project. We also made attempts to reach out to fans who wished to share their city memories. With the assistance of the City of Melbourne's Music Coordinator, Hannah Brooks, the authors organized an event at the Melbourne Town Hall – 'Retro Recall' – encouraging fans to bring their memorabilia and speak to the personal stories associated with them. On 25 February 2017, we 'interviewed' (in reality, chatted with) fans about their books, posters, t-shirts and scrapbooks. Turnout was low, but those who did show up reinforced how access to private collections provides the 'emotional, aesthetic and cultural value' (Leonard 2007: 165) of histories of popular culture. Radio and print advertising of the event, did however, bring many vinyl and photographer archivists out of the woodwork who believed the project would pay considerable sums for their collections!

The archival work listed above was supplemented by newspaper coverage of rock and pop, which was especially useful in documenting the arrival of rock and roll in the 1950s (and the usual moral panic narratives to be found in any city context globally). Beyond the interviews, PROV (Public Record of Victoria) material provided the team with potted histories of individual venues, charting their liquor licence conditions and other contexts of trading. As becomes evident in later chapters, particular venues became the focus to reveal broader changes about trading, drinking and entertainment through the decades. In 2018, Cath Strong and Research Assistant Jen Rose worked closely with the State-funded youth music organization, The Push, in cataloguing its archives and providing a timeline of its music activities. This in turn assisted the project in signifying the role of youth policies in the city's wider music histories.

Finally, we must also note that as we began our historical work, the city at large had similar ideas. Derived partly from earlier policy recommendations that the city needed a physical space in which to celebrate its popular music history, the Andrews Labor State Government provided the funding (as part of funding a wider 'Music Works' strategy) for a 'museum' of sorts to be located within the Arts Centre. The Australian Music Vault opened in December 2017, with a broader remit to showcase the 'Australian' story. With revolving themes anchored by permanent exhibitions, the Vault offers to 'unlock the stories of Australian music with immersive digital experiences, rare archival footage and see iconic music objects up close' (Australian Music Vault 2021). We appreciated the support of the Vault's Senior Curator, Carolyn Laffran, as our fieldwork crossed paths in terms of themes and music industry figures.

2

The transformed city

Introduction

While contemporary Melbourne has a well-deserved reputation as a place of artistic, musical and cultural innovation and experimentation, this is a relatively new phenomenon, a product of demographic, social, legislative and cultural changes instituted in the city – often in the face of strong opposition from religious and socially conservative groups – since the mid-1960s. Before then, the city's reputation was (rightly or wrongly) as a dull place where alcohol was frowned upon; the pubs were closed more often than they were open; shops shut at lunchtime Saturday and did not reopen again until Monday morning; and state-enforced Sabbath-observance meant that public recreation facilities and commercial entertainments were banned on Sundays. This provincial and 'wowserish' reputation was both national and international and was put on display twice in the late-1950s when the eyes of the world turned to the city. In the first instance they saw it through the prism of sport in the form of the Olympic Games staged from late November through to early December 1956. The saga of gaining and then hosting the Olympics has been well documented by historians Graeme Davison and Tanja Luckins, who have argued that anxieties in the years leading up to the Games about whether Melbourne's sporting and other public facilities, as well as its culture food and hospitality industries, most notably its liquor licensing hours, would stand up to international scrutiny. This was reflected in the long-standing national and urban 'cultural cringe', a fear that the city and Australia more generally were derivative, second-rate and provincial (Davison 1997, 2002; Luckins 2007).

Less than three years later, in early 1959, the eyes of the world again turned to Melbourne in the form of Hollywood when *On the Beach*, the film adaptation of Neville Shute's novel about mass human extinction in a post-nuclear war world, was filmed in the city centre and nearby beach resorts. From January to

March of that year, US film stars Gregory Peck, Fred Astaire, Anthony Perkins and Ava Gardner graced Melbourne's streets, restaurants, shops and hotels, bringing a touch of Hollywood glamour and excitement to a city not known for its nightlife, hedonism or fun. While the film was a critical and commercial success, presenting Melbourne and its people to the world in a favourable light, it became a public relations disaster for the city when Sydney-based journalist Neil Jillett erroneously attributed to Gardner that in her opinion, Melbourne was 'the perfect place to make a film about the end of the world'. Never completely repudiated by Gardner, more than twenty years later, Jillett finally confessed that he had in fact invented the quote, and she had never said anything of the sort (Davey 2005).

The damage was done, however, and for many years afterwards Melbourne maintained a (possibly unfair) reputation for conservatism, social propriety and cultural stodginess. A long-standing conservative State government, kept in power by the Catholic-dominated Democratic Labor Party, implacably opposed to liberalism and sexual permissiveness, bolstered and enforced a rather austere and illiberal social and cultural order. The city centre was almost entirely a place of work rather than residence or entertainment where, as depicted by artist John Brack in his famous 1955 painting *Collins St, 5.00 pm*, once the offices and shops closed for the day, grim faceless commuters took the train to their suburban homes rather than stay in town for a night out. Sundays were particularly dull and dreary, especially during the comparatively cold, wet and dark winters, further adding to this rather dismal urban reputation. New arrivals to the city were expected to assimilate to these cultural norms, as were Indigenous people who at that stage were neither entitled to vote nor counted in the national census.

Not all Melburnians were dull 'wowsers' implacably opposed to alcohol, entertainment and fun, and not everyone aspired to live in a detached home in the suburbs. The city had long had a sizeable Catholic minority, mostly of Irish extraction who, while they may have opposed social and sexual permissiveness, were mostly fine with alcohol and gambling. Many lived in higher-density inner city neighbourhoods alongside small communities of Chinese, Middle Eastern and other non-English-speaking groups. From the 1920s onwards a small number of Eastern European Jews had settled in Carlton and nearby, as did a small community of Italians. So too in the 1930s, inner urban Fitzroy became an important place of settlement for Indigenous people moving to the city from rural 'missions', looking for work and seeking reconnection with Stolen family members. Carlton's early Jewish settlers were bolstered by the arrival of German and Austrian Jewish refugees from Nazism in the 1930s and then in the early post-war years by thousands of eastern European Survivors of the Holocaust. The Italians were similarly joined after the war by tens of thousands of their fellow countrymen and women who fled the hunger and poverty of their post-war homeland for a new life in Australia. From the late-1940s through to the 1970s, hundreds of thousands of other European immigrants also settled in Melbourne as part of a national policy designed to rapidly expand the country's population and economy. Like their earlier predecessors, these immigrants overwhelmingly settled in a small number of inner-city neighbourhoods, substantially changing the demographics, culture and ambience of these areas and of the broader metropolis.

Along with their children and grandchildren, as well as the hundreds of thousands of immigrants from across the globe who have settled in the city since the repeal of the White Australia Policy in the 1960s and 1970s, these 'new' Melburnians have had a profound impact on the culture of the city, so much so that today it bears little resemblance to its mid-century self. Several generations of local-born Melburnians and intra and interstate arrivals who wanted a society different to that created by their forebears have similarly brought major social, political and cultural changes to the city. Immigrants and their children and grandchildren were particularly important to the arts, culture and hospitality industries and to the music industries as performers, promoters, venue operators and as players in the music, media and recording industries. Some of their stories will appear in multiple places throughout this book. Particular immigrant communities were also influential in the clothing and fashion industries which were elements in the emergence of the city's youth cultures from the 1960s onwards. As in other major cities worldwide, changes in the demographic profile of Melbourne in these decades combined with the growth of an economy based on services and leisure, an important aspect of which was servicing the needs and wants of young people that have had a major influence on daily life and the culture of the city.

Rather than a place of dullness and conformity, from the mid-1960s, Melbourne increasingly gained a national reputation as the leading arts, music and cultural centre, becoming a magnet for artists, writers, musicians, music fans and others wanting to be a part of the rapidly growing youth culture industry. As demographics and social attitudes changed, so did electoral politics. In the early-1970s, the long-standing conservative Premier Bolte was replaced by the younger and more urbane Rupert Hamer. In April 1982, the election of a Labor

State government for the first time in more than a quarter of a century had a profound effect on the political culture of the city. These new premiers and their governments brought new political and social ideas and attitudes and support for arts and culture, such that contemporary Melbourne is recognized as the most politically progressive city in Australia, a place where the arts, culture, heritage and personal freedoms are increasingly important and cherished aspects of urban culture. Importantly, in the post-industrial era, these sectors have become important economic strengths, selling points used to attract investment, new residents and tourists to the city.

As a prelude to the more detailed discussions of various aspects of Melbourne's music industries to follow, this chapter draws on urban historical methods, including the use of statistical sources, government policy documents and newspaper and other archival material, as well as secondary sources including books, articles as well as blogs and other multimedia to trace a fifty-year period from the mid-1960s to the 2010s. Here we are interested in Melbourne's evolution from a city with a reputation of being of and for the dull and boring, to being recognized locally, nationally and internationally as a place of culture, fun, entertainment and artistic creativity. The chapter begins with a detailed study of demographic change and argues that it was the transformation of the city from essentially an ethnic and social monoculture in the inter-war and early post-war period to one of the most multicultural in the world that was central to the broader processes of cultural change. In turn, we argue that it was these demographic changes that allowed the legislative, economic and public policy processes of openness and respect for difference, many of which were implacably opposed by more traditional religious and conservative elements of the city's population, to proceed.

Demography: Immigration, the 'generation gap' and cultural change

Immigration

When the Olympics and *On the Beach* came to Melbourne in the late 1950s, the city was experiencing the first effects of rapid growth that was to nearly double its population in the quarter century between the end of the Second World War and the early 1970s, and quadruple it by 2020. In the fourteen years between the censuses of 1947 and 1961, the city's population grew by nearly two thirds and then by another quarter in the 1960s, before expansion tailed off until the mid-1990s, when it began another rapid climb (Australian Bureau of Statistics Census 1947, 1961). A city of only about 1.2 million people in 1947 passed the five million mark in late 2018. While in the 1950s and 1960s many of these new residents were the children of the famous early post-war 'baby-boom', the major component of the growth then and now was immigration. Conceived during the Second World War as a means of defending Australia as a White European outpost in the Asia-Pacific region, the first iteration of the new immigration policy announced in early 1945 was overtly racist and exclusionary. New settlers were planned to be predominantly British, but the program was expanded to include refugees and other 'displaced persons' fleeing Communism and oppression in Northern and Eastern Europe. Skilled and unskilled migrants from Ireland were also included in the immigration program, sometimes offered paid support to migrate. Later arrivals from Western and Southern Europe were required to work at jobs designated to them by the government in exchange for free or subsidized passage. Other European migrants were sponsored by family, friends, employers and community groups. From the outset the program was open to expatriate European diaspora communities in Asia, the Middle East and Africa, but not to non-whites. Large numbers of Jewish arrivals came from Shanghai and elsewhere in Asia in the 1940s and 1950s, and Armenians and Greeks from North Africa and Italians from Ethiopia, Eretria, Somalia and Egypt in the 1960s and 1970s. This also included traders and former British and Dutch colonial-era administrators from India, Burma, Indonesia, Malaysia and other newly independent countries in postcolonial Asia throughout the post-war period. As such, Melbourne became not only increasingly foreign-born during this era, but also increasingly cosmopolitan too.

Along with Sydney, Melbourne absorbed a disproportionately large share of immigrants, particularly those from non-English-speaking backgrounds. In the early post-war years this was because the city was a major site of manufacturing and therefore a key employment node, highly attractive to new immigrants looking to secure their families' economic futures. More recently, the city has globalized and forged deep economic, social and cultural ties with cities and nations of Asian and elsewhere across the globe, again making it an attractive destination for immigrants (O'Hanlon and Stevens 2017). In the 1960s, tens of thousands of those settlers were English, Scottish and Irish, their children bringing with them knowledge of the emerging sounds of 1960s Britain, which they drew upon to become important players in the early years of Australian rock and pop. This was especially true of those who relocated to Melbourne. Glenn Shorrock of the Twilights and later the Little River Band, and Jim Keays of the Masters' Apprentices, among others, exemplify this multiple migration story, as later did Billy Thorpe. British-born migrants who settled directly in Melbourne, such as Johnny Farnham and Mike Brady, were also important in local development (Thorpe 1998; Keays 1999; Gazzo 2015; Brady 2018; Shorrock 2018). Later in the early-1970s, British-born Red Symons of Skyhooks became an icon of the city's glam rock scene, while later in that decade, London-born Stuart Grant of the Primitive Calculators was to be a key player in the emergence of the city's post-punk reputation (Grant 2017).

While the British were an important source of immigrants to Melbourne and important influences on its music scene, the largest component of the city's immigrant community, and the group that would have the largest influence on changing its culture, were the continental Europeans, especially those from Southern and Eastern Europe. By the time of the 1971 Census, only twenty-five years after the onset of the mass immigration program and barely a decade after the humiliation of *On the Beach*, immigrants from continental Europe accounted for more than a fifth of Melbourne's population, meaning that it was actively shrugging off its provincial Protestant British reputation and becoming conspicuously European and multicultural. Home to Australia's largest communities of Italians, Greeks, Maltese and Yugoslavs, by 1971 Melbourne was home to over 100,000 Italian-born residents, more than 42,000 Yugoslavs and more than 76,000 Greeks, making it at that time one of the most populous Greek cities in the world (Australian Bureau of Statistics 1971). It was also one of the largest Maltese cities in the world, with more than 25,000 Maltese-born residents, including Joe Camillieri of Jo Jo Zep and the Falcons and later the Black Sorrows (Camillieri no date). Melbourne also became Australia's most important Eastern European Jewish city in these years; a large number of these settlers were survivors of the Holocaust and their children (Australian Bureau of Statistics 2016; Graham and Markus 2018). Michael Gudinski, the child of Russian Jewish immigrants who arrived in Melbourne in 1948, was to have a profound influence on the Melbourne music scene through his record company Mushroom and other entities including booking agency Premier Artists (Stafford 2021; see Chapter 2).

While the 1971 Census was taken after changes to the Australian Constitution relating to the recognition of Indigenous people, which had been overwhelmingly endorsed in a referendum in 1967, at that time only small numbers of Melburnians self-identified as Aboriginal – just over 2,900, with another 594 identifying as Torres Strait Islanders. The 1971 Census was also taken before the relaxation of immigrant restrictions, meaning that multicultural Melbourne was at that stage still overwhelmingly 'white' and European. While just over 43,000 Melburnians had at that time been born in Asia and another 21,000 African, almost all of these were members of diasporic European communities and were thus ethnically European (Australian Bureau of Statistics 1971). While the city was increasingly multicultural, it was still overwhelmingly white and European, and was to remain so until the final abolition of the White Australia Policy in 1973, and the arrival of large numbers of non-European immigrants in the late-1970s, 1980s and 1990s. The impact of such a substantial immigrant program has been profound, and contemporary Melbourne is now widely recognized as one of the most multicultural cities in the world. Home to more than 250 different ethnic groups, the most recent national census taken in 2016 showed that just over 40 per cent of Melbourne's population (more than two million people) was born overseas, with another 20 per cent having at least one overseas born parent (Price and Benton-Short 2007; Australian Bureau of Statistics 2016). Nor is the city still predominantly white and European. Since the 1970s, increasing numbers of residents have begun to proudly identify as Aboriginal or Torres Strait Islander (more than 24,000 as of 2016), while in the same period the overwhelmingly dominant source of new migrants is Asia.

Since the turn of the millennium, Australia's two largest immigrant source countries have been China and India, with other large groups coming from North, South and East Africa, the Pacific and the former Soviet Union. Today, more than 350,000 Melburnians identify as having Chinese ancestry and just under 200,000 identify as Indians. Another 105,000 claim Vietnamese ancestry; 56,000 Sri Lankan; and 60,000 Filipino, including former I'm Talking member and singer Kate Ceberano, whose father is of Filipino and Hawaiian ancestry (Ceberano 2014). Between them, then, these five Asian ancestries account for more than 15 per cent of the city's population. Melbourne is also home to Australia's largest ethnic-African communities of Ethiopians, Eritreans, Somalis, Sudanese and Burundians. Far from being dominated by non-conformist Protestants as it was in the 1950s, in today's Melbourne, Muslims and Hindus each outnumber adherents of the Uniting Church, the successor church to the non-conformist Presbyterian, Methodist and Congregationalists who merged in 1977. The Catholic Church is now the largest single religious group with about one million adherents (nominal or otherwise); yet it is outnumbered by around 1.5 million people who profess no religion at all. Contemporary Melbourne is thus multicultural, but also secular and increasingly post-religious (Australian Bureau of Statistics 2016).

The 'generation gap'

The post-war surge in immigration laid the groundwork for the emergence of Melbourne as a cosmopolitan city, but the concurrent increase in the birth rate – the famous 'baby boom' – meant that the age profile of the city declined markedly in the 1960s, 1970s and 1980s. The rapid growth in the number of teenagers in the city at that time changed its cultural ambience, one of the reasons why it was to emerge as an important place of music and other creativity. Historians have been rightly critical of the use of 'generations' as a useful historical category, arguing that it negates the different experiences of people of similar age groups based on class, gender, race, ethnicity and geography. However, in the case of the post-war period in many places in the West and especially in cities such as Melbourne whose demography altered so radically during these years, there is an argument that for many people, the post-war urban experience was markedly different to the pre-war one (O'Hanlon 2019). Mass migration was central to this, but so too was the so-called 'generation gap' between those born before the war, the onset of the major social and cultural changes of the 1960s and those born during and just after the conflict. In common with many other societies across the Western world, there was a surge in births in Melbourne in the early post-war years which helped to fundamentally alter the age profile of the city. Immigration exacerbated this trend as many of the new settlers were in their prime child-rearing years, further fuelling the city's birth and population growth rate. With immigrants disproportionately settling in Melbourne at this time, this in turn meant that by definition the number of births there was higher than elsewhere in the country. With many immigrants having children soon after settling in Melbourne, they also increased the numbers of local births in the city (Australian Bureau of Statistics 2007).

The dual forces of mass immigration and the 'baby boom' meant that at the same time as Melbourne's ethnic make-up was shifting dramatically, so too was its age profile; the city population not only becoming more ethnically diverse, but also younger. This had flow-on effects, with the high numbers of births in the early 1950s providing large numbers of teenagers and twenty-somethings in the city from the mid-1960s onwards, again a phenomenon that radically altering its culture and 'vibe'. This growing sense of a 'generation gap' was further exacerbated by the lingering effects of a steep fall in births in the depressed 1930s: the children who should have been born in the early 1930s and thus would have been aged in their twenties and thirties in the 1950s and 1960s were simply not there, in effect, a 'missing' generational cohort. Deaths associated with the war further reinforced this phenomenon, which became especially noticeable in the mid-1960s as the numbers of teenagers surged. The 1966 Census showed that whereas in 1947 only one-third of the population of the state of Victoria was aged under twenty-one, twenty years later that figure had climbed to 37.5 per cent. In Melbourne, which by the mid-1960s was increasingly a magnet for young international immigrants and young arrivals from intra- and interstate, this figure was slightly higher at 38 per cent (Australian Bureau of Statistics 1947, 1966, 1971). The proportion of young people in the population, and hence their influence in the city's economy and culture continued to climb into the early 1970s and was, again, one of the reasons why Melbourne became an important centre of youth culture in that decade.

Cultural change

As the population increased and prosperity grew in the post-war decades, many local-born Melburnians left the working class inner city to settle on the city's rapidly expanding suburban fringe. They were joined there by some of the newer northern European immigrant communities, especially those from Britain, Ireland, the Netherlands and Germany. In the inner suburbs, these 'old' Australians were replaced by immigrants from southern Europe, giving these areas an increasingly 'Mediterranean' ambience (Willingham 2004). This was reflected in individual houses, which were stripped of verandas, painted white and opened up to the light, as were houses in Southern Europe. Demands for new foods, drinks and cultural products also increased and were provided for in new businesses opened by entrepreneurs from within the immigrants' own communities. As such, the new arrivals were to have major impacts upon not only the demography of Melbourne in this era, but also its architecture, culture and economy. European and diaspora Jews became important players in the clothing, entertainment, retail and property development industries, while Italians had major impacts upon small-scale retailing and the food, cafe and restaurant industries. So too did the Italians and the Greeks; Yugoslavs, and later the Vietnamese and Chinese also become central to food production, distribution and sales, most notably in the wholesale and retail fruit and vegetable industries. These new producers markedly broadened the types of foods and drinks on offer at markets and in retail outlets in inner suburban shopping strips as Melbourne cuisine moved away from its previous emphasis on British gastronomic traditions. Potatoes and cabbage were augmented with zucchinis, egg plant and bok choy in local greengrocers, while liquor stores and 'licensed grocers' began to feature wine and liqueurs alongside beer. Coffee also began to replace tea as the city's hot drink of choice. As immigrant communities grew in number, so too did cafes, restaurants and 'continental' food stores become a common feature of the retail strips.

Later changes in liquor licensing laws were to radically alter the economic structure and culture of these inner streets and neighbourhoods. While as we saw at the beginning of this chapter, 1950s Melbourne retained the very strict 'early closing' laws introduced as a temporary measure during the First World War, from the mid-1960s through to the late 1990s, these controls were slowly unwound. By the early 2000s, Melbourne had the most liberal liquor licensing laws and hours in the country (Kirkby, Luckins and McConville 2010). From February 1966, Melbourne's pubs were permitted to remain open until 10 p.m. from Monday through to Saturday, and could apply for a permit for certain bar areas to remain open beyond midnight on those same days, provided they offered food and entertainment to customers. Sundays were still off-limits, other than for visitors to tourist areas who could prove they were more than 50 kilometres from home and were thus classed as bona fide travellers and entitled to drink.

These licensing law changes assisted the emergence of Melbourne's pub rock scene in the 1970s and 1980s as firstly inner-city pubs with redundant dining rooms turned them over to live music, and then more famously, large outer suburban hotels set within vast carparks similarly turned their former dining rooms (home of the Australian 'counter meal') over to live music at nights and on weekends. And while the hotel dining room might now be a late-night music venue, the availability of food (no matter how inedible), if not the consumption of it, was a condition of the late licence. Nightclubs could also remain open to 3 a.m. if they similarly offered food to customers. Later, a series of changes to the liquor licensing in the early 1980s allowed pubs to open for limited periods on Sundays and extended nightclub licences to 7 a.m. Late 1980s wholesale reform, including the introduction of what became known as the 'general' licence, meant that the difference between what was a pub, a restaurant, a bar and a venue was essentially abolished. It was from these changes that Melbourne's famous small and 'laneway' bar scene emerged in the 1990s and beyond.

The other major change derived from the 1960s liberalization of liquor laws was the introduction of the Bring Your Own (BYO) licence, under which patrons could bring their own liquor to a restaurant which would either charge a 'corkage' fee or provide this service for free. This meant that the entry cost of establishing a small restaurant or café was minimal, and hundreds of small family-run establishments began to appear along shopping streets across the inner suburbs. At first, these catered to members of the same ethnic groups as the owner (often newly arrived single young men lacking culinary skills or access to their own kitchen facilities); but before long they also found favour with local residents, especially students and other early gentrifiers who became an important demographic in these neighbourhoods from the 1970s. As both Graeme Davison and Tanja Luckins have argued, the apparent 'public' and 'festive' nature of inner urban immigrant life, evident in the burgeoning numbers of cafes and restaurants, was attractive to a rising generation of young Australians who were increasingly moving into these areas while studying at Melbourne University (until the early-1960s, the city's only university and whose major campus was adjacent to the increasingly Italian suburb of Carlton) (Davison 2001; Luckins 2009). Other young people saw similar ways of life in Greek-influenced *tavernas* of Prahran and Richmond and the cakeshops and cafes of Jewish St Kilda. These were the early gentrifiers who were to rapidly alter the demographic and cultural profile of these neighbourhoods in the last decades of the century.

The movement of large, sometimes multigenerational immigrant families to the inner suburbs reversed long-standing population decline which had been a feature of these areas since the 1920s. The growth of large, shared student households also helped to stabilize the population in the 1960s and early 1970s (O'Hanlon 2004). The surge in births in the 1950s and early 1960s meant that twenty years later, there were large numbers of young adults looking to establish homes independent of their parents. The thousands of young adults who began to attend university or college in this period also flocked to the inner city and became the progenitors of widespread gentrification – the movement of wealthier, educated and middle-class residents into formerly rundown and immigrant urban areas. Just as the immigrants had replaced older Australian households in the 1950s and 1960s, they in turn were replaced by students in the 1960s and 1970s, and who were in turn usurped by smaller and much wealthier and generally local-born households in the 1970s and 1980s. By the 1990s, Melbourne's urban geography was, like that of other major cities internationally, being turned inside out, with the inner region increasingly wealthy, white and local-born; and the outer suburbs poorer and immigrant (O'Hanlon 2018). As we shall see in the final chapter of this book, all of this meant that from the mid-1970s onwards, as household size began to shrink, so too did the population of the inner city.

Decline was partly offset in this period by the construction of tens of thousands of flats in a fifteen-year building boom beginning in the late 1950s and lasting through to the mid-1970s. This saw whole streets and neighbourhoods in the inner city take on higher densities as single-family houses were replaced by townhouses, flats and apartments. While substantial numbers of these were public, built by the Housing Commission of Victoria as part of a 'slum reclamation' program that saw the inner city disfigured by unsightly high-rise concrete towers, the majority of the new flats were in low-rise blocks built by private developers (Howe 1988; O'Hanlon 2015). The residents were recent immigrant arrivals, and the large number of young adults coming of age as adults and seeking independent living arrangements, whether as singles, couples or married and heterosexual, de facto or gay or lesbian. In some wealthier areas, small numbers of private high-rise apartment blocks were also constructed in this period, often by immigrant European Jewish developers (O'Hanlon 2015), although these mostly catered to older owner-occupiers than to younger renters.

The effects of this boom were highly localized, with most of the private flats built in the inner south, and most of the public ones in the inner north of the city. As with the arrival of immigrants in the 1950s and 1960s, the coming of these new places and their new residents changed the ambience and culture of the neighbourhoods in which they were built. The public towers, combined with repeal of the White Australia Policy and the arrival of substantial numbers of Indo-Chinese refugees, meant that shopping strips in these areas took on an increasingly Asian feel in the 1970s and 1980s. In the case of the private flats, the replacement of single-family, often owner-occupied houses with blocks of ten, twenty or thirty rented flats occupied by young people brought increasing tensions over noise and other 'youthful' behaviour to what had often previously been quiet suburban neighbourhoods. As such, the culture and reputation of these areas also changed dramatically in a very short space of time. Just as the arrival of large numbers of Asian and southern European migrants to the inner city brought new business and new and more public forms of socializing and entertainment to the neighbourhoods in which they settled, so too the influx of these new younger residents who were looking for a good time rather planning to stay for a long one changed the social structures and entertainment options of these new 'flat zones'. Full employment, relatively high wages and affordable rents provided these newer, younger residents with money to spend, and they did so in new businesses, especially those associated with the emerging youth culture industry: cafes, clothes shops and 'boutiques'; music venues, record shops and other business selling products associated with leisure and pleasure. Musician Jim Keays of the Masters' Apprentices has recalled time spent in 'a small two-bedroom box in one of those typical '60s red brick three-storey blocks' in East St Kilda at this time, where he, fellow bandmembers and friends lived a life of 'sex and drugs and rock and roll' (Keays 1999: 96).

Deindustrialization, unemployment and punk rock

The rapid growth in the numbers of immigrants, young people and flat development in inner Melbourne came to a shuddering halt in the mid-1970s, when the post-war 'Fordist' economy came under severe pressure in the wake of the OPEC oil crisis and the industrialization of a number of countries in Asia (O'Hanlon 2018). As manufacturing faltered, jobs left the inner city, as did residents, especially the increasingly aging and more economically secure early post-war immigrants (Dingle and O'Hanlon 2009). While the loss of these jobs and these residents was unfortunate, it helped to consolidate the growing sense that these regions were becoming places of office work, education and artistic and musical creativity rather than places of production. As the immigrants and their jobs left the inner city they were increasingly being replaced by wealthier gentrifiers employed in professional fields such as education, the media and the finance sector; students, and from the mid-1970s, by unemployed young people, many of whom were artists, musicians and writers. While the influx of immigrants gave Melbourne its reputation as a cosmopolitan city, it was the arrival of these newer and younger 'creatives' that cemented its reputation for music, and especially live and alternative music. While there were some signs of this awakening in the 'Carlton scene' of the early-1970s when the suburb became a national music (and literary) centre, it was the emergence of punk and post-punk music in the deindustrializing city of the late 1970s and early 1980s that cemented this reputation and laid the groundwork for the emergence of the music city in the 2000s.

There were two major post-punk scenes in 1970s Melbourne, both based in the inner city and both able to thrive as a result of economic and population decline. The southern (or St Kilda) scene was a result of the cheap rents and population densities that resulted from the flat building of the 1960s. The northern scene based in Carlton, Fitzroy, Collingwood and Richmond was able to take advantage of rundown housing left empty by the exodus of people and industry in the 1970s (San Miguel 2011, *We're livin' on dog food* 2009, Grant 2017). These scenes are well documented in novels from the time, such as Helen Garner's semi-autobiographical *Monkey Grip* (1977) set in Fitzroy and Carlton in the mid-1970s, Leonie Stevens' novel *Nature Strip* (1993) set in the same neighbourhoods a few years later and in Richard Lowenstein's 1986 film *Dogs in Space*, which was filmed in the house he and others had shared in Richmond in the late 1970s (Nichols and Perillo 2019). The two scenes were also recalled in a later 2009 documentary by Lowenstein entitled *We're Livin' on Dog Food*, named after the 1980 Iggy Pop song.

As had been the case in the 1950s when the European immigrants first settled, and in the 1960s and early 1970s when the young gentrifiers and flat-dwellers moved in, the arrival of new residents in the form of young unemployed punk

Figure 1 The Prince of Wales hotel, 30 March 1996. Source: Shellie Tonkin Collection/Performing Arts Centre, Melbourne.

musicians similarly changed the ambience and culture of a number of these inner city neighbourhoods in the 1970s and 1980s. Rundown houses and flats offered cheap accommodation, and abandoned shops, factories and hotel dining rooms became rehearsal and performance venues, and record and music stores and second-hand book, furniture and vintage clothing shops became staples of then declining retail strips such as Greville Street in Prahran and Brunswick Street in Fitzroy. These rundown shopping strips, along with performance spaces in decaying picture theatres, dance halls and faded pub dining rooms, catered to a genre and generation that revelled in the shock value of dirt, filth and squalor of the semi-abandoned inner city. The strong link between punk music and drug use, especially heroin use, also meant that overt drug-dealing, street sex work and open-air drug use became a common feature of daily life in places such as Fitzroy Street and elsewhere in St Kilda at this time.

The permissive city

Moral issues

As Melbourne's population diversified and became younger in the four decades after the Second World War, not only did new ways of living and relaxing and new forms of culture, entertainment and nightlife emerge, but so too did new attitudes towards sexuality, gender norms, morality and personal behaviour, including some forms of recreational drug use. While previously these things were strictly circumscribed, with laws and customs largely informed and driven by traditional religious ideas and attitudes, from the 1960s and especially so from the 1970s, social and moral norms were at first challenged, then ignored, before being mostly legislatively withdrawn in the 1980s and beyond. Legalized discrimination against Indigenous people was wound back from the 1960s, as was discrimination against people based on race more broadly in the 1970s. Overt discrimination against women, including on the basis of matrimonial status, sexuality and sexual behaviour, dress and pregnancy became socially unacceptable in the 1970s and was outlawed in the 1980s. Access to birth control, as well as broader control over fertility and bodily autonomy, was extended through legal and legislative reform from the 1970s to the 2000s. Abortion became technically legal after a court ruling in 1969, before it was formally decriminalized in 2008. Similarly, in the realm of moral issues and sexuality, sex acts between consenting males were decriminalized in 1980 and discrimination against people based on their sexuality or gender orientation was outlawed in the 1990s and 2000s. Marriage equality (a Commonwealth rather than a State responsibility) was achieved in 2018, but 'registerable domestic relationships', including between people of the same sex, had been legal in Victoria since 2008. Most other forms of overt discrimination have similarly come to be socially unacceptable and illegal, although of course this does not mean it doesn't happen. Nor does it mean that just because women and others may have achieved legal equality, they have achieved equity economically, socially or domestically.

While documenting legislative reforms allows us to create a clear and easily digestible timeline of changing laws on moral and ethical issues, these political and legal processes have often trailed, sometimes by considerable margins, changing community attitudes. And although our sources of knowledge of these deeply personal matters must by definition be fragmentary, we do know that while the so-called 'sexual revolution' is popularly associated with the 1960s, in reality at that time only small numbers of people in Australia and elsewhere openly embraced sexual permissiveness. As historians Frank Bongiorno (2012) and Michelle Arrow (2019) have shown, as recently as the late 1970s, many people (young and old) had quite firm ideas about sex and sexuality, with sexual matters and relationships rarely discussed publicly. Arrow's work on women, relationships and marriage at this time, including the 1970s-era Whitlam government's Royal Commission on Human Relationships, alongside other studies of intimate issues, demonstrates that while these matters were being discussed more openly in certain and other public forums in the 1970s, for most people, especially women, sexual freedom and personal, monetary and bodily autonomy remained (and remain) sites of great contestation. And as Bongiorno's work shows, while there is evidence that some people (and especially younger people) were beginning to more openly and public explore and debate sex and sexuality in the 1960s, it was really only in the 1970s that premarital heterosexual sex became common and widely accepted behaviour, and mostly for couples in long-term stable relationships. Even then, the personal, social and financial costs of straying too far outside narrow moral confines remained high, especially for young women for whom an unplanned pregnancy could have catastrophic consequences. The availability of reliable contraception, especially the Pill, which became more accessible in the 1960s, helped to alleviate some of these concerns, as did sex education and access to information about sex, sexuality and the human body, which became a part of the school curriculum in the 1970s.

Censorship

As with issues of alcohol, fun and personal behaviour, until the 1970s, Australian governments not only sought to control and regulate what citizens could do, but also what they could see, hear and read. As with the prohibitions on alcohol and sexuality, state-imposed restrictions were often heavily influenced by conservative religious voices. While customs management was a Federal government responsibility, States could also censor local or imported materials (or ban them altogether), with State police forces often responsible for enforcement. Conservative Victorian governments and police were until the 1970s vociferous in their enforcement of these rules. Actor and historian John Rickard has noted that officers from the Victorian Vice Squad were punctilious in their enforcement of censorship laws, often with quite comical consequences. In one instance recounted by Rickard, in 1969 theatre impresario Harry M. Miller's Melbourne production of the play *The Boys in the Band*, in which 'all but one of "the boys" in [Mart] Crowley's play are homosexual', 'attracted the attention of the Vice Squad, who chose to prosecute … three actors for using obscene language'. A year later, Melbourne actor Lindsay Smith was fined after being found guilty of swearing and using a racial epithet about an Aboriginal man on stage in the play *Norm and Ahmad*, written by Alex Buzo. As Rickard notes, 'it was the adjective and not the noun which attracted the attention of the police' (Rickard 2005: 28).

As with laws relating to sex, sexuality and personal morality, censorship restrictions began to be relaxed in the 1970s. Bans on the production or importation of books and other literary sources were lifted nationally and within the United States in the early 1970s. As Patrick Mullins has recently documented in relation to the lifting of restrictions on the novel *Portnoy's Complaint*, this was partly in response to concerted campaigns by publishers, booksellers, academic and the literary community (Mullins 2020). A few years later, the introduction of the 'Restricted' (R) classification for films and the Adults Only (AO) rating for television allowed adults to make up their own minds about what they could watch. A similar classification system was introduced for magazines and other print materials in the early 1970s. For many, this meant relaxed regulation of pornography, with sex shops and cinemas becoming a common feature of certain neighbourhoods in the 1970s and 1980s. In Melbourne, the flashing lights and lurid window displays common to these places were notably part of the post-1960s streetscapes of the CBD and St Kilda, until they were chased off by gentrification and technological change in the 1990s. Today, censorship is called 'classification', with adults (and parents and guardians) offered advice on content to help them make up their minds about what to read, watch or download. Most contemporary evidence suggests that the majority of people in contemporary Melbourne are less concerned with the depiction of sex and sexuality on screen and in literature and more so with depictions of violence, particularly sexualized violence.

However, while tolerance of visual and literary displays of sex and sexuality became more acceptable in post-1960s Melbourne, music and musicians – and especially rock musicians – still sometimes found themselves on the wrong side of the censorship divide. While live music performances do not seem to have attracted the same sort of attention from the Vice Squad that theatre performances did, recorded music was (and is) regularly subjected to censorship or outright ban. As in Britain, the Beatles' 'Lucy in the sky with diamonds' was banned from radio airplay because of its supposed links to drug use, while six of the eleven songs on Melbourne band Skyhook's 1974 debut album *Living in the Seventies* were banned from radio because of their overtly sexualized lyrics. Cold Chisel's 1978 Vietnam war veteran's lament *Khe Sanh* was banned ostensibly because of its references to sex and drugs ('Dancing to the Music of the Banned' 2004; Daley 2014). In the 1990s, following US trends, singles and albums deemed to be overtly sexual, violent, misogynistic or thought likely to incite self-harm were not only banned from radio and television but also increasingly subject to classification and labelling with 'parental guidance' advice (Masterton 1998).

Clothes and fashion

As attitudes towards sex and sexuality and personal behaviour changed over time, so did ideas about appropriate forms of dress, for both men and women, and in public and private. Rules about male dress were always more relaxed than for women: up to the mid-1960s, men were expected to wear hats in public and suits to the office, or for organized social occasions such as dances or dinner. However, in the second half of the decade and more so in the early-1970s dress standards changed rapidly, with hats for both genders being the first to go. In the 1970s, the 'safari suit' and the cravat replaced the heavy woollen suit and tie for a brief period for men as did long hair and beards in most workplaces and social strata. For women, rules about appropriate dress had always been more strict and more rigorously supervised. In most circumstances until the mid-

1960s, across the Western world (and beyond) women and girls were expected to dress modestly with gloves and hats mandatory when out in public. Even for shopping trips, especially those involving a journey to 'town', a hat and gloves were required dress. For various reasons these rules were more strictly adhered to in Melbourne than elsewhere in the country. Partly because it was the national centre of the Australian fashion industry, with a more temperate climate and European ambience, the city had long held a reputation as a place where clothes and style were important and where dressing up was an integral part of life. The impact of the arrival of immigrants from the major fashion centres of Europe, many of them Jews and Italians who became important players in the local clothing and fashion industries, similarly meant that sartorial style was an important element of the city's post-war culture.

Other than perennial battles about how much skin was acceptable for women to expose at the beach, tensions in attitudes about style, formality and dress did not always expose differences based on generational, gender or ethnic lines, however. Rather, there was often a class element to these debates. On occasion, generational tensions did play a role, such as in the mid-1960s when English model Jean Shrimpton caused a scandal when she wore a sleeveless mini dress with no stockings, hat or gloves to Melbourne's Derby Day races in 1965. Soon dubbed the 'four-inch furore' (the dress ended four inches above her knee) by the press, the highly publicized image of the youthful, informally attired and 'classless' Shrimpton enjoying the spring sunshine at the races contrasted sharply with that of her fellow race-goers, even the younger ones, who in accordance with Victoria Racing Club Members' area rules were decked out in heavy twin-sets, complete with hats and gloves on an unseasonably hot 34 degree day. As with Ava Gardner's alleged comments about Melbourne six years earlier, the controversy over Shrimpton's dress excited glee in parts of the Sydney media and among journalists from London who had followed Shrimpton and her boyfriend, actor Terence Stamp to Melbourne who used the incident to yet again portray the city as dull and provincial. And again, as with Gardner in 1959, the incident was a source of great anguish for Melbourne boosters, horrified that their city was again exposed as not measuring up to international standards and potentially a global laughing stock. However, as fashion historian Sylvia Harrison (2005) has argued, while the 'furore' was and has been popularly portrayed ever since as indicative of Melbourne (and Australia's) social conservatism, and of a larger generational battle between youth and the 'oldies' (as represented by the Melbourne racing establishment), it was also reflective of larger forces reshaping the international industry at that time. These trends increasingly pitted on one side the expensive and exclusive haute couture fashion houses represented by Parisian designers against the new youth-oriented mass fashions and designs emerging out of 'Swinging London'. While battles about clothes and fashion were rightly or wrongly portrayed as symptomatic of a generational divide in the 1960s, they equally represented an early warning of emerging tensions within the global economy which have emerged in the decades since between older forms of capital-based production of goods to satisfy basic wants and needs, and a newer form, more focused on capturing and commodifying cultural value including ideas, brands and 'lifestyle' goods from increasingly affluent, often younger consumers.

While the 'shock' ethos of the punk era raised some concerns about young peoples' dress in the 1970s and 1980s, in the contemporary city, difference was actively celebrated rather than frowned upon. Other than in some conservative workplaces, very few people care what people wear, whether at work or at play. And while Melbourne remains a fashion centre, most of the clothes and accessories that people wear are imported, rather than produced locally (as used to be the case in the 1970s). As the world globalized in the 1980s and 1990s, successive Australian governments embraced free market ideas, especially around free trade and anti-protectionism. As we shall see in subsequent chapters, the closing down of the textile, clothing and footwear industries freed up spaces for new forms of artistic, design and musical creativity to flourish, especially in the inner city. Yet it also meant that the local fashion industry became increasingly dominated by those global styles, trends and brands that were beginning to emerge in the 1960s. While some local Melbourne brands flourished in these decades, they tended to either pitch to global markets in generic sports and leisurewear (as with Globe International, created by three Melbourne champion skateboarding brothers in 1985) or at niche haute couture markets such as Toni Maticevski, founded by the child of Macedonian immigrants in the city's western suburbs in 1999 (NGV 2021).

As the Maticeviski example illustrates, the migrant influence in Melbourne's fashion industry remains strong. While production costs remain high, low start-up design costs and access to national and global markets through social media mean that newly arrived immigrant and younger designers can establish themselves in the industry, provided they can access space and other supports. In the 1980s and 1990s, support for emerging designers was provided by the State government-financed Fashion Design Council which was closely associated with the St Kilda post-punk scene (O'Hanlon 2018), while more recently immigrant designers have been supported by the Social Studio a social enterprise based in inner urban Collingwood since 2009. Founded as a 'safe place of belonging that strives to create awareness and change public perceptions for people who have experienced being a refugee', the Social Studio draws much of its talent from young African women who, along with their families, now form a large proportion of the residents of the public housing apartment towers built in inner Melbourne in the 1960s. Like the European and Vietnamese immigrants before them, as well as the early baby boomers, the unemployed young artists and musicians and the gentrifiers of the 1970s and 1980s, these immigrant communities are now having an important impact on the demography and culture of Melbourne's inner city (Social Studio 2021).

Conclusion: Free but unequal?

While contemporary Melbourne is extraordinarily multicultural and open to new people and new ideas, tensions still exist between those who believe in more traditional forms of morality and public/private behaviour, cultures and practices, and those who are more comfortable with adults (or the market) deciding these things. For the most part, more progressive ideas and attitudes prevail, with socially progressive governments having been in power almost continuously since the early 1970s. For more than half of that time, governance has been provided by the social democratic Australian Labor Party. Even when conservative Liberal-National Party (Coalition) governments have been in power throughout the 1970s and again in the 1990s, they have mostly declined to undo most of the liberal social policies enacted by their opponents. As such, and as this journey through the city's post-1950s demographic, cultural and social history has demonstrated, the contemporary city differs fundamentally from its older self. Today's Melbourne is more cosmopolitan, more open to new people, ideas and culture than it was in the early post-war years and offers far more entertainment and nightlife options than did the one derided in 1959 as a good place to make a film about the end of the world.

It was in this evolving openness to new ideas and through the acceptance and eventual celebration of different peoples, cultures and traditions that Melbourne developed its current reputation as a music city and as a place welcoming to musicians and their fans. However, as we shall see in a number of the subsequent chapters of this book, while the city is without doubt a more open and interesting place today than it was sixty years ago, the embrace of free market, neoliberal economic ideas since the 1980s, alongside more progressive social ones, has also seen it become a much more uneven place where many people remain economically, socially and culturally excluded. In contemporary Melbourne, Indigenous people, immigrants, women, members of the LGBTQ communities and poorer people still remain far too often marginalized and excluded from the opportunities of the city, including its music, entertainment and nightlife.

3

The live music city

Introduction

As discussed in Chapter 1, a substantial part of Melbourne's claims to 'music capital' status lies in the consistent strengths of its live music sector. Since federation, the city had provided good dance halls and club circuits for various dance and jazz bands (Horne 2019). As we shall see, popular music scenes after the Second World War in the city had to contend with the increasing attention paid to the gradual emergence of rock and roll (and related media programs devoted to it), and accompanying changes to (and perceptions about) youth culture; we zoom in on venues or artists in particular periods in order to encapsulate these broader shifts. While this chapter charts key acts and known scenes, it is certainly not exhaustive: we are more interested in how industry and policy structures were constructed to accommodate the growth of a proper set of pop and rock industries.

Notions of an 'Australian' network of venues, media and recording became more evident, particularly from the 1960s. Yet we are also interested in the ways that State and city variations prevailed beyond everyday Australian experiences. The development of Melbourne's live music sector has provided distinctive infrastructure and experiences, ranging from venue structures and liquor laws to how rock/pop could be envisaged as 'leisure' by policy-makers and politicians through the week and on weekends. As with other city histories (e.g. Cohen 2007), Melbourne live music histories were informed and provoked by local parochialism. This entailed a series of fears: that (initially at least) Melbourne venues were not as vibrant as those in Sydney, and that Melburnians were not keeping pace at different periods with international perceptions of a 'good night out'. In this sense, much of the history mapped here overlaps considerably with parallel debates about dining and drinking, public order and just how much of a night-time economy its city residents would be allowed.

Beginnings

Indicating a form of reverse cultural cringe, in January 1955, *The Sun* announced that Frank Sinatra would perform on 17 January. The article was not the usual fawning homage to international sophistication, labelling 'Frankie' a 'pretty surly sort of crooner' whose 'singing style is his own … but extraordinarily effective' (Turnbull 1955: 6). Brought to Melbourne by (Sydney-based, US-born) entrepreneur Lee Gordon, the subsequent series of daily ads placed in local newspapers assuring that good seats were still available revealed perhaps a growing desperation on Gordon's part that Melbourne audiences were not keen on 'Frankie's' comeback tour. Melbourne became part of the Gordon circuit, touring acts such as The 4 Ink Spots and Nat King Cole, featuring Sydneysiders (e.g. Norm Erskine, Edwin Duff) in support slots. As he had done with Sydney musicians and audiences, Gordon's 1957 'Big Show' of Bill Haley and the Comets, The Platters, Freddie Bell and the Bell Boys, Laverne Baker and Joe Turner confirmed to local teenagers that the shift to rock and roll was on.

This shift, of course, was a matter of degree. Melbourne enjoyed a lively club and town hall circuit as extensions of post-war entertainment dominated by local dance bands. As in Sydney, many of the local musicians had substantial training in jazz and swing bands. In the early to mid-1950s, the city's premier jazz players (including Frank Traynor, Len and Bob Barnard, George Watson) formed loyal followings at sites such as Club 431 (St Kilda Road), Ormond Hall, the Atherton Club (Oakleigh), Jazz Centre 44 and the Palais Royale (St Kilda) (Horne 2019: 71, 86–8).

In contrast, cabaret venues were attempting to maintain standards, where 'Jitterbugging is banned, and so are "cuddle sessions"' ('No Cuddling on Dance Floors' 1950), while Melbourne dancers were usually well behaved, 'anything could happen in Sydney'.[1] In 1953, newspapers were commenting on the (adverse) influence of North American popular culture in signifying a 'square dance craze' ('Dangers in Liquor Bill' 1953). The cabaret promised a different setting; according to the proud owner of Ciro's, opening in October 1950, the new theatre-restaurant was modelled on the Diamond Horseshoe nightclub in New York 'on the lines of relaxed and quite good taste'; the venue was already eyeing clientele for the Olympics in 1956 (Cabaret theatre brightens city 1950). Ciro's was one of the first venues to engage indigenous singer Georgia Lee, who had relocated from Cairns and became a star on local circuits, including stints at supper dance club Claridges and a two-year contract at Ciro's.

The looming Olympics was also gradually shifting perspectives on six o'clock closing. From 1951, the State parliament began debating 'other Continental' ways to increase drinking environments without lengthening pub hours ('Late Hours Not Olympic Spirit' 1952). This entailed calls from theatre and cabaret owners for extended trading into the early hours. Others with formative experiences from elsewhere attempted a different ambience. Apart from the Moulin Rouge in Elwood, the Maas Continental Restaurant and Cabaret opened in September 1954, a venture of Helen and Robert Maas, Austrian and Polish immigrants. The attempt to produce a refined setting for dining and music based on 'Continental' principles marked a departure from their shiny CBD counterparts and influenced later entrepreneurs and performers, not least their young son Henry:

> They ran the Victory cafe, a European cafe, and there weren't many of those around, they pulled the building down and built the cabaret ... I could hear the music coming up through the floorboards [upstairs] and it influenced my whole career [as venue owner and musician] ... the live bands they had there were jazz and Latin American combos.
>
> (Maas 2020)

Other future performers who could identify with the break from post-war traditions sensed opportunities. This meant parental approval (and finances) to obtain the necessary equipment. Ian Allen's experience is typical of those we interviewed:

> My mother played piano, and we lived in Elwood in a very big house in Scott Street, and in the lounge room there was a grand piano ... And then came the '56 Olympics, and the television, and we had the first and only television in the street, so the lounge room became like a little theatrette, and mum would play a bit of music and away we'd go. And then I sort of took an interest in trying to play guitar – if I got a guitar, could I play it [aged 12]? This was influenced by music around the time of the Olympics of Elvis, Chuck Berry, Little Richard, Jerry Lee Lewis, those guys; there was no Australian guys that I was aware of on the radar then. And things just sort of snowballed from there.
>
> (Allen 2017)

Moving from earlier bands such as The Saints, The Ramrods and The Silhouettes (containing the later rhythm section of Daddy Cool and teaching a young Wayne Duncan bass), Allen replaced the bass player for The Planets, and was playing around the city at the age of sixteen.

Local experiences of US and British artists were confirmed by international touring, starting with Lee Gordon's multi-artist 'Big Shows' in January 1957, bringing Bill Haley and the Comets to West Melbourne Stadium. As Melbourne (and Australian) audiences gained access to overseas recordings, early venues that did exist catered for the gradual conversion from variety/dance to rock and roll. According to emerging singer Marcie Jones:

> They were usually old picture theatres. So you'd go down underneath, they'd take up all the seats, so they had great flooring, good for dancing, where they showed the picture, there was this huge, big stage ... [and] the huge dance floor, and it was so fantastic. And you had to be able to [jive] dance or learn pretty quickly ... the boys would come up to you and say, 'Do you want to dance?'; and if they didn't ask you like that, you'd say, 'No thanks', because we knew they couldn't dance that way ... No booze, just soft drinks.
>
> (Jones 2017)

Changes within venues didn't seem inevitable. Dances maintained the practice of rotating singers with designated house bands at a town hall or theatre, while older music traditions also had to be observed:

> So it was 60/40, so you'd have 40% foxtrots and waltzes and things like that, and then the other 60% would be rock and roll ... I started going to the dances when I was about 15 and my girlfriends Jo and Glenda, they were like my sisters ... The first dance we went to was Canterbury Ballroom and The Thunderbirds were playing ... My girlfriends went up to Malcolm Arthur – he was compering and singing with The Thunderbirds – and they said, 'My girlfriend sings. Can she get up and sing a song?' and of course, they get that all the time from girls. Probably half of them are awful, but he said, 'If she wants to, she can audition on a Saturday'. So I went down and I auditioned on the Saturday and sang 'Robot Man' and 'Lipstick On Your Collar' and got the job, and I sang with the T-Birds for about 15 months or something and Ivan Dayman ran that dance.
>
> (Jones 2018)

By the late 1950s, there was a good circuit of city and suburban dances including the Circle Ballroom at Preston, the Earls Court Ballroom at St Kilda, the Arcadia Ballroom, Thornbury, the Pascoe Vale Town Hall and the Coburg Town Hall. This often involved 'a Glenn Miller-style band, and then we would be playing popular music of the day and old rock and roll stuff adapted to the tempos that were necessary for barn dances and foxtrots and stuff like that' (Allen 2018). As unlicensed venues, the innocence of such events was not lost on performers: 'you still took refreshments in drum cases into them; wasn't any good for the punter, but it was pretty good for the muso' (Allen 2018).

In October 1953, concerns were raised about a general increase in licensing offences in general, and the number of offences linked to supposedly unlicensed town hall dances in particular ('Dangers in Liquor Bill' 1953). At the same time, publicans, fearing the attractions of theatre and cabaret venues, increased their calls for 10 p.m. closing and 'dancing in hotels' (ibid.). This was given a new urgency with the increasing likelihood of 10 p.m. hotel trading in NSW. In March 1956, the 'No' vote resoundingly won a Victorian referendum on 10 p.m. closing, with only six (out of sixty-six) electorates for the 'Yes' case ('No Late Drinks for the Games' 1956). Melbourne Town Hall was also commandeered by stations 3UZ and 3DB for lunchtime shows, providing fans with daytime opportunities to see their favourite artists, including Mike Brady with the Phantoms:

> The first show I did with The Phantoms I finished and Bruce Stewart came up to me and he gave me this roll of money and it was £13, and the average wage in those days was £17 and I couldn't believe it ... So I went and bought my mum an iron, I bought her some toaster-type thing, and I bought all these little appliances for my mum, because I'd never seen money like that. My dad earnt £17, and that was exactly how it was in those days.
>
> (Brady 2018)

Reliant upon local copies of the well-known instrument brands, musicians were frustrated with the lag in getting their hands on decent instruments. Local bands' sounds were

> Primitive. The Planets were the first rock band that worked at Sydney Myer Music Bowl, and at that time no instruments were miked up, the guitar amp was 15 watts, and people were complaining about the volume. You'd say 'what?' ... I had to get a home-made bass because I played left-handed, I couldn't get one, and I had a bass amplifier made by Peter McCarthy brand Maxim in Bridge Road, and he made the amplifier and the speaker ... But things changed. As the music shops were more willing to bring in better instrumentation, up went the standard of stuff. When the first Fender guitar came to Melbourne it was like something from heaven, it was amazing.
>
> (Allen 2018)

Figure 2 The Thumpin' Tum, 1 November 1965. Source: News Ltd/Newspix/Performing Arts Collection/Arts Centre, Melbourne.

'Go-go where?'

The cabaret spirit of the 1950s – in terms of trading hours and club-like environments, if not actual licensing laws – was to be found later in the emergence of Melbourne's discotheque scene from the mid-1960s. According to a *Four Corners* investigation of Melbourne youth culture ('Go-Go Where?'), by 1966 the city possessed 'around 40 discotheques', evidence of the city's status as 'pop capital of Australia' ('Go-Go Where?' 1966). Unlicensed, and attempting to reflect the decor of London's 'swinging clubs',[2] this circuit comprised venues such as the T.F. Much Ballroom at Cathedral Hall in Brunswick Street, Fitzroy, Bertie's on the corner of Spring and Flinders Streets and Sebastian's in Exhibition Street. This subset of venues – along with others such as the Thumpin' Tum (Little La Trobe Street), the Biting Eye (Little Bourke Street), Opus (Ormond Hall, South Yarra), Pinocchio's (Toorak) and the Mad Hatter (Little Lonsdale Street) – provided bands with a useful circuit, allowing two to three short sets per night at different times and places. An early mover was the Fat Black Pussycat on Toorak Road in South Yarra, which converted from its jazz roots to operating as a discotheque from 1963 to 1966.

With his brother Phillip, Anthony Knight established Sebastian's at 335 Exhibition Street in 1967. Operating six nights per week from 9 p.m., the venue made the most of its three levels: a stage/dance floor on the ground floor, a second level that served coffee and crumpets and a more intimate third floor performance space for bands. Alternating between playing the latest discs and live bands, Sebastian's became an important focal point for Melbourne performers and local youth looking forward to a stylish night out:

> On opening night, the queue went all the way around to Russell Street. The police came around, and asked what was it? We said 'discotheque' ... We didn't have any [permits], nobody knew what they were, legislation didn't cover that sort of thing ... [our clientele was] nice people, nice girls from nice schools – Daddy would drive them in and drop them off, which attracted nice boys; it was a pickup place ....
>
> (Knight 2017)

Travelling to the United States and then Europe, co-owner Anthony Knight did not see anything too different to Melbourne's music nightlife, believing it to be unique in its combinations of unlicensed fun that 'flew under the radar' of health and other city/State authorities (ibid.). All venues had to deal with pre-primed punters who had done their drinking until 10 p.m. at the pub, and the range of drugs on offer. A surprise visit one night from State Premier Henry Bolte and the Police Commissioner went unrewarded, according to Knight, as they could not align breaches with a venue that had no liquor licence or related permits (ibid.). Leveraging the success of Sebastian's (managed by brother Phillip), Anthony managed their second enterprise, Bertie's at Spring/Flinders Streets (with later AC/DC manager, a young Michael Browning, as band booker at Sebastian's).

Another three-storey venue at Flinders Lane, the Catcher, was very different in terms of venue policies, entertainment and its primary clientele. Established by Graham Geddes and Peter Raphael in 1967, the venue provided a looser environment for experimentation away from the pop charts. As a New Zealander seeking a breakthrough with successive Melbourne bands, Mike Rudd found the Catcher to be different:

> There was a graveyard shift you could play from midnight till whenever, which I think The Chelsea Set seemed to do a lot ... The Purple Hearts and so forth, Jeff St John and The Id ... Chants R&B, as we were then, certainly weren't progressive and were never labelled as such. We were kind of wild – we were trying to do The Pretty Things thing, if you like, just be a little wild, but our repertoire was a bit wide to actually make that convincing ... I know Broderick Smith [The Dingoes, Carson, Broderick Smith's Big Combo] mentioned that he used to see us at the Catcher and we used to do a lot of John Mayall stuff, and his particular favourite was 'Life Is Just a Slow Train Crawling Up a Hill'.
>
> (Rudd 2017)

In contrast to the 'nice' clientele of Sebastian's and Bertie's, the Catcher attracted a younger mix, with sometimes different clusters of Melbourne youth at different times of the night. It was also different in Graham Geddes' determination to provide poetry nights, film screenings and invoke a weekly club atmosphere, seeking to avoid the 'pretentious' environment of other discotheques, where his venue attracted clientele beyond the usual inner city suburbs:

> We got them from [outer suburbs] Wattle Park, North Essendon, Carrum Downs. All the Bertie's and Sebastian's people, they all came from Toorak, Armadale. And when they came, they usually came later on [in the night], they had a different way of dancing, different airs and graces ... The people who went to Sebastian's didn't like the people who went to the Catcher, and the people who went to the Catcher didn't like the people who went to the [Thumpin'] Tum.
>
> (Geddes 2018)

From late 1966, media reports revealed concern at the rise of the unlicensed discotheques, with a 'brawler van' patrol established by police in October 1966 (*Melbourne Herald* 1966). Where the Bertie's/Sebastian's enterprises escaped regular scrutiny, the Catcher encountered a series of battles with media, police and State government departments. This included Licensing Court

Disco owner resigns as headmaster

Schoolteacher Mr. Graham Geddes, under fire over his City discotheque, The Catcher, yesterday resigned from the Education Department.

"I don't want to resign, but it's obvious I'm under pressure," Mr. Geddes said. "The Minister for Education (Mr. Thompson) says in this morning's paper he is waiting for me to go.

"I was most definitely happy teaching school. I'm not interested in being anything else, but it's quite obvious I have to give it up."

Mr. Geddes, 29, the father of three children under four, has been running The Catcher discotheque at weekends while serving during the week as head master to 50 children at Macclesfield State school, near Emerald, 36 miles east of Melbourne.

The Catcher, in Flinders Lane, was described by police in the Licensing Court on Tuesday as a place where girls took drugs and couples "kissed and fondled" in the dark.

Judge Fraser refused The Catcher liquor permits.

"The licences were intended purely for private functions," Mr. Geddes said yesterday. "We hire out on other nights of the week to adult groups."

Off the streets

Mr. Geddes runs The Catcher with Graeme William Gow, another school teacher, handling his finances.

Mr. Geddes said: "In opening The Catcher we wanted not only to supplement our incomes but to give the kids a big, clean, well supervised place, so they could be safe off the streets after the other discos close at 2 a.m.

"My attendants were recruited from an organisation called Dance Supervision run by a competent young fellow, Bob Johnson."

The Catcher employs eight bands and draws 1000 young people on Saturday nights. Mr. Geddes said his staff discouraged misconduct but in any dance anywhere "one or two will kiss and cuddle."

"As a teacher of 12-year-olds I can recognise those under age and I wouldn't consider letting them in," he said.

"It is unlikely a kid of 13, 14 or 15 is mature enough to cope with being out so late."

Mr. Geddes said he watched the door and barred entry to "anyone I see who's too young.

Of these rival halls whose customers have been flowing to The Catcher, Mr. Geddes said: "All are run exceedingly well."

The ex-schoolmaster added: "That's about it — the end of my career, I've nothing more to say."

Would he launch more discotheques now he's stopped teaching? "There's no security in it," Mr. Geddes said.

Minister's view

Other city discotheques include the Thumping Tum, The Chateau, run by a Frenchman, the Prince Albert Sebastian and the The Garrison.

The Minister for Education (Mr. Thompson) said last night he knew nothing of suggestions that any official of the Education Department had suggested that Mr. Geddes resign.

"I got the idea he decided to resign himself," he said. "A teacher is supposed to get permission before he takes any other job. Then the question arises if this is suitable employment for a teacher.

"This is not the sort of thing I would expect a teacher to do.

"I don't think a teacher in charge of young children should be in this type of business."

Mr. Geddes' resignation arrived at Mr. Thompson's office late yesterday. The officer in charge of the city police district (Superintendent Hickey) said last night police included all city discotheques in their regular patrols.

"We are quite aware of their activities and the need for supervision," he said. The Director of Primary Education (Mr. John Cole) said Mr. Geddes resignation would take effect from today. A relief teacher would go to Macclesfield today to replace him.

Wheat farmers need rains

CANBERRA.— Wheat planting in Victoria for next season's crop was in "quite a threatening position," the Australian Wheat Board chairman (Dr. A. R. Callaghan) said yesterday.

Victorian wheatgrowers needed rain badly, Dr. Callaghan said, but South Australian wheat farmers were in "an even worse position."

However, good crops were expected in New South Wales—apart from some dry southern areas—Queensland and Western Australia.

"Sales made last week by the board brought the total overseas sales for the season to 277 million bushels," he said.

"With another five months to go before the end of the crop year on November 30, and with prospects for further sales quite promising, the board is now confident the season's carryover will not be excessive, but of reasonable and managable proportions, except in NSW.

Figure 3 Graham Geddes resigns his teaching role as criticism of the Catcher increased, *The Age*, 29 June 1967. Source: Fairfax/Nine.

suggestions of overcrowding and accompanying fire risks, with evidence of drug-taking, prostitution and periodic violence ('Discotheques need control' 1967) and accusations of the venue harbouring escapees from State wards, attendees as young as twelve, 'heavy petting' and lacking in proper ventilation (ibid.). From mid-1967, *The Truth* newspaper mounted a campaign, writing to the Chief Engineer and Police Commissioner asking them to cite reasons as to why the venue shouldn't be closed down (Chandler 1967). On 28 May, Geddes objected to the newspaper's photographer taking photographs of patrons asleep at tables. A City Court judge found Geddes guilty of assault and placed on a good behaviour bond ('Catcher Owner Gets Year Bond' 1967). Of more immediate concern to Geddes, *The Age* made much of the fact that his primary job was Headmaster at Macclesfield High School. Questioning whether discotheque management was a suitable occupation for an educator, the Minister of Education called for Geddes' resignation ('Disco Owner Resigns as Headmaster' 1967).

The increasing bouts of violence, and signs of increasing drug usage, became difficult to manage, exacerbated by other incidents between bouncers, and older males looking for fights, led to the demise of the venue (Geddes 2018). After this, Geddes sold the venue, which continued to exist (with a later different name, Traffik) from 1969 to 1971. While the Catcher was 'pretty wild' (Geddes 2018) in terms of ambience, music and its mix of punters, it was unique in its owner's attempts to institute a broader welfare policy towards his dancers, making links to other cultural activities that extended to inculcating a sense of responsibility among its youth. The end of the discotheque scene was evident by 1972, when the Knight family sold their city venues, witnessing changes in music genres, (fewer) clientele and fashion (Knight 2017).

As a tribute to what was already a simulacrum (London clubs paying homage to Victorian era stylization), the Melbourne discotheque era could not entirely recapture British feeling, especially without the added sophistication of a (legitimate) drink. Yet it was a novel solution for youth caught between the fading glories of the original town hall circuits, and the later introduction of pop and rock with 10 p.m. closing for pubs. The State had some cause for concern about venues that fell between the usual approved structures, especially with the time-honoured tradition of overcrowding (for example, the Catcher was licensed for 400 people, but regularly housed over 1,000 punters nightly). Yet the success of the discotheques presented councils and State governments with a visibility of youth who were prepared to engage in the trappings of perceptions of an international club scene, which at times was welded to local concerns of school children alcohol consumption, drug use, violence and sexual activity, with the call in 1967 that 'discotheques need control' ('Discotheques need control' 1967). Just as importantly, the astonishing number of venues by the late 1960s provided bands with the security of good live work, supported by consensus in media reports that Melbourne (and not Sydney) was driving innovation, where the discos allowed for diversity of approaches. In turn, the continual Sydney-Melbourne rivalry was supplemented by more interstate acts (such as the Twilights) seeking out the city, or moving permanently, in search of better wages. For some fans in other cities, there was frustration and a sense that they were on the outside of a 'scene' looking in (*Go-Set* 1967).

Ballroom baby boomers

An examination of performance opportunities away from the pub circuit is perhaps more representative of the considerable changes within post-war Melbourne. The successive waves of immigration in the 1950s and 1960s produced another set of baby boomer youth who were highly aware of their generational roots, but also keen to plug into available local music. Building on events in town halls in the 1950s, a healthy Italian subculture developed in the 1960s linking local Italian media and live ballroom performances that straddled Italian heritage with Anglo-American pop and rock. Bands found work at function rooms (Buonesara Hall in Newmarket, Torino Studios in East Brunswick, Pitrone's Reception rooms in Clayton), cabarets (Campari restaurant, the Madrid Cabaret, New Paris Cabaret, Piccolo Mondo in Bourke Street, Il Capuccino at St Kilda) and even motels (the Palmlake Motel in Albert Park, the Park Royal motel in Parkville) (Whiteoak and Scott-Maxwell 2010: 303–4). By 1970, Whiteoak and Scott-Maxwell estimate that over thirty 'cabaret ball' venues existed offering different mixes of MCs, floor shows, instrumentalists (e.g. accordionists), traditional song and Italianized versions of current pop chart hits (ibid.: 304). The former Adelphi cinema, the San Remo ballroom in Carlton which opened in 1967, was a centrepiece of the *balli italiani* circuit that also included the Catania ballroom in Thornbury (Carlton, Fitzroy, Brunswick, Coburg and North Melbourne were favoured places of settlement for first and second generation Italian migrants).

Preceding the turn to rock and roll for some, Ugo Ceresoli's Club Mokambo Orchestra was successful within fairly lucrative ballroom/cabaret circuits. A key vocalist with Mokambo, Jo Lawrence, remembers the vitality of the scene:

> I sort of fell into it. When I was singing with Mokambo Band we did Latin, French. Maybe it's a wedding: they'd say, 'the bride comes from Turkey' – so you'd learn. I'd always try to understand the words I was singing so I could put feeling into it. And I enjoyed the challenge of doing it. I got up to about 11 or 12 languages – mind you, some were one song ... The Mokambo Orchestra was very popular in those days. Not just within the Italian community, most of the guys who went were Italian, but the girls were Aussie, English, Polish etc. I think they were girls who liked Latin type guys and they were good dancers – much better than the Aussie guys. Always crowded, fun nights ... Ugo used to have floor shows ... competitions like Mr Brutto (ugly), spaghetti eating .... [and the band] could be anything from 7 to 13 piece (ibid.).[3]

The Mokambo Orchestra played combinations of mambo, cha cha cha and even calypso and Twist songs. The effort to be contemporary was not always welcomed: 'We played what was popular; I remember singing some songs I hated, such as Johnny O'Keefe's "Move, Baby, Move"' (ibid.).

Another contemporary act well known to Lawrence, Sergio G and the Flippers, is a useful example of the integration of multicultural influences in new settings. Born in Pisa, Tuscany in 1941, Sergio Giovanni arrived in Melbourne in 1960, establishing Sergio G and the Flippers as a local band in 1967. Drummer Joe La Greca left school at fifteen to begin his career with the band; guitarist Sam Manuelle[4] had enjoyed an earlier career with the Avengers, joining them at eighteen and perfecting his rock and roll sound through covers of Elvis, Cliff Richard and the Shadows, Chuck Berry and Buddy Holly; the band also supported acts as diverse as the Strangers, Olivia Newton John, Merv Benton, Johnny Chester and Pat Carroll. Managed by Sergio, and augmented by keyboard player Raffaele Pterilli, the Flippers' first gigs were residencies, playing six nights a week at restaurants: first at Mario's, and then the Palmlake Motel and the Pickwick in Toorak. They soon found work on the larger hall and ballroom circuit, headlining *Grande Ballo* nights at Broadmeadows Town Hall, the Catania ballroom or *Grande Serata Danzante* at Moonee Ponds Town Hall. Most advertisements also featured the catering service employed (usually buffet style), and the floor show feature artist, with admission of $1.50. The band's success is indicated by their ability to play at fan club pizza and 'BYO' nights at the Copacabana Hall in Brunswick. The San Remo ballroom at Carlton was a favoured gig, and the band quickly went full-time: 'We were working 4 hours a night with our suits on … and getting more [in one night] than the worker's [weekly] wage … the venues were always packed out' (Manuelle 2020).[5] For punters still finding their feet in Melbourne, the dances were also a good place to find marriage partners:

> A lot of singles would get up on the dance floor and that's how they would meet – it was very strict in those days. Quite a lot of people come up to me and say 'that's where I met my wife/husband'
>
> (Manuelle 2020)

The band played Italian standards such as 'Volare', 'Quando, Quando', 'Girando Il Mondo' and took requests, including popular 'wedding numbers' (ibid.).[6] After his earlier rock career, Manuelle describes his Flippers guitar style as 'sentimental with fill-ins … a Continental feel that wasn't rough, but melodic', and often imitating mandolin picking styles (ibid.). Even in 'cosmopolitan' Melbourne, obvious difficulties existed in maintaining links with Italian charts and popular song. The Flippers overcame this via a brother of a band member

Figure 4 Sergio G and the Flippers. Source: Sam Manuelle Collection.

recording Italian festival and radio/TV hits and mailing cassettes to Melbourne, ensuring the band was ahead of other local acts in delivering 'local' authenticity (La Greca 2020). Song contests assisted artists in establishing reputations and professional work. Sergio G and the Flippers won the Festival of Italian Song in 1983 with 'A Prestito del Tempo', a song written by Ugo Ceresoli.

Melbourne media was important for promotion of acts and venues. This included stories and advertisements placed with *La Fiamma* and *Il Globo* newspapers. The Flippers were also the house band for the *Carosello* program on Channel 0 from September 1968 that enjoyed a solid following with Melbourne audiences (the program had begun with another house band, Trio Franco, in December 1967) and continued later on Channel 7 to the end of the 1960s. Produced and financed by Franco Cozzo, the local furniture retailer also was key in the Flippers obtaining a recording contract with the W&G label, releasing ten singles and one album between 1968 and 1972 that gained airplay on both Italian media and rock stations 3XY and 3KZ. *Carosello* was a vital program for Italian-Australians, representing in some respects the liveliness of local performance circuits, and bridging traditional and pop aesthetics.

By the mid-1970s, the restaurant, town hall and ballroom circuit had petered out; dining and band packages had declined in popularity, often

Figure 5 Advertising a Flippers gig at the Copacabana, Brunswick, 1969. Source: Sam Manuelle Collection.

replaced with Italian disco nights. Sergio G and the Flippers staged a successful reunion performance at the San Remo ballroom in 2010, with 540 people dancing and dining, 'with another 300 on the waiting list' (Manuelle 2020), evidence that musicians and audiences were keen to remember when new migrant communities took matters into their own hands to ensure a dynamic hybrid of genres and traditions. Much has been made of later Australian DIY rock circuits; yet in 1960s Melbourne, a thriving conglomeration of caterers, agencies, venues, highly proficient musicians and eager audiences provided visibility for Italian-Australians well before official policies and discourses of multiculturalism.

Pub rock

The Bolte State government had taken its time throughout the early 1960s in responding to calls for extended hotel trading hours. This included a European study trip of licensing regulations by the Licensing Court Chair in 1960, and a two-year Royal Commission (1963–64) that made clear that the older hotels functioning as drinking saloons and accommodation stops for travellers were extremely outdated. With the arrival of 10 p.m. closing on 1 February 1966, hotels reconsidered their entertainment options.[7] For many, the economical path lay in presenting cabaret-lite fare with the provision of meals, floor shows and dance bands. Just in case youth did not get the message, one co-owner of five suburban hotels argued that bouncers would have to be employed to 'keep out the long-haired kids. Once we serve these kids, we're stuck with them' ('Night Life, 1966').[8] Further changes – the Liquor Control Bill of 1968 – allowed hotels to apply to trade to 3 a.m. and an extension of theatre trading. Outside of the cabaret culture in the inner city, which had enjoyed longer trading hours, these changes set the foundation for a general acceptance of drinking/entertainment options into the early morning.

By the early 1970s, earlier investments in stages, dance floors and other entertainment trappings shifted to use by rock bands (and not dance bands). The Matthew Flinders Hotel (Chadstone), the Village Green (Mulgrave), the Whitehorse Inn (Nunawading), the Croxton Park Hotel, the South Side Six (Moorabin) and the Waltzing Matilda (Springvale) formed the nucleus of a suburban circuit. For those who had enjoyed the opportunities to experiment in the discotheque era, such as Mike Rudd, the shift could be profound:

> [Spectrum] were playing at these unlicensed clubs like Bertie's and Thumpin' Tum and then all the opportunities started to arise in pubs, and we were ill-equipped to actually play pubs ... We were a sit down and listen band, and people on beer don't sit down and listen, so I thought 'we're going to have to do something dramatic here', and that's when I formed the alternative band, The Indelible Murtceps, and we played different material and used smaller equipment, but, to the casual observer or listener, we would probably be as unfathomable as Spectrum were in the first place.
>
> (Rudd 2017)

The rise of the pub circuit brought inevitable clashes with the suburban idyll. 'The beat of the drums' was clearly audible for neighbours of the Matthew Flinders Hotel, with one Parliamentary Member questioning whether *any* noise should be 'tolerated' from hotels in residential areas (Victorian Legislative Assembly 1972: 1796). A year later, the same Member stated that even after the pub had invested $8,000 in soundproofing, complaints had not ceased, and the venue was now offering bands on Sundays to 10 p.m. (ibid. 1973: 2157).[9]

Located in Greville Street, Prahran, the licensee of the Station Hotel, Frank Stanley, had agreed to allow musician Mark Barnes to book bands on Tuesday, Thursday, Friday and Saturday nights. The list of bands who played during the week included the spine of Australian and New Zealand acts who dominated the decade: Cold Chisel, Skyhooks, Little River Band, Rose Tattoo, Daddy Cool and Split Enz. The hotel was then taken over by a new owner, who (incorrectly) believed that a Theatre Licence was regulatory cover for charging punters $1.50 for pub rock in 1976, a misreading of the appropriate entertainment approval (Blake 1975).[10] In 1977, he was notified by the Department of Health that he required approval to run public entertainment in the main lounge (Rayner 1977). Subsequent alterations to the hotel were completed and approved in 1979 at a cost of $143,000 with a capacity for the entertainment lounge of eighty-nine people (Hicks 1979). This is indicative of the State government's 'catching up' with what was happening in the pubs, with a determination to ensure structures accorded with their purposes. The Station continued pub rock into the early 1980s, and its real value resided in its Saturday afternoon gigs, where bands such as The Dingoes established their core audiences through intimate settings and performances.[11]

In contrast, parliamentarians suggested that under 1975 licensing conditions, establishments with club licences 'could not afford pop stars' in the same fashion (Victorian Legislative Assembly 1975: 5428). In the Legislative Assembly in

1976, the Labor Opposition moved for another inquiry into licensing, citing the continued rise of suburban 'beer barns' and the consequences of youth drink driving to see their favourite pub rock performers (ibid. 1976: 2449). In 1980, the Hamer Government introduced 1 a.m. permits for hotels and restaurants, extended Sunday trading and increased the number of club licences.[12]

A sub-circuit was also developing parallel to mainstream rock gigs. The arrival of punk inspired a surge of DIY gigs, recordings, retail and music-media. As someone who had transferred their loyalties from devout Skyhooks-ism, a teenage Helen Marcou remembers a collision of postcodes and moral codes:

> I was with the 'progressive kids' at Camberwell, and then we moved to a blue ribbon Liberal suburb. It was 1975, the year of the dissolution. The kids at school called me a Communist ... I was immediately ostracised because of my Left political leanings, and so was seeking alternatives. I remember one girl [at school], when I had turned 'punk', sat behind the bushes, throwing berries at me, shouting 'You're an insult to Skyhooks, being into all that punk stuff'.
>
> (Marcou 2017)

Punk bands gained a foothold in venues that were afterthoughts to the regular Oz rock punters, such as the Champion hotel (Berry Street, Richmond):

> At places like the Tiger Lounge ... there'd always be the regulars drinking, who sat there all day long ... we were invading their territory. Upstairs at the Champion [Hotel], there'd be an old guy with big white hair, the quiff, serving beers. Or you think about Graeme Richmond, who ran the [Crystal] Ballroom, or Francis Bourke who was behind the bar at the Tiger Lounge ... very Australian. Gambling, drinking, men's places. It was a changing of the guard.
>
> (McLean 2017)

While Melbourne punters were influenced by the sounds of UK punk (especially the Sex Pistols) and local eruptions happening at the same time (especially the Saints), the dress code of op shop suits and short hair was a local variation that produced 'a bourgeois punk scene – very middle class' (Marcou 2017). The small scale of the original punk circuit meant that regular punters could convince those on the door to give them a shot at a gig. By the early 1980s, opportunities shifted back to venues in or near the city, including the Chevron Hotel (Prahran), the Bombay Rock (Brunswick), the Venue and the Prince of Wales (St Kilda) and the Armadale Hotel. In 1985, the new Labor Government extended cabaret licences from 3 a.m. to 7 a.m. Ollie Olsen remembers distinct punk and post-punk scenes with different methods:

Different sides of the Yarra were represented. [Whirlywirld] were in North Fitzroy with The Primitive Calculators and the Little Band scene sprung out of that. Little Bands were friends who had ideas about making a band that was very short-lived, so just one-off performances, using our equipment. The St Kilda side was more Boys Next Door ... they were very divided movements in a way.

(Olsen cited in Redlich 2020)

The election of the Cain Labor Government in 1982 produced a Premier who was determined to back his Ministers in reforms, including liquor law. In 1984, it announced economics academic John Nieuwenhysen to lead a review of the *Liquor Control Act 1968*. Encouraged by press support, Nieuwenhysen took his role seriously, relishing the job of comparing his experiences of London as a student to the Menzies-era restrictions of Melbourne nightlife. His 1986 Review, and the subsequent *Liquor Act 1987*, broke with the axiom that increased licences and outlets automatically led to public order problems, breaking the rigid dividing line between dining [restaurants] and drinking [hotels]. Determined that the State would adopt a 'European style-approach' that would have 'alcohol de-mythologised', the new Act saw growth in licences from 3,000 to 20,000 licences in just a decade. Contrary to some media campaigns and Liberal Opposition forecasts of a city awash with alcohol, 'the sky hadn't fallen', with the number of liquor licence categories reduced from twenty-nine to six (Nieuwenhysen 2018).

At the centre of the 'European-style approach' was the provision of options for meals and drinks as alternatives to the 'vertical drinking' of the hotels (Nieuwenhysen 2018). The ability of cafes and restaurants to employ the new On-Premises Licence allowed drinking without the provision of a meal. Over time, more cafes and restaurants became jazz bars, or were employing duos through later closing. Other venues provided bands or DJs through much later licences by combining existing cabaret licences with the new General Licence open to non-hotels. New CBD nightclubs (such as Razor, Hard Times, Swelter and Hardware) emerged to take advantage of the new laws (Harden 2009: 151–2).

Conversely, Nieuwenhuysen believed the larger rock pubs to be the antithesis of the emphasis upon diversity: 'I thought the beer barns were absolutely appalling, they were too big to control' (Nieuwenhuysen 2018). The 1986 *Review* made much of 'the new hotels', which were large, attracted substantial crowds beyond their local area, paid licence fees in excess of $100,000 and typically held 3 a.m. entertainment licences (Nieuwenhuysen 1986a: 266–7).[13] For local councils, the new rock pub constituted too much change:

THE AGE, Saturday 25 April 1987

LIQUOR LAW REFORM

Government acts on abuse of alcohol

Reforms to cut cost of obtaining licences

By SIMON CLARKE

The Government will try to restrict the exposure of young people to liquor by refusing to allow alcohol to be sold at cinemas and maintaining the ban on people under 18 years of age selling liquor in bottle shops.

The Government has also decided not to allow alcohol to be sold in milkbars, convenience stores or service stations as part of a bid to reduce young people's abuse of alcohol.

Tests will be carried out on coin-operated breath analysis machines for installation in hotels to decide whether they should be widely introduced to raise drinkers' awareness about the effects of alcohol.

The Government is investigating devices to lock car ignitions if the driver is under the influence of alcohol and the discussion paper released yesterday says that the Government will continue to intensify efforts to reduce road deaths related to drinking.

Under-age drinking will be made the top priority of a new coordinating council to be set up to implement a comprehensive education campaign to tell people about the dangers of alcohol abuse.

Mr Fordham: Community does not support liquor free-for-all.

The new Liquor Act will have as one of its main objects the effective coordination of government and non-government agencies' efforts to control alcohol abuse.

The Government has also decided to continue controlling the number of outlets where liquor can be bought, despite evidence that increasing them does not necessarily increase consumption or abuse of alcohol.

The Minister for Industry, Technology and Resources, Mr Fordham, said that when he announced the Government's planned liquor reforms yesterday "the community does not support a free-for-all where liquor is concerned. Any government that does not ensure that the community's concerns (about abuse) are catered for would be very foolish".

In the discussion paper, the Government says it will continue to monitor the wine cooler industry closely after the removal of 250-millilitre cooler handypacks from the market.

The paper says that if the liquor industry fails to comply voluntarily with proper alcohol advertising standards, the Government will begin talks with state and federal governments "to discuss ways of developing firmer control, particularly over advertisements for alcohol which might improperly influence under-age persons".

The measures aimed at tackling abuse were generally welcomed by the Victorian Association of Alcohol and Drug Agencies, whose president, Mr John Stuart, said it was essential alcohol should not be made more freely available if the abuse problem was to be tackled.

By SIMON CLARKE

The State Government expects to halve the cost of obtaining a full restaurant licence under its planned reforms.

Applicants will not have to be legally represented, or be present at hearings unless the application is contested. Most applications will be settled by filling in simple forms. Government officials estimate this will make the process of seeking a licence to sell liquor in restaurants about half as expensive as it is now.

Some people in the liquor industry believe that if the Government relaxes the standards of restaurant facilities required before they can get a full licence, the cost will drop by more than half.

Under the streamlined licensing scheme, there will be seven licence categories instead of 29. Applicants will be dealt with by a new liquor licensing commission, which will replace the semi-judicial Liquor Control Commission.

Objections to the granting of a licence would be possible only on the grounds that the applicant was not "a suitable person" or where granting a licence would "have an adverse impact on the interests of the community in the area".

The system gives wide powers to the chief executive of the proposed new licensing commission, and does not appear to establish a defined procedure for lodging objections to licence applications or refusals.

Neither does the proposed system set ways of limiting the total number of licences to be granted throughout the state, although the Government has said it wants to retain control of the total number of licensed outlets.

Responsibility for setting the fire, building, health and food standards at licensed premises will be vested in local councils, and the new commission will pass on to councils all documentation relating to these standards from individual applicants.

Nieuwenhuysen 'pleased'

By HUGO KELLY

Dr John Nieuwenhuysen, whose report into liquor licensing last year sparked fierce public debate, yesterday pronounced the State Government's response to his work a victory for common sense.

But liquor industry unions, hotel proprietors and liquor retailers criticised the 66-page response, released yesterday, claiming that jobs and money would be lost if Victoria's new liquor plan went ahead.

Dr Nieuwenhuysen, a reader in economics at Melbourne University, said that the Government had gone part of the way to creating a freer, more streamlined system of liquor sale and consumption. But he said the review did not go as far as he had hoped.

"I am pleased, even though there was justification for a more positive response from the Government in some areas," he said.

Dr Nieuwenhuysen: report a victory for common sense.

Dr Nieuwenhuysen criticised the Government's decision to allow licensed restaurants to sell liquor without meals provided that no more than 25 per cent of the restaurant was devoted to liquor sale.

"Who is going to police that law? It's absolutely nonsensical; there seems to be little way of policing just where this 25 per cent of the restaurant is where alcohol is to be served," he said.

Mr Darryl Washington, president of the Australian Hotels Association, said the review could cause major social, economic and employment problems.

"This is the most revolutionary change in liquor laws in 25 years, and some areas concern us greatly," he said. "We are disappointed to the extent of the changes, which seem to favor other licensed outlets to the detriment of hotels."

Mr Russell Stucki, the managing director of Coles Myer's Liquorland chain, one of Australia's largest liquor retailers, described the review as "a disgraceful misuse of political power".

Mr Stucki condemned the Government's continued limit on the number of liquor licences held by a company to eight per cent of the market.

Figure 6 The Age comments on the licensing reforms. *The Age*, 25 April 1987. Source: Fairfax/Nine.

> What was often a quiet and acceptable neighbourhood amenity too often becomes a brash and noisy entertainment centre operating until the early hours and drawing patrons from many miles away … the present legislation does not effectively recognise this material change of use.
> (North Fitzroy Residents Group cited in Nieuwenhuysen 1986b: 534)

This was reinforced by surveys cited in the *Review* revealing strong support for stricter oversight of pub entertainment (ibid.: 762). The opportunities that these 'new hotels' presented to younger clientele, however, did present diversity to older pub traditions. Another survey cited in the *Review* found '60 per cent of the population agreeing that "public bars are mostly only suitable for men" and only 18 per cent disagreeing' (ibid.: 768). In this sense, the entertainment room offered new spaces for women in particular to ignore the earlier gender 'rules' of the front bar.

Nightclubs

Alternatives to the pub circuit did exist due to the determination of those who drew upon other forms of city and family heritage. Returning from the United States and Europe as a cabaret performer in 1982, Henry Maas leased the apartment on the top floor of a building sited on the corner of Brunswick and Greeve Streets in Fitzroy.[14] Finding no vibrant cafe culture, Maas established the Black Cat Café downstairs with Toni and Brian Edwards, assisted by a $10,000 Tatts Lotto win:

> There were no cafes around the area; the council were betting on how long we would last; we didn't have alcohol until the last few years … The decor was from op shops – tables, chairs, lamp shades … It was full of people at night, because they had nowhere else to go … The music was jazz, Latin American, French cafe music, film music – no rock, no roll, fifties [vibe] (Maas 2020).[15]

Drawing on his earlier experiences constructing cabaret characters and signifying styles from the 1920/30s to 'punk jazz', Maas established the Bachelors from Prague in 1986, a jazz/funk outfit with a Friday residency at IDs nightclub in Prahran.[16] Another simultaneous venture was the Purple Pit in the Champion Hotel, until co-establishing the Night Cat in Johnston Street, Fitzroy. Beginning with a 1 a.m. licence, and eventually gaining a 3 a.m. licence, the former Greek restaurant was converted in the hope of constructing 'a more sophisticated adult place, more funk/jazz orientated; we used op shops to furnish, painted the floors with new designs every 6 months … our only [competition] was the Bullring [with Latin American bands, also situated in Johnston Street]' (Maas 2020).

Maas's professional and personal histories reveal the different intersections of cultures. Earlier memories of his parents' 1950s Maas Continental Restaurant and Cabaret in St Kilda, and its distinctly European sensibilities, were certainly carried through in his insistence that Melbourne should do more to provide artistic communities with interesting food and decor. These intersections are also evident in wider immigrant networks: Mario Maccarone, the co-founder of the Continental Cafe (1993) and Mario's Cafe (1986), managed the Bachelors from Prague. For Maas, 'I didn't see myself as an entrepreneur, I was just following my passions' (ibid.). In comparison to Sydney, 'the city was close'; buildings were available in the right city positions, and were relatively cheap, providing opportunities before later higher costs of rent and ownership (ibid.).

Venues were also able to trade later (past 3 a.m.) by exploiting club laws relating to membership-based environments. Situated in Hardware Lane, the Hardware Club was established by RRR workers Andrew Maine, Paul Jackson and Jules Taylor, who wanted alternatives to commercial discos:

> We started to get really disillusioned about places to go in Melbourne … It was time to put better music into clubs. We didn't want to set up a venue that that tried to please everyone musically – our bias is fairly heavily towards disco and funk.
>
> (Maine cited in Guilliatt 1983)

1960s club veteran Brian Goldsmith was the first to be granted a 7 a.m. cabaret licence for the Underground (King Street) in 1985 (with Inflation nightclub granted one a little later). Not granted widely, the 7 a.m. option was described as the 'most significant change in Melbourne's nightlife since the six o'clock swill' (Guilliatt 1985: 30). Goldsmith was proud of the various innovations in opening the Underground in 1977, including its operations as a member-based club:

> I created a new [drinks ordering] system … we charged them a minimum at the door to guarantee they attended to eat here … we charged $1 an hour which they paid on the way out to drink as much as they liked … They clocked in and out with a Bundy clock … I'd eliminated the stupid shouting system, we had less [problems with] drugs; they drank less.
>
> (Goldsmith 2019)

With a capacity of 400 people, the Underground also established female bouncers at the door, began the TC Club[17] for teenagers on Saturday afternoons and ensured that the sound system was more attuned to the dance floor than other sections of the club, enhancing conversations (ibid.). Queried about the unique drinking payments system, Goldsmith argued to the Licensing Commission that he was operating akin to existing laws for functions (Goldsmith 2019).

Having operated Swelter nightclub, Gavin Campbell opened Razor in 1986, leasing the site (and its private club licence) from the Light Car Club. This meant a membership and guests system similar to the Underground, and became quickly known for its unique DJ mixes of soul, funk, house and disco; and for media and music stars to attend without hassle from the clientele:

> It was close to St Kilda so it drew all the band people in, that was crucial. We knew the space would work. It was like a big old house. It wasn't like a nightclub. It was perfect for us. We put the cocktail bar in upstairs, then we had a projector outside screening the film *Robocop* on the balcony. The summer of 1988 we had a heatwave … Eight weeks in a row of beautiful hot Fridays and the balcony rammed with people every week when the sun came up.
> (co-owner Gavin Campbell cited in Johnston 2012: 48)

Having gained valuable experience in operating Peanuts Gallery (having bought it from Brian Goldsmith in 1976), Sam and George Frantzeskos obtained the Commodore Hotels administration building at 60 King Street to establish Inflation in 1979, based upon a Studio 54 aesthetic (Fleckney 2018: 29–9). According to the Models' Sean Kelly, who worked as an Inflation barman, 'It was a music scene, a dance scene, a fashion scene. It was haircuts, photography, models' (cited in Fleckney 2018: 41). Approved for 438 patrons in total (with 254 in the dance floor basement), it made the most of its 3 a.m. restaurant/cabaret licence before the brothers sold the nightclub and moved on to establish Metro (Bourke Street) in 1987.

Rock at this time extended its strengths in the suburban pub/club circuit: the Chevron Hotel (Prahran), The Club (Collingwood), Her Majesty's Nightspot (South Yarra), the Central Club Hotel (Richmond). Bombay Rock (Brunswick), the Armadale Hotel (Armadale), Prince of Wales and The Venue (St Kilda). Venue bookings nationally were dominated by the Gudinski-owned Harbour (Sydney) and Premier (Melbourne) agencies, the Sydney-based Dirty Pool[18] and Nucleus in Melbourne, who catered more to 'indie' bands and audiences. This arguably represented the peak of success for the more visible bands who toured

Figure 7 The Sports, 1987; venue unknown. Source: Ruth Maddison Collection.

on the back of album releases to an agency circuit of pubs, registered clubs and RSLs:

> There were so many good venues to play, but the downside of that was that groups got fucked up pretty quickly. They were playing too much and weren't as imaginative as they could be. We got really tired, worn down from playing long sets. We weren't like [Cold] Chisel, we were a bit offbeat, poppy and we probably seemed a bit stuck up in those places [the pubs] … It was exploitative, because the agencies could make a lot of money if they just kept you working … If you've got a group that's successful, it's easy if it's all going ok. You just turn up with your worksheet. You didn't have to think at all (the Sports' singer/songwriter Stephen Cummings, cited in Homan 2003: 128).

1990s: Global conversations with local scenes

Live circuits continued to be healthy into the 1990s, particularly in the inner city: Punters Club (Fitzroy), Esplanade Hotel (St Kilda), the Empress Hotel (Fitzroy North), the Tote (Collingwood) and the Royal Derby (Fitzroy). By

1994, *Billboard* was proclaiming inner Melbourne as a central incubator for global stardom, citing a mixture of older and emerging talents: Paul Kelly, Kate Ceberano, Stephen Cummings, the Black Sorrows, Chris Wilson and the Mavises (among others) (Duffy 1994: 1, 24). For journalist/writer Jeff Jenkins:

> When I started to go and see more bands, when I would have been 17 or 18, [it was] the Punters Club on Brunswick Street. Brunswick Street was a real mecca, so certainly the Punters Club opposite the Evelyn Hotel …. You could go and see gigs at both venues, so in between bands you'd shoot across the road to the Evelyn, then back to the Punters Club. That was really exciting.
>
> (Jenkins 2018)

Billboard makes a textbook claim for that of a scene, and how well its interdependent parts work together:

> Still, the most cohesive scene in Melbourne can be found in Brunswick Street, a short distance northeast of downtown. Here, a critical mass of pubs – the Royal Derby, the Punters Club, the Evelyn Hotel, and others – is supported by the Poly Ester [sic] record and book stores, the Fretted Instruments guitar shop, and a seemingly endless string of cafes. As an indie record outlet, Poly Ester is complemented by shops elsewhere such as Gaslight Music and Blue Moon Records. The Brunswick Street vibe recalls such American music districts as Sixth Street in Austin, Texas … Melbourne offers not one, but two public radio stations that support local and alternative music … The latter [RRR] earns particularly high marks among the local scenesters.
>
> (Duffy 1994: 24)

The point is reinforced by maps of St Kilda and Fitzroy offering international readers key venues and other infrastructure, with older players (such as Michael Gudinski) commenting on the longer history of Melbourne as a 'music-oriented' city (ibid.).

Frente! is offered in the *Billboard* piece as an example of the Fitzroy scene's ability to produce global stardom, citing their 'two year' rise 'from the Punters Club Hotel on Brunswick Street to US success on the Billboard 200' (ibid.: 1). Underage, Angie Hart explored the Fitzroy circuit, including the Dan O'Connell Hotel, and her sister worked as a barmaid at the Punters Club, who recommended her to Simon Austin as a singer for a new band. The band's first gigs in 1989 were at the Punters when acts cancelled, playing originals (Hart was 17). Initial success with their first EP meant a place on the Premier management roster:

We were soft and gentle and fitted certain venues. Premier [agency] had a template of how they tour their bands and you are on a roster and you support any of the bands on the circuit. We had an interesting time trying to tailor our gig. We were quite eclectic and people gave us a pretty good go – [there were] only a few gigs when we were a really bad fit. We toured with Hunters and Collectors and with Violent Femmes, which was a pretty good fit, but the crowd were awful.

(Hart 2020)

The band's rapid rise meant a fairly abrupt shift in attempts to capitalize on US/international chart[19] success:

It was really great to do the first couple of EPs. In the studio, we never had anyone looking over our shoulder, it felt really creative. Could be how we felt it might go – inventive, creative ... [Once we started touring overseas] You are gone for 3 to 6 months at a time. We relocated for a while to the UK to make that possible. It was ungrounding. I didn't love it. But, playing to international audiences was great ... The backlash, tall poppy syndrome hit – 'we were dubbed the most annoying band in Australia' – and so it was a great time to leave. There was no internet, so we could just be ourselves and start afresh. UK audiences are pretty tough, very discerning music fans, intimidating but also staunch and regional touring there was exciting ...

I can hear the influences of music I liked [in the early and late 90s] in our songs – for example, harsh insistent guitar, serious drum beats. I've become quite romantic about bands of that era. In the 80s and 90s there was a separatism. When I came back, I felt like Melbourne had worked its shit out – we are a supportive group. Everyone is very supportive and wants to help each other out (Hart 2020).

The global exposure of Frente! made it seem possible that local and 'quirky' had potential, underscoring the scene's alternative credentials. This also applied to indigenous bands, such as Tiddas, where North Melbourne venues allowed for a sense of community (see Chapter 7).

Conclusion

The emergence of rock and roll in the 1950s certainly loosened the prevailing nightlife entertainment options for youth, as had been the case in Sydney, late 1950s town hall circuits revealed that 'harmful'/'harmless' youth leisure also meant the beginnings of a viable career path for aspiring rockers. The input of increasing Southern European migration to Melbourne provided key differences in what live circuits looked like in the 1960s: newly arrived musicians from Italy, Spain or Greece looked to Elvis and the Beatles as much as their homeland stars (and in fact enabled productive careers by blending both influences). Well before punk, the DIY attitude to finding gig spaces provided the city with a structural looseness in allowing scenes and innovation to be fostered. Later, the suburban sprawl of the 1970s introduced the 'new hotel': the monster rock pub that fed the national Oz Rock movement catering to singer-songwriters such as Richard Clapton as much as to AC/DC and Cold Chisel. This was in direct opposition to the 1986 liquor reforms that promised civilized drinking contexts in keeping with the city's self-image as having got the liquor law settings 'right'.

Yet sufficient gaps appeared between law and practice to enable other options. The exploitation of the 'club membership' liquor licence in the 1980s is a good example in converting unlikely spaces into rock/dance clubs. The importance of individual entrepreneurs in different periods (such as Andrew Knight, Henry Maas, Brian Goldsmith, Dolores San Miguel, Graham Geddes) cannot be discounted in their determination to provide something new for fans and musicians. This was a regular refrain from venue owners we interviewed: that a largely unregulated venue sector thrived due to local councils and State government either having little idea what was occurring within the walls of the city's venues or simply not caring too much.

By the late 1980s and into the 1990s, the city's musicians were aware that Melbourne encompassed a series of micro-communities that not only could be packaged and sold internationally as 'vibrant scenes', but also represented a central sense of support and identity. As with other Australian major cities, licensing, noise and planning law had caught up with the live sector. Noise complaints were increasingly recognized as the central problem that the city was not ready to grapple with, given the overriding discourse that venues were 'problems' to be managed. How Melbourne dealt with this is discussed in Chapter 7, along with a discussion of how the idea of Melbourne's connection to music has been constructed in comparison to other places.

4

The media city

Introduction

The relationship between media and Melbourne's music goes well beyond representation. Media are woven into the cultural, political and economic fabric of the city. In this chapter we show how innovations in program formats, organization and media technologies have impacted upon music in Melbourne. In 'music city' discourse, media is generally limited to functions, in terms of tourism, marketing or as part of a 'cluster' where a 'broad artistic, cultural, and entertainment economy can provide demand for musicians' (Florida, Mellander and Stolarick 2010: 786). Mainstream media, however, has not always allowed musicians access to viable incomes; the idea of the 'struggling artist' has been one of the defining notions of urban music (see Chapter 6). In popular music studies this notion is related to 'authenticity': too much media exposure can corrupt artists or lead listeners to consume, rather than appreciate, music and musicians. Authenticity is often counterposed to alienation generated by music-as-media-product.[1] In this chapter, we challenge the functional view of media with regard to popular music by highlighting how innovations within Melbourne's mainstream and alternative media have allowed space for the expansion of musical knowledge and audience. We also address the historical context for the relationship between that city, music and media.

In the early popular music period of swing and jazz during the 1950s, the city's newspapers linked music and vandalism, generating a panic about juvenile delinquency. Radio, and then television, appealed to young consumers – teenagers – and changed the relationship between musicians and audiences. Record sales, not sheet music, became the critical product promoted by marketing. New copyright arrangements for recordings favoured publishers, rather than composers. The consolidation of mainstream broadcasting led to the impoverishment of musicians while becoming battlegrounds for music industry tiffs between Melbourne and Sydney. However, in courting consumers, electronic media also played a role in empowering fans and a youth culture that was open to innovation. Partly in response to increasing broadcasting 'hype', in the 1960s a group of Melbourne university students developed the first national cultural newspaper produced by and for young people. From the late 1970s, hundreds of volunteers, including fans and musicians, worked to promote local music through Melbourne's community media, which were early adopters of digital platforms. Fans also provided new forms of distributing music and knowledge within and about the city. In contemporary pandemic times, mediatized music streaming is crucial to the city's scene, which has been hit hard by health-related lockdowns. The chapter offers case studies of television and radio programs, and discusses print, audio and digital media to reveal formats related to changing historical contexts. It begins by discussing the 'mainstream' context for contemporary popular music before considering how media innovations have influenced music in Melbourne.

Early popular music: Cultural conservatism, media and modernity

As the capital of Victoria, Melbourne shared the State's cultural conservativism. In 1955, state censors banned screenings of *Blackboard Jungle* – the movie that, for Australians, ushered in rock and roll music – despite the Commonwealth film censor being satisfied with edits made to the original film. The Victorian censor argued that the film should be screened to adults only ('Children can't see this' 1955). Public entertainment was a particular focus for conservative values. While in 1955 New South Wales had changed liquor laws to provide for later closing hours, Victoria maintained 6 p.m. closing regulations for another decade. The *Theatre Act* (1958) that prevented places of entertainment opening on Sundays was extended in 1967 to cinemas and music venues through the *Sunday Entertainment Act* (repealed in 1993). In July 1952, young dancers drew attention to the restrictions on Sunday entertainment by staging a 'mass rebellion' street dance. In a tone typical of the time, *The Argus* reported that 'fifty hysterical bodgies and widgies ... jived, jitterbugged and chanted to the rhythm of a juke box' ('Bodgies jived a protest' 1952). A spokesperson for the rebellion 'promised it would be a weekly feature until dance halls were reopened'(ibid). This was one of the few times that reports of popular music provided for a reasoned voice of youth and an early sign that cultural values would be a site for generational tensions.

While the Victorian censor's ban of *Blackboard Jungle* indicates a general concern about how the combination of film and popular music would impact on youth, conservative media's view of music predates the introduction of rock and roll. In 1951 the *Herald* sent John O'Shea into the night to join 'the thousands of young people, mostly in their teens or just out of it, who nightly throng the halls where modern music is played' (O'Shea 1951: 9). The 'popular music craze' O'Shea reported on that night was jazz and swing music. At the Malvern Town Hall, watching jazz trumpeter Paddy Fitzallen, the journalist captured the impact of the music on the Saturday night crowd:

> The dark curly-haired young man standing on the stage raised his silver-plated trumpet to his lips. He tapped lightly with his foot, four times slowly, and breathed a note into the hall. Packed on to the crowded dance floor hundreds of young couples swayed to the slow rhythm of the young man and his orchestra. They did not dance – unless moving from one foot to the other in the same spot is called dancing. The young man with the trumpet blew a high note, they held their breath, and sighed as he came down the register. Then, on a note that seemed to quaver, they wriggled as if he had sent a shiver along each of their spines.

O'Shea's article was generally sympathetic to 'hepcats' and their music, yet his writing demonstrates themes that conservative print media adopted to discuss youth and music in the 1950s. First, there is the idea that young people are in the 'grip of this modern music'. The crowd is enraptured, such that music becomes a sensation that travels throughout the listening mass. Within this frame it becomes legitimate to consider, as O'Shea does, 'what does the music do?' While reflecting a common sense, that music impacts upon audiences, the question belies its class component. Whereas European art music allowed for sublime reflection, modern jazz and swing provided frenzy – an unpredictable unsettledness, characterized by its description as a 'craze'. In these ways, Australia's conservative press justified linking youth, music and a loss of sense.

Secondly, and relatedly, the article conveys the challenging language of youth. Young people's loss of sense is demonstrated by their unintelligibility. O'Shea is just one of a number of journalists that feels they need to explain to their readers the modern, urban language that youth adopt: '"Jive," "Bop," and "Bepop" (sic). "Squares", "Morons" and "Logs" are all uncomplimentary terms for devotees of music other than the "modern" kind. "Bugs", "Hepcats" and "Solid Meat-balls" are modernists. Anyone daring enough to decry the actions of any hepcat is a "Peasant". Later that year, the *Herald*'s police reporter provided an interpretative vocabulary that included: "beachings" (beach parties); "rave on" (talk if you must); and "nothing makes me sick" (I'm still listening) ('A "widgie" describes her cult to a "peasant"' 1951).

Commercial radio, however, catered to the tastes of modern music fans. Radio reflected modern language through using slang and modern idioms; Bob Horsfall called his 3AW modern music program 'Easy does it'. Like many of Melbourne's early media personalities, he came from variety theatre and always maintained close connections to the stage (Horsfall 1993). In 1949 he compered a regular 3KZ 50/50 dance (half old time, half modern music) at the Yarraville parish hall. By 1951, he was 3AW's most popular 'disc jockey'. He presented the *Night Owls Club*, a specialist dance program which, like most radio programs, was tightly managed. *Night Owls* attempted to replicate a dance hall, with fifteen-minute sets consisting of three tunes. In 1953 Horsfall moved to 3UZ and became the busiest dee-jay in Melbourne with a show every night, including an early *Hit Parade* program, a precursor to the Top 40 formats that developed in the late 1950s. 3UZ was the top popular music station in Melbourne until 1958, when Stan Rofe began his innovative broadcasts on 3KZ.

The popularity of post-war musical styles did not stop Victorian newspapers – in particular *The Argus* and *The Sun* – conducting a campaign that linked 'delinquent' youth and music. News reports on the policing of public space showed young people being chased from beaches ('Police declare war on bodgies' 1951), record bars ('Police hunt bodgies and widgies from city store' 1956) and concert halls in the 1950s. This report captures the spirit of the time:

> Jitterbug music sent bodgies and widgies wild at the Melbourne Town Hall last night. 'Splinter' Reeves's swing band was playing 'Blowing Up a Storm' when three policemen came in. Bodgies and widgies had been jitterbugging in the aisles for about an hour before 2000 people who went to hear a jazz and swing concert. The police strode down the centre aisle and were cheered as they quietened a youth in front of the bandstand ... The police stayed in the hall until it was cleared after the concert ended.
> ('"Hepcats" go wild at Town Hall concert' 1953)

The moral panic about music, youth and delinquency was fed by conservative moral opinion (see Bessant 1991; Stratton 1984, 1992). It peaked around 1956: the year television was introduced to Australia. That year, the State government allocated £20,000 for the Youth Organisations Assistance Committee to develop more efficient youth clubs. Dr Fritz Duras, the committee chair, was prominent in the Eugenics Society of Victoria.

The 1956 Olympic Games in Melbourne coincided with the introduction of television. Both these events generated anxiety about social change in the city. Newspapers, in particular, presented themselves as bulwarks for middle-class values against the perceived threats posed by relaxing social hierarchies. Lifestyle and news stories linked the growing economic and cultural influence of the young to American-influenced affluence and moral corruption that, the argument went, was transmitted by a range of non-news media products from comics to films, from radio serials to modern 'jungle music'. Later, in the mid-1960s, as we discuss below, new print outlets and innovative formats in Melbourne television and radio captured this youthful cultural synthesis of audio, image and text. These innovations were born from an incessant attack on youth and its relationship to music in Melbourne's newspapers. Later editors also refused to take popular music seriously. Music journalist Jeff Jenkins, who worked for one of the city's best-selling papers in the 1990s, recalled, 'I had a chief of staff who was kind of like […] "If I catch you writing music stories on my time, I will hit you," [and] he was the type of guy who probably would have punched me' (Jenkins 2018). For Jenkins, the free street papers – *InPress and Beat* – which relied on music industry advertising were more accommodating: 'Most people work their way up from street press to a daily paper or to something bigger. I kind of worked my way down to street press' (ibid.).

By the early 1960s newspaper proprietors had bought into radio broadcasting to manage the competition around news. Radio's immediacy threatened publishing's pre-eminence in information. Consequently, they were happy for radio to focus on entertainment. Photographers were the link between radio and newspapers, taking publicity shots of radio and entertainment personalities for news and lifestyle stories. In the process, several photographers developed reputations for capturing Melbourne celebrities. Laurie Richards, a *Herald* photographer, left a legacy of images that documented 3DB (owned by the *Herald*) and its on-air personalities (now held by Melbourne's Performing Arts Centre). Later, music promoters were happy to facilitate music photography and it became an important genre (see for example Carroll et al. 1991).

Talented teenagers: Media innovations and popular music

If newspapers were intent on presenting an adult point of view, broadcast media catered to the new youth market and provided exciting new career prospects for the young. Far from being unruly, the youth radio addressed was more like the subject of the pop song, 'Teenager in Love'. Although confused, they recognize their social dilemma – 'one day I feel so happy, next day I feel so sad' – and resolve to 'learn to take the good with the bad'. In their entreaty to 'the stars up above', they ambiguously engage a metaphysical, even religious, sentiment while metaphorically acknowledging the romantic authority of new 'stars' of film and other media. In Melbourne, this song was recorded by Heather Horwood, whose career charts the opportunities that broadcasting afforded youth in the 1950s. Horwood also came to radio and television from vaudeville and variety theatre. She began performing at three years of age. By thirteen, she was a regular on the 3DB's popular *Swallow's Parade* which was parlayed into a television program in 1957, when Horwood was seventeen. She appeared on the live music program, *Teenage Mailbag*; mimed hits on a television version of *Hit Parade*; and became the house singer for HSV-7's variety program, *The Sunshine Club*. Her picture appeared in *The Sun*, the *Herald* and on the cover of *Post*. In 1958, she cut two early pop songs, including 'Teenager in Love', at Melbourne's W&G studios. In 1959, at nineteen, Horwood gave it all away to marry (Pennell 2007, 2020).

Radio, as we noted, reflected the voice of youth addressing young people as a specific audience who enjoyed popular music and who would buy dance tickets, records and related products. In early radio, sponsored programs 'blocks' addressed diverse audiences, including women and children, but as arrangements were formalized with content providers, the structure of radio changed. In the late 1950s, sponsored segments gave way to spot advertising that targeted working people and purchasing influencers – generally a woman who was assumed to make decisions about household budgets (Tebbutt 2007). Children's shows were replaced by teenage programming that courted young wage earners. Melbourne radio catered to the teenager more than any other Australian city (Oram 1966: 119). As Michelle Arrow (2009: 64) suggests, 'teenager as consumer undermined notions of teenager as vulnerable or dependent'.

One of the most enduring formations of mutual interest between audiences, music and media is the 'talent show'. Electronic media thrives on public participation and talent shows allowed radio to provide opportunities for new stars to emerge. 3UZ's *Radio Audition* claimed to be the longest running talent show in the world (1943–83) (radio and television star, Barry Crocker, had a start there). Later, in the 1960s with the 'beat band' movement well in place, Hoadley's chocolate bar company combined with a new hip, Melbourne publication, *Go-Set*, to produce an annual Battle of the Sounds. This band talent quest, which lasted until 1972, was an important platform for many of Australia's emerging post-Beatles 'beat' performers. The prize was a trip to London; the catch was that the band played for free on the ship that transported them to the mecca of pop stardom.

Melbourne broadcasters maintained a strong integration of youth and variety programming into the late 1950s. *Swallow's Parade* allowed young pop singers such as Gaynor Bunning and Ernie Sigley (later a popular television host) to begin their careers. In 1957, as Top 40 radio took hold, these variety shows provided some of the earliest youth music programs on television. On Melbourne's HSV 7, Sigley, Horwood and Bunning were regulars on *Teenage Mailbag*, singing songs requested in viewers' letters, although participation tended to be more symbolic than actual as the program producers selected songs to suit the singers (Pennell 2020). One of the earliest live music programs on Australian television, *Teenage Mailbag* aired from 1957 to 1958 and was later expanded to become *The Teenage Hour*. Horwood and Bunning also contributed to *Hit Parade*, but performers did not consider it highly because the songs were mimed (Pennell 2007, 2020). Nevertheless, *Hit Parade* was popular with viewers, introducing music to new audiences. Marcie Jones – who later formed the popular women's group, the Cookies – remembers watching *Hit Parade*: 'My girlfriends and I … when television first came to Australia, we'd watch the *Hit Parade* […] I can remember sitting there and saying, "I'm going to be on television one day and I'm going to be singing and I'm going to do this and I'm going to do that"' (Jones 2017). Rae Dixon also remembered *Hit Parade*, but television was out of reach for her family:

> The local milk bar where we used to meet saw the potential and installed a 14" set for our enjoyment and a large share of our meager earnings. We flocked down and jammed in to feast our eyes on the amateur miming skills of the performers as the top ten was replayed in black and white. All ended up with stiff necks and full stomachs, leaving the shop owner counting his till, bulging with our hard-earned pounds, shilling and pence.
>
> (Dixon nd)

Later, when Rae could afford a television set, music programs had a similar effect upon her family. Her son, Bruce Milne, recalled that in the 1970s, morning music programs led to jockeying to be in front of the television first: 'we'd have big fights on a Saturday morning, I think it was, because I would want watch some music shows, *UpTight* or *Happening 70* or something like that … and my youngest siblings would want to watch some cartoon shows' (Milne 2017). Rae Dixon had been a singer in local theatrical troupe, the United Entertainers, and later Milne, inspired by 1950s and 1960s rock'n'roll, pursued his passion in music by innovating with fan-based media to produce Melbourne's *Plastered Press* fanzine and *Pulp* which covered east coast scenes (Melbourne/Sydney/Brisbane) as well as the cassette magazine *Fast Forward* (see below).

In the 1950s, live singing programs such as *The Teenage Hour* provided exposure for other performers as well. In 1959, Horwood invited George Bracken to sing on the program after seeing him with his band, the Blue Jeans, at a dance in Dandenong (Pennell 2020; 'The quiet Aboriginal; the greatest fight is for his people' 1959). Bracken, a lightweight boxing title holder, was an Indigenous man originally from Palm Island off the coast of northern Queensland, where his father played in the Palm Island Mission band and his mother sang in a choir. Bracken performed his own songs and impressed Ron Tudor, a talent scout for W&G Records, who invited him to record in W&G's studios. Bracken's recordings of his own songs ('Blue Jean Rock' backed with 'Why don't you write?') were unusual in a time when imported hits were foisted upon new singers. His songs were among the first Indigenous rock and roll recordings and, along with Sydney-based Jimmy Little's more country-tinged 'Frances Claire' – a song about his daughter also recorded in 1959 – were likely to be among the first pop music titles composed by Indigenous Australians.

In Sydney, *Bandstand* was first broadcast in 1958, with its format copied from the original American program of the same name. Festival Records teamed up with the program to promote their artists, forming the 'Bandstand family', an informal name that referenced the close association between broadcaster, artists and label. This connection maintained a stranglehold on televised pop music – *Bandstand* continued for fourteen years – and made it difficult for Melbourne bands or singers to break into the Sydney market, at a time when media was largely city-based. It took a decade before there was a comparable program to promote Melbourne acts. When it was established, the *Go!! Show* consolidated a pop aesthetic that was at odds with *Bandstand*'s family appeal. A decade on, in 1974, the Australian Broadcasting Commission, Australia's public service broadcaster, based another music television show with a youth orientation – *Countdown* – in Melbourne. *Countdown* had a decidedly national character that deliberately transcended parochial city cultures and launched a national resurgence of charting Australian pop and rock acts that had international reach.

Radio formats and Stan Rofe

In the late 1950s and early 1960s, Stan Rofe was recognized as Melbourne's pre-eminent dee-jay. After training at the Vincent School of Broadcasting, Rofe found work in 1953 at Davenport, Tasmania, on 7AD. He soon came back to Melbourne when his father walked out on his family. On his return, Rofe was unable to find radio work until alumni from another broadcasting school in Melbourne assisted him. Rofe had the good fortune to befriend an announcer in Tasmania who was happy to recommend him to the Lee Murray Broadcasting School's network (Rofe 1980). The informal system of school 'pals' and alumni, oiled by favours and return favours as much as reputation, was a critical aspect of consolidating the radio industry for men, in particular. While the connection with variety and theatre had led many female performers into early music broadcasting, 1960s radio was largely a male domain and remained so well into the next century. In 2017, Amanda Keller was the first woman presenter inducted into Commercial Radio Australia's Hall of Fame.

After seven months on air at 3AK, Rofe moved to 3XY before finally settling at 3KZ in 1955. 3KZ was an unusual station. With premises at Trades Hall in Carlton, it was established by the Industrial Printing and Publicity Co-operative, who believed the labour movement should have a role in media. The Co-operative supported the newspaper, *Labour Call*, and in 1926 they began exploring options for radio broadcasting, securing a licence in 1930. While never simply a union broadcaster, with its roots in labour, 3KZ was less likely to pander to corporate interests. Later, in the 1970s, the model of a cooperative that brought together labour and community interests for radio broadcasting had an even greater effect when a federation of union and community activists established one of the early alternative broadcasters, 3CR. 3KZ, with a more sceptical view towards marketing, provided space for an important innovation in broadcasting.

In the late 1950s and early 1960s, broadcasting pop music was generally managed through a tightly controlled format that provided for the repetition of a specific list of songs. On Melbourne radio, as we saw earlier, pop music formats began to develop in the mid-1950s. Bob Horsfall on 3UZ was an important precursor, selecting dance and swing music and playing a 'hit parade' of the eight best-selling songs. In 1954, Mike Williamson played the eight top hits on 3AW where a local airline, TAA, sponsored a half hour *Hit Parade* on Sunday. Stan Rofe, on the other hand, found that at 3KZ he had the opportunity to develop a pop music program without the restrictions of formatted radio. Initially 3KZ copied Sydney's 2UE *Spin with the Stars*, but Rofe's popularity prompted a rethink and the *Platter Parade with Stan Rofe* was initiated in 1958. The three-hour session from Monday to Friday set Rofe's program apart from other popular music broadcasters. The latitude 3KZ provided to Rofe gave him an unprecedented platform:

> My program on KZ had developed [...] into a free-for-all, open house type program where you didn't even ask to come on the air, you just walked through the door ... and ... you got on the air regardless [...] I started finding all sorts of people coming up; would-be groups and singers [...] It was helping me build my name and giving them the opportunity of exposing their names to the public.
> (Rofe 1980)

Rofe's innovative free-flowing format became his trademark at KZ. It differed from the tightly formatted Top 40 broadcasts on rival pop music stations in Melbourne and Sydney and audiences loved it. Rofe used the platform to stoke parochial concerns around local pop music.

The parochial industrial rivalry between Sydney and Melbourne evident in the media was grounded in real conditions. The major recording company, Columbia/EMI, had been based in Sydney since the 1930s and developed a stranglehold on music production in the country. The corollary was the poor recording facilities in Melbourne. Heather Horwood (Pennell 2020) remembers attending the White and Gillespie (W&G) plastics factory in 1958 on weekends to record amongst the machinery. Yet, there was also evidence of a professional inter-city camaraderie in broadcasting. When his management asked Rofe to take on contemporary music programming in 1957, he visited Sydney to talk to dee-jays there, including Bob Rogers, John Laws and Tony Withers. According to Rofe, Rogers passed on a contact that could assist importation of recently released American recordings (Rofe 1980). On his return to Melbourne, Rofe arranged to receive records from the US and convinced KZ to subscribe to the industry journal *Cashbox* to provide up-to-date industry information, and so had the bones of a Top 40 program. Such generosity was possible because capital cities in Australia had largely hermetic markets and advertising conditions; ratings were not the force that they came to be. At this time, the major advertising agency, J. Walter Thompson (JWT), supported a McNair rating service that favoured survey-style data gathering, while Sydney-based ratings company, Andersons, argued for a diary system.

Figure 8 Stan 'The Man' Rofe at the 3KZ studios (seated) with performers (left to right) Lonnie Lee, Johnny Devlin and Johnny O'Keefe. Source: Laurie Richards Collection/Performing Arts Collection/Arts Centre, Melbourne/RSN.

While individual camaraderie existed, systemic rivalries were inevitable. Bob Rogers has said that Melbourne was a 'rock'n'roll enigma' (Rogers and O'Brien 1975: 163). Reflecting on his career in the 1950s and 1960s, Rogers could not understand why so few stars emerged from Melbourne but gave no credence to the idea that Sydney broadcasters favoured Sydney artists. Stan Rofe, however, believed that Sydney was getting all the breaks, arguing that rival Melbourne Top 40 station 3UZ was a conduit for Sydney performers (Rofe 1980). While access to American recordings and a subscription to *Cashbox* gave Rofe the makings of a Top 40 show, his 'open house' approach gave him much more. It allowed him to build deep connections with local Melbourne musicians. He shared their aspirations, was generous in his support of their ambitions, and provided his import records to new performers who came through his studio, often with a recommendation to record it, if he believed it suited them. He also listened to musicians' complaints that Sydney was closed to them. When performer and entrepreneur, Johnny Chester, approached Rofe to advertise his new dance venue at Preston Town Hall,

Rofe asked if Chester would let him become the dance compere, to which Chester agreed (Johnstone 1991: 156). As well compering, Rofe promoted the Preston dance on air to great effect – for no money according to Chester (ibid). Dance promoters were becoming significant advertisers on 3KZ and Rofe's status with the station grew as his role as a booster for local music developed, compering dances in Malvern and other suburban venues. By the end of 1960, with his standing at 3KZ secure, and his popularity in the city at an all-time high, Rofe set out on a mission to support Melbourne performers: he stopped playing Sydney recordings, with the exception of the recordings of his mate, Johnny O'Keefe:

> We kept the embargo going on the Sydney acts, and we wouldn't touch them [...] If you didn't record in Melbourne then you weren't played on the Stan Rofe show unless you were Johnny O'Keefe [...] I used to get very cheeky and go on the air and plead with the kids and tell them not to go out and buy any Sydney acts at all ... I thought, well if I can't use that microphone as a piece of political material in the battle with Sydney then I shouldn't be here.
>
> (Rofe 1980)

The intensity of Rofe's commitment to Melbourne artists galvanized support from the music community in the city. To make good on his commitment to Melbourne, Rofe convinced Ron Tudor from W&G to record local performers. The company's facilities were just not good enough, however, to compete with the Sydney studios. It was not until 1966, when the Go! label began in Melbourne, that adequate representation for the musicians and singers was possible in the city. Benefiting from the obvious tie-in with television's *Go!! Show*, and improved recording conditions at Bill Armstrong's studios in South Melbourne, Rofe concluded that 'We finally broke through, but it took a TV show to do it, not a radio program' (ibid.). In 1963, after eight years, Rofe left 3KZ for 3UZ where he also enjoyed considerable popularity, even while his format changed to a more traditional Top 40 style.

Television innovations: The importance of the *Go!! Show*

Melbourne television experimented with music programming in their formative period. *Blues, Studio One*, which included live-to-air segments and some mime, was broadcast for five episodes in 1957, starring popular Melbourne blues singer, Joan Bilceaux. As noted earlier, *Teenage Mailbag* was probably the first live pop show regularly broadcast on Australian television. Both shows were on HSV-7 which, with connections to 3DB and the *Herald*, represented the Melbourne establishment. HSV had prepared for television's introduction in 1956 by running pre-broadcasting dummy programs in a large exhibition hall on the Melbourne Showgrounds for over a year in the lead up to broadcasting (the first licences were awarded in 1955; broadcasting began later). These programs forged a tight-knit group of performers and technicians although a 'learning-as-you-go' approach was prevalent long after broadcasting began. Singer Jo Lawrence (nee Muhrer) performed with ABC radio as well as fill-in roles for commercial television. Television, she found, generally had regular performers who all knew each other and who managed musical arrangements to suit (Lawrence 2020). This was also reflected in early Sydney television. As we saw, *Bandstand* actively recruited a 'family', making it difficult for Melbourne performers to participate. In Melbourne, popular music programs on television did not continue beyond the 1960s. HSV-7 attempted a popular variety program with *Bandwagon* in 1959 but, despite performances by international acts such as Johnny Ray on his tour that year, it was short-lived. *In Melbourne Tonight* (GTV 9), hosted by Graham Kennedy, had huge audiences and ran until 1970 but did not feature pop or rock music. Melbourne acts had to travel north, to Sydney, to break into television and reach broader city audiences. This pattern continued until 1964 when a new broadcast service, ATV-0, scheduled the *Go!! Show*.

When ATV-0 began broadcasting in August 1964, it was the first new station in a capital city in almost a decade of television (other capitals and regional cities followed over the next few years). Radio listeners would have to wait another two decades, before the launch of new capital city stations, when FM was opened to radio and EON-FM began broadcasting to Melbourne in July 1980. After the consolidation of broadcasting, existing stations, largely controlled by traditional media interests, lobbied government to ensure there would be a slow roll-out of any competitors (Herd 2006). As in radio at this time, Australian television was largely based around city markets. The broadcasting industry initially had a disruptive influence but by the mid-60s, it had settled into conservativism. New licensees, however, had to establish a profile with new programming.

Melbourne's ATV-0 set out to capture a young audience, taking a chance that a pop music show could do that. Music shows had tended to be shunted aside to less important time slots, such as weekend mornings or afternoons when there was no sport. When ATV-0 launched, the *Go!! Show* became a flagship program. It was the station's first live program, broadcast in primetime on a weekday night.

The show was produced by one of the industry's earliest independent production houses – DYT Productions – an innovation in early Melbourne television which was established when key personnel left TCN-9 to form their own company. Horrie Dargie, a jazz musician and performer who ran the talent department at TCN; Arthur Young (musical director) and John Tilbrook (sales manager) formed the basis of DYT (Dargie, Young, Tilbrook). When they left GTV 9 they took with them a young Dennis Smith who had been working 'traffic' – scheduling advertisements – and managing the production of 'live-reads' on GTV's variety programming (Smith 2019). When the new television channel was mooted for Melbourne in the early 1960s, DYT met to decide what kind of program to pitch:

> We said, 'Well, the biggest thing that's missing in Melbourne is a musical teenage show'. There were two in Sydney at that stage – *Bandstand* and also Johnny O'Keefe's *Sing, Sing, Sing* … they were musical, but they were [for] an older audience. I thought that we needed … something to cater for the younger [audience].
>
> (ibid.)

When the *Go!! Show* aired, Dennis Smith became the program's floor manager and producer and ATV-10 adopted 'Go!' as a defining slogan for the new youthful broadcaster. From the beginning, the program had a live audience. Smith recalls there was 'an extraordinary fan base' that created an incredible atmosphere in the studio: 'the moment they walked in through the studio, they started screaming … and they'd be throwing things – teddy bears and stuff, all those sorts of things that fans did, but it was amazing … our shows were … excitement from the moment we started' (ibid.). The highlight of the program's first year of broadcasting occurred in November 1964 when a live concert at Melbourne's Myer Music Bowl attracted 40,000 fans. This was also the last Melbourne-only program as from 1965 the *Go!! Show* was also distributed to Sydney. Over the next decade, ATV-0 in Melbourne consolidated its commitment to cater for teenage viewers and live audiences, commissioning a sequence of popular and influential local live pop programs including *Kommotion* (1964–67), *UpTight* (1968–70) and *Happening '70, '71* and *'72*.

The program was important to Melbourne music for a number of reasons. Firstly, it supported the Strangers who, as the house band, performed in 130 episodes between 1964 and 1967 and became valued studio musicians (Johnston 2010: 149–50). Further, the program promoted live music performances and artists' careers. The suburban dances were an important source for talent on the *Go!! Show*. Many of these performers did not have recording contracts as

Melbourne only had one significant label in W&G. As Dennis Smith recalled, 'it didn't make a lot of sense to promote them on television and have their names [on air] and nor be able to follow up with a record, so we started our own label' (Smith 2019). Thirdly, the television spawned a local label in Go! Records, which was managed by DYT's Dargie. As the only formal televisual tie-in in the Australian music industries at the time, the label expanded recording opportunities for Melbourne-based pop performers (a recent box set of the label collected over 130 recorded performances by more than fifty artists), and provided valuable custom for Bill Armstrong's newly renovated studios which were also starting to attract Sydney-based performers to Melbourne (see Chapter 5).

In 1967, after three years' production, the *Go!! Show*, along with *Kommotion*, was cancelled by Channel 0. The station had begun by funding Australian productions but found that it was unable to make a profit. Like other Australian television stations, it increasingly came to rely on imported product (Hall 1976: 45–6). Nevertheless, the program had for the first time provided a profile for Melbourne-based bands. The independent company that produced the program for ATV-0 was able to draw on the experiences of its principals, especially musician Horrie Dargie, and take advantage of improvements in recording infrastructure to develop a companion recording label that allowed emerging Melbourne artists to record songs. As a popular program broadcast in primetime television, the program grew an audience for Melbourne-based music and Australian performers generally.

Go-Set: Innovations in Melbourne print media

By the time the *Go!! Show* had run its race, the independent cultural newspaper that reflected its name – *Go-Set* – was just one year old. From its first issue in February 1966, *Go-Set* had directed itself at a youth audience, with its masthead declaring it was a 'teens and twenties newspaper'. Tony Schauble, a twenty-one-year-old editor, told ABC TV that the main thing its readers would take with them from the newspaper was that 'young ideas and the young outlook is something that could be taken seriously' (*ABC TV* 1966). In this they were related to the *Go!! Show*, which had developed a pop aesthetic that reflected youth lifestyles. *Go-Set* took up the cause of ATV-0 in its third edition when Schauble lambasted the Myer Music Bowl's refusal for the *Go!! Show* to stage a pop concert at the Bowl during the upcoming Moomba Festival in March 1966.

It became a line to draw around what was or was not possible under Melbourne's conservative establishment:

> Just who is it that is drawing up the definition of culture in this country? Does culture exclude the tastes of people under 30 by definition? The Myer Music Bowl was planned to provide entertainment for the people of Melbourne and surely this includes all of them ... in any case, either directly or indirectly we, the go set are contributing as much as any other section to the upkeep of the Bowl.
> (Schauble 1966)

The editorial prompted readers' letters – as Schauble had requested – decrying the decision and in the end, the ban on pop at the Bowl was overturned. The *Go!! Show* Moomba concert in March attracted 85,000 people and *Go-Set* reported that despite teeming rain, 'the audience danced and screamed through each particular act ... Police lined the front of the stage to stop girls from rushing the artists' (Healey 1966). The success of the combination of *Go-Set* and the *Go!! Show*'s pulling power clearly demonstrated a shift in the terms in which a youth constituency could confront the agenda of cultural conservatism, using youth-friendly media. The establishment was prepared to push back however; three years later, a 3UZ concert was halted due to a brawl and pop and rock concerts were once again banned from the Bowl.[2]

Just a year later, in 1967, Victorian conservatism had reached its inevitable apogee with the death sentence carried out for Ronald Ryan, the last man hanged in the State and the last execution conducted in Australia. NSW had abolished the death penalty in 1955; while Western Australia and South Australia had carried out death sentences a few years earlier, there was strong public sentiment against the penalty. Michael Hyde (2010: 13–18) suggests that this event, in February 1967, signalled the beginning of local social and political upheaval. Resentment at the conservative establishment had been growing with the introduction of the *National Service Act* in 1964, which used a lottery system to select young men for the war in Vietnam, and anti-conscription and anti-war groups formed soon after. By 1970, the First Moratorium demonstration against the war in Vietnam drew 100,000 people to Melbourne's streets. Anti-war compositions – 'Rachel' (sung by Russell Morris) and 'Smiley' (sung by Ronnie Burns) were charting nationally in Australia. The latter was composed by Johnny Young, a former *Go!! Show* host, about the impact of the war on fellow performer-turned-soldier, Normie Rowe (Johnston 2010: 284).

Go-Set's innovation in content and presentation was a radical departure from how newspapers had been presented. The masthead was a synecdoche of the imagined readership – the go-set – in the way of Rupert Murdoch's contemporaneous new venture *The Australian*, also an attempt to break with traditional print media. *Go-Set*, however, went much further in shaking up content: placing motor sport and men's fashion side by side, using differing layout styles and presenting a curated television guide of recommended viewing for the go-set. Gossip and news were often indistinguishable. Personality news was prioritized and presented as an on-the-spot, new journalism style. Observation was bundled into often real-time descriptions of events and people in coffee shops and performance spaces. In an interview with Billy Thorpe, a former teenage heart-throb who had become an inspired blues performer, Ed Nimervoll (1970) begins with a deconstruction: 'I don't run the greatest of interviews … my system is very inefficient. My way I cannot possibly report to you faithfully on all that is said and done. I can only account impressions'. While this description certainly reflects Nimervoll's interaction with Thorpe and the Aztecs, it also allowed the reporter to distance himself from his output. Musicians often did not take well to critics. In Nimervoll's encounter, Thorpe's then guitarist, Lobby Lloyde, took the chance 'to settle an old score' from a previous review (ibid.).

In immersing itself in the consumers and subjects of their enterprise, *Go-Set* took its commitment to youth cultures much further than television or radio, which had previously been the most successful media to co-opt the language and music of youth. One of the newspaper's primary impacts was to break radio's hold on Top 40 charts. Ed Nimmervoll may not have been a professional interviewer, but he certainly had a head for technical solutions, collating a national chart by following sales in all States. *Go-Set's* national chart provided the first opportunity for artists to measure success beyond single city markets. Nimervoll went on to be editor at the paper's death in 1973. In 1975, he founded *Juke* in Melbourne, a more mainstream newspaper that reported on youth cultures while also taking a role in promoting emerging music, including Indigenous bands who came to play in Melbourne from northern Australia. Grant Hanson, an important Indigenous music entrepreneur, recalled: 'as a teenager, we'd go through *Juke* Magazine, to look at who was playing where' (Hanson 2020). The newspaper was eventually taken over by its Sydney-based publishers and discontinued in 1992.

Community radio and alternative distribution platforms

After an initial flurry of innovation, the conservatism of broadcast media was noticeable by the late 1960s. Billy Thorpe moved to Melbourne at this time and found audiences 'had their own flavours and styles ... a far cry from the ... pop schlock that radio and television was trying to sell ... There was a definite tangible scene taking shape' (Thorpe 1998: 135). In 1968, *The Age* carried a letter to the editor that would, in another ten years, lead to one of the most important developments in Australian media: a third sector of broadcasting managed and presented by the communities it served. Written by a committee established by audio technician Brian Cabena, the letter announced the formation of the Music Broadcasting Society ('A third programme of serious music' 1968). MBS aimed to promote serious music broadcasting, not commercial pop music. Nevertheless, the idea of listener-supported radio with specialist programming spread quickly. As the 1970s developed, a number of student groups established experimental broadcast services and when the first post-war federal Labor government was elected in 1972, they promised to create volunteer-based public broadcasting alongside the State-funded and advertising-driven sectors. In 1979, the first community licences were issued (in 1992, federal legislation formally designated the sector as community broadcasting with the 'public' tag reserved for government-funded services). From its inception, community broadcasting in Melbourne played music from independent and marginalized performers that could not receive radio play on commercial stations.

Fans were critical to these media innovations. Community radio developed in conjunction with other novel platforms for the dissemination of music and information that gave fans control of the distribution of music – both locally and internationally. Cassettes were introduced into Australia in 1967 and sharing pirated, home recordings (from radio or from personal collections) provided for an expansion of musical knowledge at a time when commercial radio was obsessed with narrow Top 40 formats. In the 1970s, as a teenager living in Melbourne's outer suburbs, Cameron Paine listened to John Peel's famous BBC radio program with a friend who regularly received a cassette of Peel's show. Paine went on to become an audio technician in Melbourne's community radio (Paine 2018; Tebbutt 2020). A decade later, in the 1980s, Mary Mihelakos, a student at Swinburne Technological College, shared cassette tapes with another student who was in a band. This connection led to Mary managing her friend's band and eventually becoming an influential music band booker, radio presenter and journalist. In 2020, Mihelakos was inducted into the Music Hall of Fame for her services to music. Another important radio personality and avid mix tape distributor was Mick Geyer, who took the opportunity of community radio to present his own esoteric program, drawn from his personal collection, on PBS-FM. Geyer was influential at the struggling station and encouraged numerous volunteers by passing on tapes to them. He did the same for musicians and Nick Cave credits him as an influence, dedicating his album *Abattoir Blues* to Geyer (PBS 2006; Tebbutt 2020).

Experimental public radio was often run from student services. Colleges of Advanced Education (such as Swinburne Technological College), technical colleges for trades, teaching colleges and universities all had their funding increased in the 1960s to cope with the significant influx of students after 1955 (Abbott and Doucouliagos 2003). In the 1970s, these institutions supported an active youth media network of campus newspapers and radio stations. As universities expanded, an extensive campus network emerged for bands playing lunchtime and evening gigs. For school students like Bruce Milne, this provided a chance to be a part of the city's music scene:

> Community radio started up. 3CR started. So, I did a few shows there. Also, Swinburne had … an on-campus radio station. So, I started doing shows on that, even before I started going … there and I was still at the community school. I was doing a bit of radio and Swinburne had a newspaper, so I'd write articles for that and interview bands who were playing at lunch-time.
>
> (Milne 2017)

3CR reflected the earlier union cooperative that held the 3KZ licence, but this station formed by the Community Radio Federation was decidedly non-commercial. One of Melbourne's earliest community broadcasters, they played music that related to their commitment to social justice, including rock bands made up of Indigenous musicians. Milne recalls the 1970s as a period in the music industry when 'hype' was prevalent – a term that draws from the hyperbole of publicity but also links to a 'hyper', US slang for a conman. Popular commercial music appeared 'overblown' by its mainstream media marketing, especially when compared with the tangible, dynamic urban scene he was in touch with through the campus networks and city venues. Inspired to document the Melbourne music scene he was immersed in, Milne started *Plastered Press*, a fanzine that could be postered up or distributed as a roneo-ed copies to music shops and cafés. He soon joined forces with similar guerilla publishers in Brisbane

(Clinton Walker) and later in Sydney to produce *Pulp*, a zine that put a spotlight on new music that was emerging in these cities:

> *Pulp* existed from, I guess, mid-'77 until Easter, '78. A very short period of time. So, if you look at what was happening in Melbourne at the time, there was the Young Charlatans and News and The Boys Next Door. Sydney, of course, had Radio Birdman and all the offshoots of that funhouse scene. Brisbane, of course, had the Saints, who very quickly within that period put out a single that had gone crazy in England.
>
> (Milne 2017)

Later, after building up presentation and editing skills in a community radio program, *Demo Derby*, that broadcast tapes from new bands, Milne, his co-host, Andrew Maine and graphic designer Michael Trudgeon developed a cassette-based zine, *Fast Forward*. A number of the local bands they were covering began to look for audiences outside Australia; *Fast Forward* was a critical conduit for overseas music outlets to get a sense of what was happening. Independent international labels Rough Trade and Sub Pop began distributing the zine:

> There's definitely a crusade with *Fast Forward* … we needed to expose that music. … [T]hat generation of bands that moved overseas … realised that their audience in Australia was a really, really tiny percentage of the music-buying public or concert-going public and […] they either had to go mainstream or they had to […] try and find that infinitely small percentage of people in as many countries as possible to build up some sort of a network – and they did.
>
> (Milne 2017)

These bands carried with them a sense of Melbourne's culture and *Fast Forward* became an important cultural marker of the vibrant local scene.

While community radio provided a basis for an internationally recognized format adopted for *Fast Forward*, it also supported local music communities. Volunteering in community radio provided an outlet for passionate fans who wanted more than just something to listen to. Musicians, intrigued by 'the other side' of broadcasting, also became on-air presenters. Importantly, community radio provided a space for women to develop their interests in the industry. Mary Mihelakos, from a Greek immigrant background, discovered music when she was young. At school and at university she continued this interest and found community station 3RRR where she was able to leverage her passion into a lifelong commitment. When Mihelakos began volunteering at 3RRR in Fitzroy, an inner city suburb, she was given the job to compile the gig guide on one of the station's typewriters. An onerous task often assigned to 'newbie' volunteers, making up a gig guide involved studiously following up advertising and newspaper listings (in a pre-internet world) and calling venues to confirm performances. Mihelakos came to be on first-name terms with many of the venues' band bookers who respected 3RRR's role in promoting local gigs and often offered to put Mary's name 'on the door', should she want to see the show *gratis*: 'Many didn't realise I was underage' Mihelakos later recalled (eighteen was the legal drinking age) (Mihelakos 1999). After being mentored by influential Melbourne booker Linda Gebar, the founding booker of the Punters Club, Mihelakos was employed as a band publicist before she was legally allowed into hotels (ibid.). In the 1990s, as a band booker with the Evelyn hotel on Brunswick Street in Fitzroy, Mihelakos 'worked closely with fellow bookers, including Richard Moffatt of The Punters Club, to create events across multiple venues and in collaboration with community radio stations' (Woods 2020a). From the 1990s, Mihelakos became the music editor of the street paper *Beat*, and contributed to the 'Sticky Carpet' column in *The Age*, one of the few serious music outlets provided by mainstream newspapers. *Beat* was one of the free music papers that circulated in major cities that relied on venue and trade advertising: 'In the days before internet we relied on the street press, newspapers, radio and word of mouth to navigate our music consumption' (Mihelakos 1999). The street papers continued to provide important information on scene events and performances; by the turn of the century, however, information accessed through the internet became the primary source for gigs and gossip.

As the 1990s ended, one of the most important media developments for music in Melbourne was the formation of the Indigenous broadcaster, 3KND (Kool'n'Deadly). While KND began broadcasting in 2003, the groundwork had been going on for some time. Community stations such as 3CR and 3PBS, which produced an important live album from Bart Willoughby's Indigenous outfit No Fixed Address in 1979, provided crucial early support for local Indigenous musicians. Commercial broadcasters had taken up the music of Yothu Yindi and the Melbourne-based Tiddas in the 1980s but in general, the vibrant Indigenous music scene in Melbourne was not well represented in media. The Indigenous-run Songlines Corporation (formed in 1994) promoted music through mentorships and concerts (Hanson 2020), but it was not until 3KND that black Australian music was consistently featured in Melbourne, which was the last capital city in Australia to be provided with an Indigenous-run community station. KND was operated initially by the South East Indigenous Media (now it is managed by First Aboriginal Media Enterprises – FAME) and committed to 70 per cent Indigenous music content. *An early program, Songlines National*, providing local music broadcasts from diverse indigenous communities, linked Indigenous stations from Townsville and Darwin to Halls Creek and Sydney (3KND 2006: 1–2). Currently, the station has been estimated to reach a diverse audience of around 300,000 listeners a week (Hanson 2020).

Digital media

Since the close of the 1990s, media has changed quickly. A recent report found that while radio remains a primary focus for accessing music in Australia, one in five Australians and around 30 per cent of 'heavy' record buyers and those attending live events used YouTube daily to access music (VMDO 2020: 13). The streaming service Spotify has a similar audience if their paid and free listener numbers are combined (ibid.). From early in the internet period, radio broadcasters adopted online platforms. In community radio it was easier to move to an internet-based platform to stream live broadcasting (once copyright issues were dealt with) because there was no need to consider splitting audiences that were sold to advertisers. One specialist music broadcaster, 3PBS, has recently moved to new studios that will allow them to stream live concerts from their own facilities. Music journalists were also early adopters. After the demise of *Juke*, the irrepressible Ed Nimervoll established *HowlSpace* in October 2000 as an 'open encyclopedia' of Australian and New Zealand music that encouraged fan contributions (not to be confused with Howl Space, an experimental vocal learning resource). *Beat* also moved online and a recent feature celebrated Melbourne bands, including the Getaway Plan, that used the early social media platform, MySpace, to launch themselves into international recognition (Overell 2010; 'The iconic Melbourne bands who rose during the MySpace Era' 2020).

In the period of pandemic music, streaming has been one of the ways that musicians have been able to keep in front of their fans, given the health issues raised by live venues and contagion. Music Victoria has been working to support bands and musicians badly affected by the pandemic and providing online platforms has been an important part of this. Digital platforms are also offering bands further opportunities for innovation. In 2020, the Victorian Music Development Office (VMDO) established an initial pilot for their project Indie

Bands x Indie Developers, which partners indie musicians with indie video game creators. The pilot resulted in 'Hope', a collaboration between Melbourne band Cable Ties and local independent game designer, Cecile Richards. Cable Ties provided the soundtrack to 'Hope', a free game that 'challenge feelings of hopelessness and confront[s] issues of anxiety and self-criticism' (Woods 2020b). The Victorian Government, through Creative Victoria and the VMDO, has further supported links between music and games through its support for the online symposium 'High Score Composition and Sound Art for Gaming', an online symposium presented by APRA AMCOS (the Australian Performing Right Association and Australasian Mechanical Copyright Owners Society).

In this chapter we have looked at the way in which accidental and opportunistic (as well deliberative and provocatively creative) forms of media innovation have contributed to sustaining music communities and expanding knowledge of popular music in Melbourne over time. In doing so, we look to contribute to the way in which media is considered with regards to 'music city' discourse. In putting the relationship between urban music and media into a longer historical view, we argue that media is more than a marketing adjunct to a music city. Media in its various forms at time is antagonistic to music and musicians, yet it is also able to provide important forums for reviving traditions as well as expanding new music. The long story of the relationship between music and media in the city has been the ways in which passionate fans have attempted to use media forms to their own ends – promoting the music they love. In this way, alternative or minor forms of media have had important defining roles in supporting music communities – musicians, listeners and audiences, bookers and venue staff – in the city.

5

The recording city

Introduction

Since Federation, the story of the Australian recording industry had been a mixture of struggles to obtain the requisite equipment to record, master and distribute albums – fears of 'new' entertainment forms and technologies (theatre, radio) diminishing company profits, fears of the dominance of overseas recordings and consequent regulation in fostering local production (Laird 1999). In this chapter, we examine the development of recording companies and studios in Melbourne during and after the arrival of rock and roll. Some of the themes explored here are similar to Laird's (1999) account of the early 1900s, in tracing the local industry's lack of confidence about replicating international sounds and standards of recording to enable decent sales here and overseas. Some older studios now constitute part of historical tours of Melbourne Music: one label owner interviewed for this book, Bruce Milne, incorporates various recording studios into his historical bus tour of key Melbourne music iconography (Arts Centre Melbourne 2019).

An emphasis upon recording structures, people and practices can tell us much about how such a fundamental sector of the music industries interacts with the broader cultural conditions at play. Recording studio histories 'reveal much about how music, space and musicians interact: it is through a composite and always evolving way that recording studios come to be viewed as vital spaces of music in the city' (Gibson 2005: 192). This has implications not only for production settings, but related sectors, such as tourism and record retail. Further, musicians become attached to particular recording studios, due to a room's ambience, its ability captures a particular drum sound or group sound or the vibe and efficiency of studio staff. These sources of inspiration are at the centre of studio mythologies, which of course also lend themselves to wider built environment myths. In examining some of Melbourne's pop/rock recordings histories, we take up Gibson's (2005: 205) assertion that 'causal relationships between musicians, audiences, city landscapes and technologies are complex and always produced and re-produced through networks of association, power and influence'.

'We admit that American artists are nearly as good'

The arrival of rock and roll in Melbourne meant that resources – and the accompanying expertise – had to be found to capture local stars on tape and on vinyl. As with the rest of Australia, Melbourne was largely dependent upon local branches of multinational labels (particularly EMI) in providing vinyl of overseas artists. There were valuable exceptions, such as Bob Clemens' Jazzart in 1948 (Clemens ran jazz dances, clubs and Downbeat concerts at the Melbourne Town Hall). A series of recording companies existed prior to the Second World War, catering to dance hits, sentimental songs and recording local crooners and dance bands. Local recording studios, however, lacked access to the same equipment deployed by producers and engineers in the key US and UK markets, where artists and companies yearned to replicate the standards of international recordings.

In some ways, the history of local struggles with technical proficiency can be told through the life of Bill Armstrong and a thirty-five-year career across engineering, producing, manufacturing, studio, radio and public broadcasting management. Experimenting with his own tape machines, Armstrong's first technical employment involved recording performances at the 1949 Jazz Convention at Prahran Town Hall, and a little later, at 3UZ as a music producer (Armstrong 2018a). At this time Armstrong also established his own recording labels (Magnasound, Paramount, Danceland), through later distribution arrangements with the W&G label, with the presence of mind to import a Neumann disc cutting machine from Germany. In a 2013 interview on ABC radio, there is a claim to Magnasound offering the first rock and roll song written and recorded by an Australian act: the Schneider Sisters' 'Washboard Rock n Roll' in 1956 (ABC Radio 2013).

Armstrong was subsequently offered a production job at W&G, recording music and radio advertisements in a church studio, installing their disc cutting room and studio, with later work at radio station 3DB for one year. By 1961 he was lured to Telefil Studios – 'it had a very good two-track cutting machine' (Armstrong 2018a) – for commercial recordings and advertising work (the original site of Telefil is now the Memo Music Hall). Telefil was consumed (and financed) as much by television and advertising work as single/album recording.

The decision to establish his own studio in December 1965 was contingent upon finding the appropriate site. Two properties were found at 100 Albert Road in South Melbourne, allowing rental for £18 per week; the houses were restructured to accommodate a studio and an office. Armstrong was well placed to cater to interest from Melbourne television in capturing rock and roll performances that were part of live circuits:

> Well, I started there mainly on my own, and then Roger Savage joined and became a partner of it as well. And, at the same time, rock and roll was sort of starting to emerge in Melbourne, and then we had ultimately *The Go! Show* and *Kommotion* [see Chapter 4] and these things. If you wanted to go on *The Go! Show*, you had to pre-record, because they mimed everything ... Eventually the unions sorted that out and said 'Well no, you've got to do things live or record them there' ... Then you had the movement in advertising, thinking if the advertisers want to get to a younger audience, they're going to have to start hearing things that the young audience listen to. So we were getting new songwriters – Peter Best was one of them, John Hawker and John Farrar, [of] the Strangers. And, we had a lot of younger people in the writing department at agencies that were with it. And so, we sort of became part of another school or part of a people that understood each other, what they were doing, and regular recording studios wouldn't understand that ... Armstrong Studios was ... a feeling of everybody got along and understood what the market was all about, and what people wanted and what sort of sound. And there was sort of no fixed rules about anything.
>
> (Armstrong 2018a)

Armstrong consolidated a group of good engineers and producers around him, including Roger Savage, John Sayers and Ernie Rose, and expanded buildings and real estate accordingly. Obtaining the first 8 track desk in Australia in 1968, the studio became the dominant recording complex in Melbourne and was often favoured by Sydney bands and producers who preferred the Melbourne way of doing things. From the mid-1960s, the studio capitalized on the emergence of a suite of acts and quality songwriters including Zoot, Russell Morris, Brian Cadd, Spectrum and the Masters' Apprentices. In 1972, the company converted a former butter factory in Bank St, South Melbourne, enabling the construction of five studios. This was achieved through a substantial loan of $250,000 from the Commonwealth Bank, based on the hit track record (pun intended) of the studio (Armstrong 2018b). The company continued its successes with Daddy Cool, Little River Band, Johnny Farnham, the Aztecs and others.[1]

An early commercial recording label was Planet, owned by King Crawford and Marcus Herman that had established premises in Bourke St in 1951. The label had enormous success in retailing a range of standards, country and novelty records, including local cowboy Kenny Arnott's *Hillbilly Classics* in 1954. In 1958, they produced the country's first rock and roll album, *Rock and Roll Dance Party*, featuring the Henri Bource All Stars, Peter McLean and Beverly Dick ('Over 40 Rock and Roll Classics'). The label recorded many of Melbourne's contemporary live circuit stars including Bource, the Blue Bops, and Malcolm Arthur. In a cheeky nod to the prevailing cultural cringe, Planet's placard at one annual Moomba march proclaimed that 'We admit that American artists are nearly as good' ('Planet Records finale' 2017). After the demise of Planet in 1961, Marcus returned with Crest Records, producing *Georgia Lee Sings the Blues Down Under*, the first indigenous album of blues, jazz and rock and roll.

The early labels and studios were confronting a cultural battle on two fronts. There was interstate rivalry, competing with the sounds and national sway of the Sydney (male) rock and rollers: Johnny O'Keefe, Col Joye, Dig Richards, Johnny Devlin, Alan Dale and others. Melbourne artists and labels also struggled to imitate original US recordings, providing different technical and musical challenges. Sydney labels, such as Festival Records, enjoyed the benefits of setting up earlier, and profited from the rock and roll boom in Sydney that produced O'Keefe, Dale, Joye, Lee and others in the late 1950s. For MPD's Mike Brady, 'probably within five years, we were on a par with American studios in terms of sound, and then, I suppose, we had to catch up as producers. So most people in those days brought American producers out to produce their records' (Brady 2018).

There was also the problem of ensuring that contemporary recordings were locally available. For Bobby Bright, duo partner Laurie Allen's vinyl collection was a major advantage:

> Well, Laurie had an incredible collection of records. He must have been buying records for years. He had drawers full of singles and stuff like that, and albums,

where we got a lot of material from, and also we used to tape radio shows from England … the BBC were doing stuff with The [Rolling] Stones, The Faces, PJ Proby, long before they had records out there, so we knew what was going on in their scene.

(Bright 2008)

Ian Allen (2017) recalls 'records made on cardboard, vinyl and cardboard and sold by Coles'.

Branching out from its hardware enterprises as electronics manufacturers, Astor moved into content production, establishing Astor Records in 1960, signing Betty McQuade, the Masters' Apprentices, the Seekers, the Town Criers, Normie Rowe (later) and Matt Flinders. The label had a notable first local release in Pilita Corrales's *Pilita Tells the Story of Love* (1960).

Obtaining the right equipment for recording and performing was also difficult: it was one thing to see international stars in the media with the latest Fender guitars and Ludwig drums; but finding these in downtown Melbourne was quite another:

> We didn't have the equipment to get the sounds that [international bands] were getting, of course. But gradually, slowly but surely. And when we did get them, they were very expensive. I know [guitarist] Bill [Dale] – I forget how much he paid for that guitar, but it was a lot of money. And then to get the amp and the Dynacord [amplifier] on top of it, was lots of money.

(Chester 2008)

Rising expenses were often offset by real wage increases. Recording success not only provided the opportunity for interstate visibility; it meant a jump in the performance fees: 'I remember after the first year of recording I'd had three top forty records, I think they all made close to top ten, and in 1962 my price went up to £6 a spot – so I'd had a fifty per cent increase with three top forty records' (Chester 2008).

W&G was an important local label that also benefited from Armstrong's input. From 1957, W&G recorded and signed many Melbourne acts including Diana Trask, the Seekers and Johnny Chester, with Ron Tudor playing crucial roles in A&R and producing. In turn, Tudor's Fable Records from 1970 provided a training ground for artists who would become producers. Brian Cadd was a house producer at Fable, gaining valuable production experience across a wide range of acts, and also studio time for his own work (Cadd cited in

Kruger 2005b: 113). Notably, W&G recorded perhaps the first indigenous rock and roll recordings, with Palm Island boxer/singer George Bracken, who in 1959 released 'Turn Me Loose', a US Pomus/Shuman composition, and 'Blue Jean Rock' written by Bracken (backed by Bruce Clark and the Rockers).

A Melbourne sound?

Radio stations also played a role in completing basic recordings, either live to air or recorded for later transmission. Johnny Chester remembers his first recording with the Thunderbirds at 3KZ at the urging of Stan Rofe:

> With the Thunderbirds, it was all in together. There was no editing, there was no overdubbing, any of that stuff, it was all 'ready-set-go' and you record three songs, or get three takes. And I think, at the audition, I probably only got one of each. Anyway. So, after I'd done 'Hokey Pokey' which was the first thing I recorded, which was done in a real rock-and-roll sort of beat, Stan [Rofe] turned to Ron – and Kevin McClellan told me this afterwards – he said, "What do you think, Ron?" and Ron said, 'He moves well, doesn't he?'. Because I'm bopping around, the mic's there and I'm [yells and bangs] – no idea. Anyway, in spite of that, they gave me a contract and we came back in and we got three goes at both sides and the best one was the one they released. And, as I said, it wasn't fiddled with at all. Lindsay Morehouse got the sound and that's what they released. There wasn't even a vocal booth … just plywood partitions … But I think Harold [Frith] had an overhead mic and a kick drum mic. I don't think there was anything on the snare or anything. We only had six channels … They had a great big, I think, a big plate echo in the back of the dunny somewhere and it was straight on to the tape through this thing. And I'm sure it was only six channels so it might have just been an overhead mic for Harold, because it was the five-piece band and me.
>
> (Chester 2008)

For some, the Sydney-Melbourne rivalry intensified through a belief that Sydney recordings were of a higher quality: 'what we made up for in the lack of production we made up for with enthusiasm' (Chester 2008). According to manager Gary Spry:

> Well, the records made in Australia were as good as anything made overseas, but what wasn't as good, was the mastering of them and the cutting of the discs.

> With the Twilights, we had them cut overseas because they had a better – didn't lose any quality off it from the cutting. Here, in Australia, we lost a bit of quality off the records in the cutting, it wasn't in the recording ... But the cutting is done by the record company, like EMI, so we requested that EMI use Capitol to cut the actual record.
>
> (Spry 2009)

Bill Armstrong credits the arrival of English engineer Roger Savage in providing local recordings with 'an international sound ... with all of the engineers who were under Roger's influence, or Ernie Rose or John Sayers or whoever' (Armstrong 2018a). Beginning as a freelancer, Savage was the engineer for early Bobby and Laurie recordings, along with MPD Ltd, Lynne Randell, the Easybeats, the Spinning Wheels, the Twilights, Axiom, Spectrum, Marcia Hines, John Farnham and the Master's Apprentices. For Armstrong, Savage 'could make things sound like they weren't Australian' (Armstrong 2018b).

This is an interesting observation, where cultural cringe meets technophilia. This was arguably less about a particular house style, and more about ensuring gradual yet constant innovation (paying attention to room setups, microphone choices and regarding the console as an important long-term investment in a studio's future). Musicians were prepared to travel interstate to obtain innovation; and in the 1960s and 1970s, studios such as Armstrong and TCS (Channel Nine) successfully lured Sydney artists to record in Melbourne (David Mackay (the Twilights, the Mixtures, Cliff Richard, the La De Das), for example, often preferred Armstrong Studios to EMI's Sydney setup).

The sense of requiring perpetual investment in the latest technologies and/or credentialled staff has never receded. For example, Chris Corr, whose formative engineering experiences were through observing Channel Ten record *Young Talent Time* in 1978/79, argues that he can 'date an era by the drum sound'; by the mid-80s, studios were investing in standard international equipment: 'At the end of 1984, there was one solid state 24-track console, and that was at AAV ... it was a quantum leap, they were so expensive. [Richmond Recorders bought] a console in April 1985, the second one in Melbourne and Australia' (Corr 2017).

This accelerated the drawing power of Melbourne for aspiring producers and engineers. After serving various apprenticeships in London, Jim Barber, for example, cites the lack of 24 track studios in Adelaide as a major reason for settling in Melbourne in 1981 (Barber 2017).

The Go!! label

An offshoot of the successful television program that began on Channel 0 in August 1964, the Go!! label was important in signing local talent and providing a base for interstate stardom. Talent for both the program and label was initially derived from Melbourne's live music circuits, with scouts spotting singers such as Marcie Jones and granting them a TV contract of £18 for fortnightly performances on the TV show (Jones 2017). Mike Brady remembers the local aura of the program:

> We [MPD Ltd] were going to sign to EMI – in fact, EMI paid for our demos – but our manager said, 'No, you've got to go with the Go!! label because it's so cool and so now and it'll look better' and all that stuff. EMI would have given us a better international shot, I think, if we had gone with them, but the exposure was fantastic. I mean, all of a sudden, this little band – my band in Melbourne, MPD – were known all over Australia. We could go to Perth and fill a dance. So it was the *Go Show* more in those days than anything else that did it.
>
> (Brady 2018)

An interesting stand-off developed in 1970 in relation to the interdependence of the local recording and radio sectors. A long-held complaint from the commercial radio stations – that they were providing recording companies with free promotion of their product – became a serious dispute.[2] From 15 May, Australian stations ceased airing Australian and UK acts due to the stations' refusal to pay mechanical royalties to the recording companies. This particularly affected the multinationals (Decca, Parlophone, Columbia) and the larger Australian labels, such as Festival. Reports of ways around the 'ban' included rumours of a pirate radio station ship to hit the seas in Sydney Harbour (Munson 1970: 17), while other media took sides: 'It hardly seems a good idea to dispute with radio stations when that's how you earn your bread and butter, but maybe the record manufacturers have other promotions stints up their sleeves. It will be interesting to see' (ibid.).

Another solution was to produce local covers of international hits that had yet to receive Australian airplay, providing local hits for Liv Maessen ('Knock, Knock, Who's There'), the Mixtures ('In the Summertime') and Autumn ('Yellow River') among others. While Fable and other Australian independents were presented with a wider window for local airplay, the ban had other consequences. Upset with Fable Record's decision not to join the ban, owner Ron Tudor argues that EMI leant on Fable's distributor, Polygram, to end their lease deal; worse, instructions went out to deny Fable access to pressing plants throughout the country (Tudor in Stapleton 2010). Lasting from May to October, the inadvertent effects of the ban for smaller labels meant that 'a reset button had been pushed on the music scene' (Nichols 2016: 157).

The prevailing blues, psychedelic rock and country rock strands prevailing in Melbourne in the early 1970s produced memorable albums from a range of acts: Chain, Carson, the Dingoes, Spectrum, the Coloured Balls, Axiom and Country Radio. The success of Daddy Cool's single ('Eagle Rock') and album (*Daddy Who? Daddy Cool!*) in 1971 proved the commercial value of local recordings (Walker, Hogan and Beilharz 2012: 116), confirmed with the local sales for Johnny Farnham and Billy Thorpe and the Aztecs. EMI enjoyed success with local signings (the Masters Apprentices, the Twilights, Russell Morris, Flying Circus, Johnny Farnham). Other local labels invested in local signings, including Sparmac, Fable and Festival (Thorpe and the Aztecs, Country Radio, Wild Cherries, Chain). Other international labels – RCA, Phillips, CBS – also invested in local acts. This was in part propelled by Australian consumers playing their part in the growth of record consumption; 'Between 1972–74, LP manufacture increased by seven million units, easily beating the 1969–72 rise of four million' (Baker 1981b: 483).

The independents

While 'indies' – independent recording companies – became more of a focus internationally in the 1980s, they formed an important component of Melbourne's growth in the 1970s. These companies are broadly defined by their smaller structures in relation to the 'majors', promising some level of creative autonomy to their artists, with 'no ties to vertically integrated corporations' (Hesmondhalgh 1999: 35).[3] A crucial factor is also the DIY management structures. The willingness of enthusiasts to back their favourite artists in terms of financial and organizational structures was a feature of Melbourne popular music from the 1970s. The subsequent undergrowth of smaller recording outfits provided alternatives for local artists regarding pathways to success, and even redefining 'success' in more local terms.

With Consolidated Rock, Adrian Barker, Michael Browning and Michael Gudinski had successfully achieved a near monopoly of venue bookings in

Melbourne; by 1970, Gudinski was thinking about establishing a recording label. Leveraging the artists within his management/booking company Evans Gudinski (a merger of Consolidated Rock with Australian Entertainment Exchange), Mushroom Records was launched in May 1972, with Festival Records supplying financial, recording and distribution support (Coupe 2015: 22–30). In similar ways to Motown's mythical salesmanship as 'the sound of young America', it has been argued that 'Mushroom may have been aspiring to be "the sound of young Melbourne"' (Coupe 2015: 33). The debt that Melbourne owes to Gudinski/Mushroom is undeniable; yet its contractual arrangements have often been submerged within the mythology. One can acknowledge its achievements while also recognizing that its competitive instincts were part of the furniture:

> That place was a conflict-of-interest minefield; there was a string attached to so many acts in Melbourne that came from that [Mushroom Records/Premier Artists] building. You had the record company and the booking agency, the management, the people making the posters – everything, all run by the same people, all representing almost every artist in town.
>
> (artist Renee Geyer cited in Coupe 2015: 38–9)

Like other labels, Mushroom developed through close attention to local live circuits, signing acts that dominated the pubs, such as Chain, Madder Lake, Mackenzie Theory, Carson, the Dingoes and Buster Brown. It was Skyhooks, however, that cemented the label's survival. Their first album, *Living in the 70's*, charted at number one nationally for sixteen weeks. Their success was built upon a combination of factors: an art-rock sensibility derived from inner city Carlton bohemia, the production and song arrangement nous of 1960s/1970s musician Ross Wilson and a stage act that went far beyond the pub rock mannerisms of the time, borrowing from theatre (see Nichols 2016: 223–33). One description of the first album also describes their entire output and ambitions: 'primarily white Australian, political, and socially aware' (ibid.: 229). Melbourne 'indies', nonetheless, did rely upon corporate structures in various ways. It has been argued that 'Between 1973 and 1978, for perhaps the only time in history, local labels were calling the shots over the transnational conglomerates, but only because they were already in bed with them' (Walker, Hogan and Beilharz 2012: 119).

Melbourne was also beginning to produce retail stores that acted as vibrant conduits between fans and recording labels. A number of retail entrepreneurs developed import networks that ensured locals were aware of international genres that in turn influenced local scenes and labels. Situated in Manchester Lane, the Archie and Jughead's record store began in 1971. Interviewed by the ABC TV's *GTK (Getting to Know)* program in 1971, owners Keith Glass and David Pepperell explained that they wanted to be ahead of the curve in 'selling the minority stuff' such as David Bowie, Hawkwind, Velvet Underground and John McLaughlin; 'we get excited with a new shipment of records ... We don't have people who just want to spend $3.95 on a [German big band musician] James Last LP' (Pepperell in ABC TV 1971). The retail stores were important sites of connections even in later eras (networking in very fluid, looser forms): for Thrush and the Cunts' Jules Taylor, 'you just had to stand for a day in Climax Records and you met everybody ... when people knew that the [reggae and ska] shipments were arriving, you'd see these hordes of black-coated op-shop dressed people arriving' (Taylor 2020: 68).

As companies such as Mushroom began to look more like an Australian 'major', others found value in the micro-local. Au Go Go Records was founded by Bruce Milne and Philip Morland in 1979, setting up shop in Fitzroy. In time, the label released a diverse array of acts including the Young Charlatans, Mungabeans, Marching Girls, Clint Small, Scapa Flow, Little Murders, the Zorros and Dorian Gray, the Moodists, Spiderbait, the Meanies and Magic Dirt. Well before establishing Au Go Go, Milne was an avid (under age) patron of the late 1960s/early 1970s venues, had hosted some music programs on Swinburne Tech radio and on 3CR, established *Pulp* fanzine with Clinton Walker and worked on *RAM* magazine. He had also undertaken an apprenticeship of sorts with Keith Glass at Missing Link Records:

> Keith was thinking about working with some newer bands and said to me, 'Look, if you're getting 50 bucks a week on the dole, I'll give you 50 bucks a week and you can just work out of here and help me with things' ... he signed the Go-Betweens and The Boys Next Door, that became the Birthday Party, and the Laughing Clowns and a whole lot of other things ... Keith was a great mentor. Of course, he'd put out so many records before, so he taught me the mechanics of recording through to manufacturing through to distribution and that was a really fabulous time.
>
> (Milne 2017)

Glass nominates several challenges in establishing Missing Link, including the inability of existing record pluggers and distribution chains to recognize the motives (and value) of non-mainstream recordings, and the refusal of banks to grant loans to grow the business (Glass 1994). Profits from the import/export

Missing Link store were soon depleted in running the recording/distribution operation:

> We couldn't have made those records without the shop to put them through, and the [independent] radio stations that played them. They fed off each other. Virtually anything in that market that was quite good would sell a thousand, two thousand singles.
>
> (ibid.)

In the earlier years, Glass's 'network' consisted of committed individuals, rather than retail. The story of the company's efforts to sell the Flying Lizards' 'Money'[4] in 1979 after Festival had passed on distribution is emblematic of the existing environment. Offers made to the major companies for distribution deals for 'Money' met with either 'total disinterest' or 'no awareness of the market at all' (ibid.).[5] Glass also believes that the cultural cringe remained: 'the syndrome was if it's punky and alternative from England, it was alright, but if it's home-grown, it's not good enough' (ibid.).

For Au Go Go, capitalizing on the relatively cheap leasing costs of the inner city meant the label was situated in the heart of changing scenes. In discussing the formative years of the label, Milne has emphasized the local ecosystem:

> I think the challenges of setting up an independent label in the early days were – well, obviously, financial. Lack of experience, because we're all still feeling our way, although we certainly were building up networks – distribution networks and contacts around the world. The landscape in Australia was very different than it is now, in that you knew your records would get played, if they were good ones, on RRR and PBS. So you knew inner city Melbourne, you had some grounding. But outside of that, where was the radio that was going to play your records? Where was the television that was going to expose? Well, there was none. So that was out of the question, I think. The divide between the Australian music industry and what we thought we were doing was a chasm. That disappeared later on, which I celebrate. At the same time, I miss in some ways, that 'them or us' attitude that we had.
>
> (Milne 2017)

Milne was also running a record shop at the same time as Au Go Go and managing some of the label's acts. For Milne:

> [The meaning of] "independent" changed dramatically. In my mind, really independent – I mean, I just stopped using the word because it took on – it's

like "alternative". It just took on this life of its own. "Independent", to me, meant outside of a set of networks. We were independent from commercial TV and commercial radio and we were independent from the [media owners] Rupert Murdochs and Kerry Packers.

(ibid.)

Into the 1980s, Milne also had a job at Virgin doing A&R, and was then approached by Roger Grierson to establish a small label within Polygram (Reliant Records), and then set up another label of his own in 2002, In-Fidelity Records with Waterfront Records' Steve Stavrakis, with distribution through Shock Records (Milne 2017). For those running smaller labels from the Melbourne suburbs, viability amounted to territorial expansion: 'we knew that our acts only sold to 0.001% of the record buying public, so what we've got to do is find that percentage in England, in Finland, In Canada' (ibid.).

Later labels reinforced the strength of catering to local artists. Established by Paul Elliott, Polyester Records signed bands such as I Spit on Your Gravy and Little Murders. Linked to the record store on Brunswick Street in Fitzroy, the label operated from 1983 to 1991. Established in 1988, Shock Records benefited from the prior retail and distribution experience of its founders, Andrew McGee, Frank Falvo and David Williams, releasing a range of Melbourne acts while also acting as a distributor of international acts on a larger scale.

Richmond Recorders (RR) benefited from the talents of Tony Cohen, who had undertaken an apprenticeship at Armstrong Studios in 1975–76. Beginning with Models in 1978, Cohen came properly into full producer duties at the studio, working with Peter Lillie, Serious Young Insects, the Boys Next Door, the Ferretts, the Go-Betweens, Paul Kelly and the Dots, the Sacred Cowboys and Pel Mel (among others). According to a biography of Cohen, the employment conditions were certainly unusual: the Recorders' owner provided Cohen with a house a few doors from the studio, and paid him primarily with drugs and cash, with continual disputes with recording companies about royalties owed (Blair 2016: 74–98). Cohen is credited with providing the time, affinity and ear to ensure an emerging set of Melbourne bands were captured properly on tape:

Its hard to imagine the music scene without Tony's input at that time. If Tony hadn't been around to do it, there just weren't any other engineers around who could work at the same intensity that Tony did, night after night. I just don't think any other engineers were, frankly, as good really. I think the kind of ideas bands were trying to articulate in the punk thing or post-punk thing or whatever it was, there was no-one else who could do that except Tony ... He is just central to the sound of that music.

(Models keyboard player/songwriter Andrew Duffield cited in Blair 2016: 82)

The Boys Next Door and the Birthday Party also assisted in sustaining Missing Link, founded by Keith Glass in 1977, who saw himself as not a 'producer so much as an intermediary and organiser' in the studio (Baker 1981a). Reflecting on the local hierarchy, Glass observed that York Street studio (Fitzroy) catered for those on a budget; bands with slightly larger means would book in Richmond Recorders; and the more lavish acts (especially those with multinational backing) would record at AAV (Glass 1994). Quincy McLean remembers his Richmond Recorder experience:

> Back in those days you'd try and get midnight to dawn sessions at Richmond Recorders – our first experiences with an in-house engineer who got the keys to the building to sweep up and would track a bit of your stuff. Then gradually we eventually, with Blue Ruin, ended up with Phil Calvert in the band, and of course he'd had all that experience with the Boys Next Door and the Birthday Party, and he worked with Dorian Gray a bit, and then Psychedelic Furs. So he came to us with a wealth of information and he said 'We've got to record with Tony Cohen', so the first album was done with Cohen. But again it was midnight to dawn sessions. We recorded that album in two nights, and with Tony's production and the fact that we worked our arses off to get it, I think we did a pretty good job.
>
> (McLean 2017)

The more established labels did attempt to grab a piece of the punk (and later, new wave) action. Mushroom's attempt, the offshoot label Suicide Records, signed a clutch of acts (including Wasted Daze and the Boys Next Door):

> I actually went to the launch of Suicide Records ... which was really a blatant attempt to cash in, and I don't think a lot of the artists who were signed to it had a lot of respect for the Barry Earl aspect, but it was a foot in the door. I think bands like the Models, who formed out of Teenage Radio Stars, and the Boys Next Door, who pretty quickly evolved into the Birthday Party ... A lot of those bands were evolving pretty quickly, but the launch pad of that I think was great, at least for those two bands. There were other bands that came out of that, like JAB, and members of that split off into other bands.
>
> (McLean 2017)

David Vodicka founded Rubber Records (Ice Cream Hands, Jet, Even, Underground Lovers, etc.) in 1989 (proving that 'bedroom labels' were not new in the 1990s) as another example of the cross-pollination of Melbourne media: Vodicka for a time was a breakfast host on RRR.

For some studios (such as Armstrong/AAV), advertising revenue was important in longer-term viability. Advertising work lessened as a result of broader media deregulation undertaken by the Hawke/Keating Labor governments in the name of opening up local fiefdoms to international competition. Radio and television advertising was no longer compelled to have a local production component. According to Wendy Stapleton, this seriously affected a source of income that shored up more precarious touring and recording revenues for artists:

> It was the end of jingles because what that meant was that anything that was already recorded overseas they could just use, whereas everything used to have to be recorded or re-recorded in Australia. And then at the beginning of deregulation, just to appease certain parts of the entertainment industry, they said, 'Well, we still have to have Australian voice-overs', and that was basically to appease Actors Equity, because they were quite strong. It did nothing for the musos. It did a lot for the people that did voice-overs, and I used to do voice-overs as well, so I had one foot in each camp, but that was the end of it. That was the end of it for recording jingles.
>
> (Stapleton 2017)

Advertising jingles had also been important as training grounds for aspiring producers, and valuable income for fledgling studios.

In 1984, 'there was one solid state recording console [in Melbourne], and that was at AAV ... it was a quantum leap, they were so expensive'; Richmond Recorders purchased the second in 1985 (Corr 2017). However, serious investment could lead to substantial revenues. According to Sing Sing Studio's Kaj Dahlstrom, typical fees were '$17,00 to $20,000 per day ... sessions [then] were longer, framed by the record companies, and we got more mixing work in those days' (Dahlstrom 2017). Working at Richmond Recorders in the early 1980s, Jim Barber reflects that beyond recording costs, 'video costs were taken out, of course, before royalties were added ... one in 20 bands made back the cost of their recordings' (Barber 2017).

Melbourne luminaries (managers Michael Gudinski and Glenn Wheatley and radio's Lee Simon) formed part of an industry panel convened by the Hawke

Labor Government's Trade Minister, John Dawkins, as part of an export push driven through Ausmusic. The Minister's 1986 press release revealed the bare economic considerations: export income was estimated at $8.5m, while royalty payments overseas amounted to $63m (Dawkins 1986). The Minister also noted the imbalance between the larger multinationals based in Australia, and the 50 'indie' companies representing only a 10 per cent share of the local market (ibid.). Companies were to be provided further support at key international trade fairs (such as MIDEM in Cannes), while more workshops and guidelines were to be produced for aspiring local acts. In the same year, Export Music Australia (EMA) was launched to promote Australian popular music in select markets, co-funded by APRA, AMCOS and ARIA. As Breen (1999: 81–7, 160–1) has argued, conflict about strategy between Ausmusic, Austrade, industry sectors and government departments reduced the ability of the push to be really effective.

By 1990, journalist/historian Glenn A. Baker proclaimed in *Billboard* that CBS Records Australia was looking to Melbourne, rather than Sydney, for future local growth, noting that Mushroom had enjoyed an 'unobstructed first stab at area talent for 15 years' (Baker 1990). By 1994, the same publication pronounced Melbourne as the crucible of creativity; its secret lay in the tight connections between its 'critical mass of pubs' and indie record stores and labels (Duffy 1994a: 24). Under the depressing heading 'Business is Boomeranging', a 'Billboard Spotlight' at once noted the diversity of Australian indie labels and sounds, and the majors' determination to capitalize on them (Duffy 1994b: 65).

Blues rock outfit Blue Ruin's singer Quincy McLean provides a useful description of a gradual immersion from artist to entrepreneurial efforts driven by the lack of local infrastructure:

> I was looking for somewhere for Blue Ruin to rehearse. I stumbled across this old warehouse. A female friend was looking for somewhere to do a dressmaker's building and had stumbled across an old recording studio [older name?] that had become derelict, and she knew I was looking for somewhere to rehearse. She showed me and I was blown away. I loved the idea of having somewhere that you could record as well, but it really had been gutted. This is the studio in North Fitzroy [York Street and Silkwood Studios] ... Daffy Williams had set it up in 1977/1978. Actually, it had been the studio where people like Paul Kelly and the Dots; Australian Crawl; I think possibly The Sports; [Whirly World], Primitive Calculators – a whole heap of those bands [had recorded]. But then the York

Street people sold it to the Silkwood people, and eventually, unfortunately it got run into the ground, and it was ripped apart. So when I stumbled across it I was really just looking for somewhere to rehearse. I couldn't really afford to rent the whole building, so I got a friend to take upstairs, and I just got a whole heap of other bands in to help cover the costs, and I ran it as a rehearsal studio, and then evolved it back into recording, and it's just continued to evolve from there. That was from late '91. Then about eight years later I heard that Stable Sound on Hoddle Street was closing down. The bands from there were trying to come to me to rehearse. I got curious: 'Why is it closing down?' … I was told that Stable Sound couldn't get more than 20 or so bookings a week, and I was turning away – I was doing 20 plus in just three rooms, and turning away probably the same amount of bands again. So I thought, 'I'm going to give it a go. I took it over', and it really was very, very run-down. I've spent the last 20 years evolving it and trying to make it better.

(McLean 2017)

The recording sector reflected the live and management sectors of Australian music in its over-representation of (older, white) men. Recording with Sweet Jayne, Chris Scheri adopted a determined DIY approach to sharpening her skills. Scheri was determined to learn recording techniques, progressing from bedroom equipment to observing engineers and producers, to setting up her own studio in the building deserted by Regency Recording:

I set up in there and we patched everything in and I got a desk and I borrowed some money and bought myself a $15,000 freestanding tape machine and just paid it back gradually when I got clients. So basically the studio, there was Music Recording Studio 7 and I took in paying clients, but it also worked on the barter system … and the barter system was you play guitar for me – because I wasn't, I played acoustic guitar, but my electric guitaring's okay but there were better players than me that I could use. And drummers and things. I'd mike up the drum kit and stuff like that. Or I'd use a Linn drum. If I was programming the drums it was the Linn drum and if I wanted a live sound I'd get a drummer in. And then I'd do their demos. So they didn't charge me and I didn't charge them. It was a good system. It worked really well.

(Scheri 2017)

By the end of the 1980s, in addition to the earlier 1960s innovators, Melbourne hosted other studios (Sing Sing, Flagstaff, Stable Sound) that catered to the different needs of recording budgets, producer aesthetics and other commercial outputs (such as advertising).

Contemporary recording contexts

In the late 1990s, a number of factors coincided to wring changes to the older 'major'/'indie' label structures, and the circuit of recording studios promising to deliver the right ambience and sounds. Already facing greater global competition for the youth leisure dollar from other electronic consumer items (Laing 2004; Leyshon 2009), the arrival of digital download stores (iTunes in 2001; Spotify in 2008), along with a range of other curated digital record services (Bandcamp, Soundcloud), presented several challenges to recording companies and studios. The decline of physical sales since the late 1990s, and the subsequent rise of illegal downloading precipitated a consistent decline in recording sales globally, although this has been contested elsewhere (see Rogers 2013). It has taken much of the 2000s (spiked by the 2008 Global Financial Crisis) for legitimate streaming services to recover sales back to 1990s levels. According to the International Federation of Phonographic Industries (IFPI), recording revenue declined from US$25.2 billion in 1999 to US$14.2 billion in 2014 (IFPI 2018). In relation, 'software as an economic of agent of change' (Leyshon 2009: 1310) has been crucial in transferring the expensive studio experience to the bedroom, lounge room or garage. While the more famous studios have retained favour for the 'buzz' of the recording room, or through invoking historical successes, the emergence of software such as ProTools has made recording a much more intimate and individualized experience. This, in turn, has seen the range of associated activities – A&R, mentoring, pre- and post-production – of labels reduced in scale. Of equal importance, the accompanying decline in record retail has robbed punters and industrial figures alike of invaluable social spaces.

The 'traditional' recording studio is fewer in number, replaced by more smaller setups that are mixtures of freelance and independent structures serving a number of purposes.[6] Yet a number of labels are continuing the tradition of ensuring that new music is heard. After the uneven 1970s and 1980s 'indie' experiences, Moodists' drummer Claire Moore believes the baton has been passed on to contemporary labels with the same spirit:

> That's probably got something to do with giving people at least their first start, or even people staying on indie labels now for the whole trip, which is great that they can do that now without having to go to the majors if they don't want to … Milk Records have done amazing things – Jen Cloher and Courtney [Barnett] …

I put out a solo record with Chapter [Music] and they've just gone on to do great things, put out lots and lots of records.

(Moore 2018)

A cluster of other labels – such as Sunset Pig, Spoilsport, Flightless, Mistletone, Two Bright Lakes, Listen – play important roles in providing non-mainstream genres and acts with local exposure.

North Melbourne has always possessed different mixes of venues, record retail and recording outfits. As the boundary of gentrification (marked by housing price rises and levels of working/middle class affordability) pushes northwards beyond Northcote (see Courtney Barnett's 'Depreston'), new intersections have developed that constitute overlapping scenes. Soul/funk (e.g. the Bamboos, Saskwatch, Clairy Browne, Cactus Channel), indie rock (Barnett and other Milk! artists) and punk are serviced by venues (the Workers Club, Northcote Social Club, Coburg RSL, the Gasometer, the Tote), labels (e.g. Milk!, Bedroom Sucks, Hope Street Recordings), retail (e.g. Northside Records, Polyester) and community radio (e.g. Vince Peach's Soul Time on PBS; Chris Gill's Get Down on RRR). According to Chris Gill, establishing Northside Records (including providing regular gigs and album launches in-store) was a matter of individual enthusiasm catering to demand: 'A lot of people are into the music but there wasn't a place that was dedicated [to "groove based music"] – call it a church' (Gill in *Now Sound: Melbourne's Listening* 2018). The 2019 Vinyl Lovers' Tour Guide (*Diggin' Melbourne*) lists eighteen vinyl stores in Fitzroy/Collingwood/Carlton, and ten stores across Northcote/Thornbury/Preston/Brunswick and Coburg (*Diggin' Melbourne* 2020).

A constant refrain of those interviewed for the *Now Sound* (2018) documentary was the fear of the city losing spaces not just for performance and recording, but the associated venues, cafes, late night trading pubs and clubs that allow for chance encounters to meet (romantic, business and creative) partners. Clearly, the 1970s/80s convergence of retail, recording and performance has its contemporary versions (and entrepreneurs). To the extent that scenes inform understandings of networks, clusters and hyper-locality, the collective plea remains that the mix of different spaces and activities remains crucial for local actors to produce records that are commercial and non-commercial. The set of 'underground incubators' (Straw 2015: 481) discussed above also require wider 'public contexts of sociability, conviviality and interaction' (ibid.: 483) to bring layers of subcultural capital to the surface.

Figure 9 Bakehouse Studios, Richmond. Source: Quincy McLean.

As some retail stores return to serving as performance spaces, and star community radio DJs air their favourite records in the venues, recording studios are also offering new mixtures of roles. Bakehouse Studios, operated by Quincy McLean and Helen Marcou, have been consistent in their intent on the studio serving multiple roles as rehearsal rooms, recording studio, art forum/exhibition space, music event launching pad and policy centre:

> I think we've really responded to the hybridity of art, really. Musicians aren't any longer just musicians. People will do all sorts of things that complement or are part of their art form. We have everything from people doing VR, 3D videos in there, to little showcases. We've collaborated with everything from the symphony to fashion to live art, performance art, theatre, and even visual arts. So when we did the Bakehouse Art Project in 2014, we invited ten local

visual artists and makers and craftspeople to come, put a permanent installation in these old, grungy rehearsal rooms, and provide this space where musicians could come and create that next generation of the art. That's been pretty much our ethos: that we don't isolate contemporary music or popular music, and it's part of all of those larger art forms.

(Marcou 2017)

For Marcou, the multi-development of Bakehouse was a logical response to wider industrial shifts:

The way I like to see it is that independents have won the race, by default, as the majors have either collapsed or are winding down, or moving to non-traditional roles, like facilitating more management and media and publicity. The artists are empowering themselves, and really taking a lot more control. I think Bakehouse has come in at that really exciting time. We've seen ourselves more as fulfilling part of that role, and facilitating people and enabling them to make the most of their art. Whether they come to us as musicians or film-makers or dancers or people doing an event, we get really excited about helping people recognize their vision.

(ibid.)

Figure 10 Amanda Palmer performing at Bakehouse Studios. Source: Quincy McLean.

Bakehouse also seems to be performing the crucial role of 'public sociability' (Straw 2015: 483), providing the chance encounters that lead to other creative forms:

> It's not an overly technical space. It's about – aesthetic is really important, and hospitality, and community. A lot happens in that courtyard space. Bands pick up other bands, other members. It's a really interesting anthropological viewpoint, when you stand back and see what happens there, from day to day, and that – I hate this word, it's a weasel word – cross-pollination of people. But coming together and the interactions there are incredible at times.
>
> (ibid.)

In the 2000s, set-up costs for studios were confronted with the realities of contemporary prohibitions. For example, Metropolis (formerly Armstrong) Studio closed in 2005, and Sing Sing Recording Studios's Cremorne site was sold in 2016, prompting relocation to Box Hill in concert with the TAFE music industry courses located there. As large spaces, studios have been targeted for residential redevelopment, exacerbated by inner city housing booms (Sing Sing's Cremorne property was sold for $4.55m (Tan 2016)). For Bakehouse Studios, 'over the last six years we've seen a 400 per cent increase in our rental' (Marcou 2017).

Having sold 49 per cent of Mushroom to Festival Records in 1993, Gudinski sold the remaining 51 per cent to Rupert Murdoch's News Corp. in 1998, although retaining the Mushroom title. It is suggested that the first sales tranche was designed to provide funds for UK investments, and the second to provide greater transition to touring as recording revenues globally soured (Coupe 2015: 254). In 2005, 'the Festival-Mushroom Group (FMG) ceased trading and its carcass was acquired by Warners [Music]' (Walker, Hogan and Beilharz 2012: 129). While Gudinski resurrected his usual concerns with the promotion and recording of Melbourne acts through his Mushroom Group, the News Corp transactions signified in some ways the end of a particular 1970s way of doing things.

Diversification is also evident in other means to encourage different studio experiences. The Push, a youth music initiative that has been operating since 1988, has established its own label. Beyond the signing and promotion of local young Melbourne artists, its six-month program 'provides both industry and artist participants with an opportunity to gain practical experience and establish their networks within the industry while being mentored by record label professionals and other experienced artists, recording engineers and producers' (The Push 2021). Supported by Creative Victoria, The Push label is important in developing training experiences for aspiring label owners that in turn provides access to key local networks.

Conclusion

Through a process of importation – of key people as much as technologies – local recording infrastructure managed to overcome various insecurities about sounds and international worth. Led by Bill Armstrong and AAV, Melbourne developed a strong reputation as pop headquarters in the 1960s, backed by its flourishing live music circuits (see Chapter 2). By the 1970s, a range of innovative independents (such as Fable and Mushroom) played a crucial role in harnessing the shift to greater visibility on radio and television (see Chapter 4) that was reflected in vinyl sales. This has arguably been the city's remaining strength into the 1980s and beyond in producing 'amateurs' with deep knowledge of local subgenres and scenes able to transpose their enthusiasm to start small labels. If there has been/is a 'Melbourne Sound', it perhaps lies in the quirks that emerge from the DIY-ness of wider local scenes. Yet the changing role of the recording studio in not simply diversifying its recording clientele, but catering to other music and cultural sectors, may not be enough to stem the loss of bricks-and-mortar businesses and the important social milieu that accompanies and feeds off them.

6

The legendary city

Introduction

While the specifics of policy, social change and economic fortunes are essential in understanding how Melbourne's status as a music city has been established, it is also important to consider how the stories that are told about what Melbourne is, or is not, play a role in creating the city. This chapter mainly relies on the accounts of interviewees, and discussions in the Melbourne music press, to construct a more bottom-up account of how Melbourne music came to be framed the way it is. Despite no clear 'Melbourne Sound', and a variety of scenes within the city and changing styles over the years, there are certain tropes and discourses that have developed in discussions of Melbourne's popular music that may help to explain the strength of its claims to be the music city of Australia. In examining these, this chapter considers music in terms of its 'fixity' and 'fluidity' (Connell and Gibson 2003); that is, the way in which music can be simultaneously something that is constantly moving and changing, while also having strong associations with particular places, or particular times. In this instance, the story that plays out is one where Sydney is the most common point of contrast and is used as a key tool in framing how Melbourne is understood. Sydney is undeniably the business centre of music in Australia throughout most of the period under consideration in this book, but Melbourne is able to use the discourses associated with rock, circulating at a global level, to frame itself as the home to more 'real' musical expression. While there is a period in the late 1970s and early 1980s when Melbourne's dominance is challenged by the emergence of a cluster of commercially (and in a number of cases internationally) successful rock bands based in Sydney, narratives of the decline of Sydney's music scene from the 1990s – in comparison to the revitalization of the Melbourne scene in the wake of the Save Live Australian Music rally in 2010, which will be discussed in detail here – are deployed to reclaim Melbourne's status as Australia's pre-eminent music city.

In utilizing interviews with people from the Melbourne music community conducted during the course of this project, we are relying on and drawing from the collective memory of this community. These recollections are possible to be understood as not recounting the history of Melbourne music, but helping to construct what it is. The common themes and threads that run through the accounts of respondents do not simply show us that some 'truth' has been uncovered about the subject being discussed, but are more likely to have arisen because of shared experiences in the Melbourne scene(s), and exposure to the same media (including the music media discussed in the previous chapter, but also key documentaries, movies and books). Using media reports from throughout this history therefore helps us to see where some of these common threads have originally emerged, and, more interestingly, places where the current collective view of Melbourne's past may differ from accounts that were written at the time the events we now look back on were taking place.

Melbourne v Sydney: The second city?

We'd rather live in Melbourne though some folks say it's faulty
Sydney's got its strippers but we've got Henry Bolte
We've got Australian Rules and the Melbourne Cup each year
Sydney's girls are way out front but we've got stronger beer
'Melborn and Sideny', The Idlers Five, 1968
I want to see the sun go down from St Kilda Esplanade
Where the beach needs reconstruction, where the palm trees have it hard
I'd give you all of Sydney Harbour (all that land, all that water)
For that one sweet promenade
'From St Kilda to Kings Cross', Paul Kelly, 1985

The lyrics of these two songs, written two decades apart, help to illustrate how the ideas of what Melbourne and the Melbourne music scene are can only be fully constructed by making it clear what they are not. This is true of all cities, which are always understood to a greater or lesser extent through comparisons with other cities, whether nationally or on a global level. This section will examine how Melbourne's musical identity is positioned mainly in relation to other Australian cities, and Sydney in particular. Melbourne's framing as a global city, and in comparison to overseas centres, will be explored in a following chapter.

In the music press during the *Go-Set* years, a sense is conveyed that the major cities in Australia have quite separate scenes to one another. It was only in 1966 that *Go-Set* published the first national music chart, which, along with the later development of shows like *Countdown* in the 1970s and 1980s and the nationalisation of Triple J through the 1990s, helped to strengthen the idea that there was a national music scene, and a distinctly Australian musical identity. In the mid- to late 1960s, however, *Go-Set* compares and contrasts the major cities' music scenes to one another on a regular basis. For example, an article in April 1968 gives an overview of Australian east coast cities' music scenes through the eyes of rock group Wild Cherries, and shows a series of tropes that will persist across the decades already emerging ('Wild Cherries: Thoughts and Opinions' 1968). Wild Cherries' experiences with having shows shut down led them to declare that 'fascism is alive and well, and barely hidden in Brisbane', a telling statement only months before the election of Premier Joh Bjelke-Petersen, whose corruption and violent opposition to youth culture in Queensland have since become touchstones as a low point in State relations with popular culture in Australia. Sydney gets a mixed review, with promising new discos contrasted with 'disc jockeys who are so lacking in musical taste we can't believe it' and 'Discotheque owners who would rather cater for their own tastes and those of their friends than those of the people who pay'. Canberra is described as 'a beautiful city with what appears to be a dormant pop scene', and it is worth noting that the nation's capital is almost never mentioned elsewhere in any music publication examined here or by interviewees. Melbourne is given a favourable review by the Melbourne-based band, who also note 'some mysterious and monstrous force doing its best to hold back progress' in the city.

Perth and Adelaide, separated from the east coast touring circuit, tend to be mentioned less often and usually in the context of discussions of musicians who have relocated to Melbourne. This inevitably frames the move as being in some way about the deficiencies of the music scene that had been left behind, and the relative benefits of Melbourne. For example, in 1968, Vince from the Valentines explains the band's move from Perth to Melbourne:

> Melbourne is where it's all happening, where you can make money, and the only city where you can become internationally accepted […] There are no dances or discos for the under 21's in Perth, and if we were to go over we would have to play smaltz music in hotels and we don't wish to do this … We feel sorry for the kids as no-one seems to care whether they are provided with pop entertainment or not. We would dearly love to go to Perth to see our fans again but Melbourne has now become our home.
>
> ('Valentines Slam Perth Scene' 1968: 6)

Despite occasional mentions of bands moving away from Melbourne to find work in other Australian cities (in addition to the steady stream of artists who move overseas, mainly to the UK, to try their fortunes in other markets), by the end of the 1960s, the idea that moving to Melbourne or Sydney is an important career move for bands in Australia had become firmly established in the journalistic discourse.

As references to other cities become less common, Sydney becomes established as the clear point of contrast to Melbourne. This is in the context of a broader rivalry between the two cities which has been present since the foundation of Melbourne in 1853. Controversial Australian historian Geoffrey Blainey (2014: 230) has declared that 'Rarely in modern history have two big cities competed so strenuously, so evenly, for so long as Melbourne and Sydney ... it is difficult to find another pair of cities which for more than a century have sought supremacy and not been far apart'. Kaji-O'Grady (2006: 61) notes that:

> As early as the 1880s Marcus Clarke, in his 'The Future of the Australian Race,' spoke of Melbourne becoming the 'intellectual capital,' while Sydney would be the 'fashionable and luxurious capital.' Manning Clark formulated his understanding of the different cultures of the two cities in the 1960s, portraying Melbourne as earnest, humanist and socially optimistic and Sydney as libertarian and elitist.

While the parameters of this rivalry have shifted significantly since the invasion of Australia and have been shaped by the economic and political fortunes of the States and the nation, these broad lines of 'intellect' versus 'fashion and luxury' have continued to resonate. These themes emerge when comparisons are made between Melbourne and Sydney in a variety of creative areas, from advertising (Crawford 2015) to architecture (Kaji-O'Grady 2006) to television (Bye 2008) and are clearly present in the discussion of music below. These themes can be connected to the positioning of Melbourne as a 'second city' in a variety of ways. While there have been times when Melbourne has clearly dominated Sydney in specific areas (for example its rapid growth and affluence during the gold rush in the late 1880s, or its period as Australia's capital between 1901 and 1927), it has long been positioned as Australia's 'second city'. Sydney is of course Australia's literal first city (with Melbourne being the fifth of the country's State capitals to be founded), and has generally been the seat of economic power, as well as the 'face' of the nation internationally as its most 'global' city throughout the twentieth century (Searle and O'Connor 2013). However, understanding how being a 'second city' might impact on Melbourne life cannot only be thought about in terms of economic and population metrics. Leone (2014: 8), while noting the complexity of the term, defines second cities as existing only as part of a relationship:

> One might say that first cities are such because the complex network of economic, political, and sociocultural agencies that shape their identities encourage individuals and groups not to conceive them in relation to other cities but in a purely intra-systemic manner. On the contrary, it could be said that second cities are such because the same complex network encourages individuals and groups to conceive their urban identities in relation to those of other cities, and in particular in comparison to those of first cities.

Highly mobile populations, and the way in which cities have become places that one can choose, mean that second cities can find ways to use their 'secondness' to their advantage, for example by developing those characteristics that set them apart from the 'first city', and in this way presenting themselves as attractive alternatives:

> Melbourne's not being the financial capital city of Australia is considered not in terms of a previous economic primate stripped by Sydney, but in terms of Melbourne urban community's choice to construct its identity as centred on different, alternative values.
>
> (Leone 2014: 16)

This way of drawing on specific points of uniqueness to construct an idea of Melbourne popular music that clearly sets it apart from Sydney emerged in materials collected for this project and will be explored in detail here. It should be noted that of course there has never been just one notion of what Melbourne is, and that significant divisions and rivalries exist within the city itself (as will be demonstrated in Chapter 7), and that the 'second city' concept is itself fluid, incorporating ideas of how cities can be both global and 'second' in various ways, and that in different contexts a second city can become a first, and vice versa (Correia and Denham 2016). In addition, it has been argued that the Sydney-Melbourne rivalry is 'exhausted and boring and from the point of view of other cities in Australia, is solipsistic and provincial' (Kaji-O'Grady 2006: 60); in the same vein, the materials captured here are mainly Melburnians talking to themselves about their city and so should be treated as somewhat of an inward-looking conversation.

Regardless, the centrality of Sydney as a point of reference for understanding Melbourne was demonstrated throughout the interviews we conducted for this project, where for most interviewees describing Melbourne involved invoking Sydney in some way. This is exemplified in this exchange from the interview with Stephan Schutt:

> Q: What do you think at that point it meant to be a Melbourne band, do you think that that meant anything or –
> A: Yeah, there was always a difference in the sound between Sydney bands and Melbourne bands. There was a consciousness that Sydney bands were slicker and perhaps a little less "authentic" – inverted commas, right.

(Schutt 2017)

For Schutt, the first thing that needs to be understood about being a 'Melbourne band' is that it is *not* a Sydney band. Interviewees discussing all eras similarly use qualities of Sydney as a way of establishing the position that Melbourne holds. These qualities – Melbourne as authentic, Melbourne as rock and the possibility of a Melbourne Sound – will be elaborated on below, but we will first present an overview of the changing dynamic between Melbourne and Sydney, as this provides an important context for the rest of the discussion.

The main points of contrast that are made between Melbourne and Sydney are along the lines of Sydney being glamorous/tacky and rich/money-obsessed, in comparison to Melbourne's realness/roughness and intellectualism/snobbishness. These existed within an overarching understanding that Sydney dominated Melbourne economically in the music realm, with the physical location of the offices of major record labels in Sydney being fundamental to this. These tropes were in place as far back as the 1950s. For example, Wendy Stapleton talked about how in the late 1950s:

> Sydney was the headquarters. Even for television, you know, like the Johnny O'Keefe show and what was the other one – *Bandstand*. Everything was out of Sydney. But it was still slightly cabaret. It was pop but it was still a bit more your Col Joyes and all of those people. It was a little bit poppy-corny.

The establishment of Bill Armstrong studios (as discussed in Chapter 5) is noted by the press at the time and interviewees as changing the dynamics between the cities. With bands no longer required to go to Sydney to record, and the development of television shows such as the *Go!! Show* and *Kommotion* broadcast out of Melbourne, a commentary emerged that positioned Melbourne as fresh and exciting in comparison to complacent Sydneysiders stuck in their ways. This persisted through the 1960s, with artist Reverend Black articulating a common viewpoint expressed in *Go-Set*: 'The trouble is that Sydney record producers are too far removed from the Melbourne scene ... In fact they are out of touch with what's happening with the modern pop scene' ('Reverend Black loses his cool' 1968). At the turn of the decade, radio broadcaster Stan Rofe (1970) went further in extending this critique to the entire Sydney music scene:

> Can I be a little unkind to the majority of Sydney groups by saying I believe them to be moulded in the same image, with little variety, little imagination and little originality, and I say it despite my lack of knowledge of the Sydney scene. It is an older scene playing to an older generation and it has nothing to stimulate Australia in 1970.

Despite the parochialism that doubtless underpinned remarks like this from a Melbourne-based commentator, interviewees with different perspectives also echoed this assessment of the music scenes at this time. Mike Rudd (2017) described how in the 1960s:

> ... we had elected to come to Melbourne because Tony McCarthy, my friend who had come over to check out Sydney and Australia, said, "Well, Sydney's really clubby and Melbourne's got a few more interesting things happening", and I just found that held true. Still does.

From Rudd's perspective, this difference could be traced back to different influences on the evolution of the music scene in each city, particularly visiting American servicemen:

> Melbourne's always seemed to be different from Sydney. We never got the R and R [Rest and Recreation leave] situation, the Vietnam situation, so we didn't get that American thing here, so it seemed to have been less kind of clubby and less exploitative than perhaps Sydney was.
>
> (Rudd 2017)

The shift from 'pop' to 'rock' as the dominant paradigm in Australian music during the 1970s reconfigured the relationship between the two cities again. Melbourne initially staked a strong claim as the Australian rock capital, with its claim to bands like Chain, Daddy Cool and Spectrum, thus for a time consolidating the idea that it was the trend leader musically. *Go-Set* explicitly attempts to shore up this claim, for example publishing a two-page spread entitled 'Winds of change on the Melbourne rock scene' (MacLean 1971) that documents the venues, media and industry infrastructure in the city that it credits with having created a vibrant rock scene from almost nothing in a short space of time. Part of this article contains interviews with prominent bands explaining why they have moved from Sydney to Melbourne. This moment also sees the emergence of narratives that attempt to naturalize the relationship between Melbourne and rock by connecting the music forms to aspects of the city, and contrasting these to Sydney:

> Melbourne has tended to produce more great rock bands than Sydney because the southern city is more like the emotions of rock music. It's hard, grey, cold. It's an industrial city, whereas Sydney is a cosmopolitan city. Think of Sydney and you think of the tall skyscraper, but you also think of the miles of beach along which the city squats. Sydney's the surfing centre of Australia. Melbourne is the rock centre.
>
> (Crabshaw 1976)

Quotes like this in the press clearly lean into Melbourne's 'second city' status by making an artistic virtue out of less-than-ideal characteristics of the city ('hard, grey, cold') even while emphasizing some of the more appealing elements of Sydney. Indeed, the idea that that there is a relationship between the physicality of Melbourne and the music that is created there emerged often in interviews and media, sometimes expressed somewhat vaguely. Bruce Milne, for example, stated that:

> Melbourne music is – in some ways is defined by our weather. I really believe that we are the only mainland city that we're – soon as Easter comes around, we certainly putting on – certainly sweaters, but probably long johns, as well, and you don't strip them off until sometime in late October or November. Whereas everyone else is still sitting around in their backyard in their T-shirts and thongs, drinking a beer. When you've got that sort of lifestyle, you tend to have things develop out of that sort of lifestyle.
>
> (Milne 2017)

For Clare Moore, the fundamental differences she ascribed to the cities led even to different types of music:

> Sydney bands were sort of like Radio Birdman and those kind of groups. We used to love going to see them, but they definitely sounded completely different. See, the choice was you go to Melbourne or Sydney, really. You had to get out of Adelaide, you had no choice about that. And the bands who went to Sydney

had kind of maybe, possibly, less success and more barriers. Sydney was where the business was and Melbourne was more where the artiness and the weirdness was, and you could experiment more if you came to Melbourne and maybe do things without people seeing so much. But in Sydney, it's all out there. If you don't hit it off straightaway, you've had it. We got that sense, so we went to Melbourne.

(Moore 2018)

This account again shows a reframing of what might be considered the advantages of Sydney into potential problems, and also gives an indication of how by this point in the late 1970s other cities, such as Adelaide, were not even considered options for people seriously considering a music career. This consideration of Melbourne as important musically – particularly in the rock area – was also found in government. The Dix inquiry on 2JJ in 1980 noted that when the station was initially established in the mid-1970s:

… it was also management's intention to relay JJ to Melbourne and that eventually Melbourne should have its own radio station 3JJ. At that time it was recognised that Melbourne was the centre of the pop/rock music industry and that 3JJ would in some ways be even more relevant there.

(Dix 1980)

However, the position of Melbourne was threatened by the development of a strong and very successful rock scene in Sydney in the late 1970s and early 1980s. A gig review of Cold Chisel in 1979 suggested that:

There are some things that it's just no use denying, and one of them is that these days Sydney has a monopoly of the country's best full-on rock bands. There are no competitors in Australia's one time music capital for the likes of the Angels, Rose Tattoo, Midnight Oil or Cold Chisel when it comes to delivering with flair and noisy aggravation. What makes things even harder to take is that all these bands appear so infrequently in Melbourne, leaving the southern punter with a diet of grungy heavy metal, disco and stale Carlton 'sophistication' which perhaps accounts for his reluctance to pay to see any band at all these days.

('Cold Chisel' 1979)

The negative references to the 'stale' Melbourne scene that begin appearing at this time indicate that this is a point where Melbourne becomes more clearly overshadowed by Sydney in the music stakes. During this period, stories emerge in the music press of bands moving to Sydney rather than the other way around, and including critiques of the Melbourne scene in these pieces. By 1982, music journalist Christie Eliezer is describing the Models as 'the great white hopes of the Melbourne scene, desperate to fight back with something to break Sydney's stranglehold on the Oz scene'. The framing of Melbourne as pretentious or snobby also becomes more pronounced, with a specific trope of 'Melbourne-as-obsessed-with-hairstyles' emerging. In the early 1980s in particular, it was not uncommon to see articles and reviews make statements like 'most [Melbourne] crowds are more intrigued by the variety of hairstyles at a venue than the band and where most bands are interested only in refining some form of almost pure pretension through their music' ('Safehouse build a secure future' 1983).

Over time, however, there is a reassertion of the 'commercialism as degraded culture' narrative in the Melbourne community that gives some scope for a return to presenting Melbourne in a more positive light in comparison to Sydney. Drummer Helen Smart highlights both of these impulses in this period in the following way:

> Sydney was kind of the big sister because Sydney had the kind of Albert [recording label] scene with Dragon and those kind of big hit bands, whereas with Melbourne, we had a kind of snobby hipster vibe going on. So there were the kind of – there was the start of that kind of rootsy culture that we have now where we have a billion kind of Americana and country and that kind of bands, but it was more – in those days it was more kind of, 'Oh, we're more intellectual than the Sydneysiders with their Dragons and their Ice Houses and that kind of thing. We're more cerebral and we've got the Go Betweens', because we co-opted the Brisbane scene, so we kind of adopted the Laughing Clowns and the Go Betweens as our own, like they were ours. I don't know whether they'd see it that way, but we felt that they were ours, that was our kind of music, and that was more – we were kind of snobby about our music as opposed to the mainstream Sydney kind of stuff.
>
> (Smart 2018)

The pivoting of rock to 'roots' as a genre easily framed as more authentic and, at this time, more innovative in the Australian context is noteworthy here, as well as Smart's canny acknowledgement of the possible negative framing of the Melbourne scene as both 'snobby' and prone to taking credit for the work of artists whose Melbourne-ness is questionable. (The Go-Betweens are an interesting example here of the fluidity of music and its relationship to place, as during the 1980s the press did indeed refer to them as a Melbourne band, but Brisbane has since consolidated its claim to the group, not least through the naming of a bridge in the city after them.) Notable here though, and indeed, throughout the period under consideration in this study, is the tendency to use genre terms that are racially coded – blues, roots, r'n'b – as a way of claiming authenticity. This is an obvious tension in a scene where the artists represented in the pages of the music press are overwhelmingly white, particularly throughout the 1970s and 1980s, and where, as will be shown in the following chapter, Indigenous musicians in particular were long actively excluded from participating. People of colour who were present in the music press during the early decades of rock and pop were almost exclusively from outside Australia.

By the mid-1990s, Sydney is declared 'well in front of Melbourne in the music game' in an ABC television investigation into the industry (Adams 1994). However, during the 1990s, the discourse increasingly shifts back in Melbourne's favour as Sydney's success is reframed as inauthentic (in a similar manner to the 1960s). Key figures in the Melbourne scene responded to the ABC report by emphasizing the strength of Melbourne's live scene and its local music media, meaning 'people can listen to alternative things that are very fresh … Sydney haven't got anything like that' (agent Mick Newton, cited in Adams 1994). This perception was framed even more stridently in Melbourne-centric discussions. For example, in the mid-1990s, Melbourne zine *Form Guide*, produced by the Punters Club, summed up the perception of the musical divide between Melbourne and Sydney, and between 'pop' and other types of music:

> Wanna be a pop star? Fire the rest of the band, move to Sydney and hire a bunch of soulless muso hacks to back you live. Record an over-produced ep of bland pop and do interviews with Rolling Stone and Juice in which you talk about how much you've 'grown' and 'matured' since your 'early days'. Sit back and watch the money strewn into your record company's bank account. Develop a nasty and expensive habit that requires a daily trip to Cabramatta. Die broke, lonely and forgotten in a gutter in the Cross. Receive a tiny obit in the music papers.
> ('How to succeed in rock'n'roll' 1995)

Despite the continued concentration of major record label offices in Sydney, the narrative put forward in publications and by interviewees – and which has indeed become embedded in the national imaginary in various ways – is that Sydney's live music scene has declined significantly since the 1990s. The narratives associated with threats such as 'the pokies' (the introduction of poker machines in large numbers in licenced venues, also an issue in Melbourne) have framed Sydney as a live music scene in crisis. This was greatly exacerbated when in 2014 the O'Farrell Coalition Government in NSW introduced new lockout laws in certain areas of Sydney in response to night-time violence, and in particular a number of 'one punch' attacks that left young men either dead or severely injured. Comparing the different approaches to their respective city live music sectors taken by NSW and Victoria leads us to a further discussion of liquor licence laws; the divergent paths the cities have taken over this issue have laid the groundwork for Melbourne's to reframe itself as a global music city, rather than 'second city' to Sydney.

Discord and accords

In Melbourne, media and government concerns with CBD violence that had been simmering through the 1980s and 1990s (as discussed in Chapter 2) increased into the 2000s. By 2008, the City of Melbourne contained 1,400 liquor licences, and their number had increased by 61 per cent since 2000 (Padula 2016: 3). While some noted that the initial Nieuwenhuysen reforms of the 1980s (see Chapter 3) had encouraged excess, the original architect argued that the new club culture (in King and Queens Streets) had much to do with the CBD problems, and went against the earlier aims of diversity of functions and sites: 'Despite the sixfold multiplication of licences over the past twenty years, per capita alcohol consumption has remained stable. The problems ... [are] heavily associated with the large nightclubs in the city' (Nieuwenhuysen 2008: 21).

It is significant that the city looked to replicate 'lockout' laws that had been trialled elsewhere as a means of targeting venue and street violence. A trial 2 a.m. lockout that began in June 2008 was successfully diluted by venue owners who were granted exemptions by the Victorian Civil and Administrative Tribunal (Houston 2008). The Director of Liquor Licensing's own attempt to be granted powers to establish 2 a.m. lockouts upon specific venues failed in the Legislative Council. In their place, the State Government and Melbourne Council established various measures (a Safety Summit; undercover venues taskforce; a Safe Streets taskforce) in 2008.

While added security measures were part of some venues' operating late hours, the changes wrought in 2009/10 were different. Even without infringements or histories as 'troublesome' venues, licensees had measures placed on their licences that assumed 'high risk' activity when entertainment was provided. For those venues operating beyond 1 a.m. and/or providing 'live or recorded amplified music', the Director of Liquor Licensing stipulated that crowd controllers (security guards) be hired at a ratio of two for the first 100 patrons, with one additional controller for every further 100 patrons, in addition to the installation of CCTV cameras. While the exact number of venues affected was hard to discern, the retrospective conditions fell upon a bewildering array of venues and genres: e.g. the Oakleigh Bowling Club, the Lomond Hotel (Brunswick), the Emerald Hotel (South Melbourne) and the Railway Hotel (North Fitzroy); the Greek Deli and Taverna (Chapel Street, Prahran), providing rebetika music also found themselves categorized as 'high risk' (Bruce-Rosser 2009). Similarly, the Arthouse, a North Melbourne hotel providing a range of 'indie' music, faced the option of abandoning its post-1 a.m. licence, or retaining it with reduced capacity, while a Nigel Kennedy violin performance at Abbotsford Convent was accompanied by two security guards (Williams 2010: 16).[1]

The Railway Hotel proved an interesting case of the absurdity of the new conditions. Offering blues and jazz bands to mainly older clientele, bands set up in the corner of the front lounge, with punters having the choice of either standing at the bar or grabbing a table (usually used for meals). For Rick Dempster of the Brunswick Blues Shooters who enjoyed residencies at the pub:

> Our crowd were mostly regulars, people who had been turning up week after week, year after year, to eat, drink, talk and dance. It was a wonderful atmosphere. Most of the customers were aged between forty and seventy-odd (our drummer, by the way, is seventy three, and has been playing in bands since 1957)[2].
>
> (Dempster cited in Homan 2010: 108)

That the intention to simply provide live music triggered a 'high risk' label, and accompanying changed licence conditions, stirred local industry sectors. Anger increased at the news that the Tote Hotel in Collingwood, 'indie central' for a range of tribes and genres, looked likely to succumb to the new conditions. 'The potential of losing Melbourne's CBGB' (Marcou 2017) spurred a rally outside the venue on 17 January, filling Wellington and Johnson Streets. A small group – studio owners, promoters, academics, musicians and lawyers – began to meet regularly at the Railway Hotel in Brunswick to discuss strategies and options.

The Save Live Australian Music (SLAM) organization, established by Bakehouse Studio owners Helen Marcou and Quincy McLean, was pivotal to placing a public face on industry discontent. Building on the famous AC/DC video of the band playing 'Long Way To The Top' around city streets in 1975, SLAM arranged for the RockWiz Orchestra to play the song on a similar flatbed truck from the State Library to Parliament. Wearing 'Don't Kill Live Music' t-shirts, an estimated 20,000 marched to Parliament House to hear speeches from Claire Bowditch, Tim Rogers, Dobe Newton and Paul Kelly (among others). The Brumby Labor Government, keen to forestall criticism, negotiated an agreement with SLAM, FairGo representatives and other industry advisors – the Live Music Acord – which, crucially, promised to decouple the Government's rhetoric about 'alcohol-fuelled violence' from live music, to reverse the condition placed on licensees providing live music, to look at a peak body representing all stakeholders and to undertake research on the sector. This did not prevent the planned rally proceeding after the Accord had been signed, with Marcou and McLean determined to retain the pressure upon the Government, as the Premier bizarrely proclaimed the rally as a 'celebration' of the industry:

> While we were waiting for the Live Music Accord paperwork to be edited and photocopied, [Ministerial staff] asked us again how many were attending [the rally]. We said Facebook says 10,000, but we couldn't be sure. They then asked who we had speaking, and I said 'Paul Kelly'. And everyone opposite on their side of the table went 'Oh God, we're fucked'. And they were.
>
> (McLean 2017)

The subsequent march on 23 February 2010 of musicians, fans, publicans, school children, parents and music industry workers achieved several outcomes.

Figure 11 The SLAM Rally, 23 February 2010. Source: Zo Damage Collection.

With an election looming, it forced the Brumby Government to negotiate to remove the debate from the front pages.³ And, not least, parties on both sides of the aisle realized that the local music industries had become proficient in providing a unified front and narrative that could be symbolized and reinforced by action.⁴ A new Director of Liquor Licensing was appointed in May 2010, who proclaimed his support for live music, and subsequently approved the Tote's new liquor licence (under new management that included FairGo4Live Music's Jon Perring). The State government allocated $250,000 for the establishment of Music Victoria, with *Age* journalist Patrick Donovan being appointed founding CEO in July 2010. In June, the government commissioned an independent consultancy firm to produce an evaluation of the economic value of music to the state.⁵ A Live Music Committee was also established to address longer-term concerns.

Consensus rock

The Live Music Accord provided the local music industries with a seat at the policy table, although the industry representatives who had signed were highly conscious of the need to work hard in ensuring the Brumby Government followed through on its promises. A series of initiatives strengthened the consensus that live music represented a national and global advantage in creative industries and branding strategies. Yet actioning this would have to wait until the end of the conservative Baillieu Coalition Government in 2013. A $22.2 million Music Works package announced in 2015 by the new Andrews Labor Government created 'Quick Response' grants for export/touring; a Good Music Neighbours program assisting venues with acoustic design and soundproofing; the Music Under Wings program providing mentoring/development assistance; housing for the Melbourne Music Vault in the Arts Centre; and established the Victorian Music Development Office.

There was also eventual movement on the longstanding issue of venue noise complaints. The health of local pub circuits had been increasingly threatened by noise complaints from residents. A central case was the Esplanade Hotel, an iconic piece of architecture looking out to Port Phillip Bay, and which had provided some form of music since the 1920s. By the 1980s, its large, multi-storey structure allowed multiple bars (mainly 'indie') band rooms and dining options. As part of the wider redevelopment of St Kilda, in 2000 developer

Figure 12 'Please leave these premises quietly'. The Prince of Wales hotel, 30 March 1996. Source: Shellie Tonkin Collection/Performing Arts Collection/Arts Centre, Melbourne.

corporation Becton sought to purchase the hotel and build a thirty-eight-storey apartment tower behind the venue (Shaw 2005: 165). Acknowledging music industry and locals' resistance to the redevelopment, Port Phillip Council 'prepared an amendment to its planning scheme that decreased the height limit to 10 storeys, protected the heritage-listed buildings on the site, and attempted to specify planning strategies that would allow the hotel to operate for as long as it has cultural and economic viability' (ibid.), with further controls to safekeep its cultural significance and heritage. Noise complaint disputes could also extend to other fields of engagement. Situated in 27 St David Street, Fitzroy, the Rainbow Hotel had experienced successive problems in providing live music as residential redevelopment was built opposite the venue (Shaw 2009). According to Horne (2019: 256–60), the Rainbow's owner, Chick Ratten, faced a new apartment development behind the pub in Young Street in 1996, driven by crime syndicate leader Alphonse Gangitano. Ratten's connections to Gangitano's father allowed some room for 'negotiation', with Gangitano agreeing to State planning changes to ameliorate future noise problems.

In the wake of the SLAM rally, the suggestion of 'Agent of Change' legislation was dusted off from the 2003 Live Music Taskforce report that went beyond a prior Planning Practice Note that stated that the 'reasonable expectation of the existing land users should be respected'. Labor's Planning Minister, Justin Madden, seemed to provide stronger reassurances in asserting that 'where somebody might do a residential development near an existing venue, you cannot complain if that venue has been operating for some time' (Parliament of Victoria 2010). As an admirable sentiment, venue owners and musicians believed that Maddern's statement did not hold up to (sub)urban scrutiny. In September 2014, the Andrews Government announced *s.52.43 – Live Music and Entertainment Noise* – of the Victorian Planning Provisions:

> In planning, the agent of change principle assigns responsibility for noise attenuation measures to the 'agent of change' – a new use or development that is introduced into an existing environment. In practical terms this means that if a new or an existing live music venue seeks to establish or expand, they will be responsible for attenuating any noise effects that are caused by that change on nearby residential properties. Similarly, a new residential development close to an existing live music venue will be responsible for noise attenuation of its building to protect future residents from the live music venue.

In many respects, this was deemed the first legislation globally that provided a much wider context in considering noise complaints in emphasizing that conditions and uses went both ways. While it did not provide de facto protection for existing venues and their trading conditions, it has proved to be of significant use at local council mediations, and has added further to Music Victoria's campaign for all stakeholders to acknowledge that venues have social/cultural benefits. Asked to examine the broader contexts of the recent Agent of Change for the State Government, FairGo4Live Music's Jon Perring believes the planning amendments do not encourage the use of greenfield sites as venues:

> You [still] won't get through the planning system in under a year. You'll then have to apply for a liquor licence – they'll probably want to put you on "L Plates" first up, which means a 1 a.m. licence, which threatens the viability of the actual business, before you get really into a mode in which you can operate. So why wouldn't you look around for a failing pub with a 3 o'clock licence, where you can go from Day One?
>
> (Perring 2020)

For Nick Tweedie, who has lent his considerable barrister experience in planning law to various venue complaint cases since the SLAM rally (and as a member of the State Government's Live Music Roundtable), Agent of Change retains some key advantages:

> I think it's been generally successful ... It does two things. It says that if you introduce a residential use into an environment, and someone causes a nuisance in that residential use, it's their job to fix it, and reverses that principle, and tries to avoid the conflict before it happens. It has also drawn the issue to the attention of council planning officers and given them a tool requiring [venues] to be protected. It's a red flag they have to look out for, and they can't ignore ... One of the most effective means of dealing with this is the developer not necessarily spending a lot of money on its own development, but making a contribution to the venue to take steps to reduce its emissions – reducing emissions at its source ... So, a smart developer will say to a venue, 'I'll give you $10,000 to clog up the holes in your roof, or for an airlocked doorway, as opposed to me spending $100,000 on glazing all the windows on every apartment'.
>
> (Tweedie 2020)

Its global import has been recognized; other cities have followed the Victorian lead or are in the process of adoption (e.g. Austin, Texas). From 2018–19, England, Wales and Scotland all amended their planning laws to introduce local variants of Agent of Change.

City contrasts

To return to our consideration of the relationship between Sydney and Melbourne, the response to lockout laws in Sydney was very different to that in Melbourne. While Sydney live music advocates rallied to protest the laws, their activities did not resonate in the public imaginary in the same way as the SLAM rally did, and the laws resulted in the closure of many venues and nightclubs. While these laws were eventually rolled back in January 2020 (just in time for the industry to close down because of the coronavirus), they had a highly detrimental effect on the city's night-time economy, with estimated losses of $16 billion per year to the state ('Sydney's lockout laws ... ' 2019).

A number of interviewees fit this into an ongoing story of Sydney failing to effectively deal with the same sorts of challenges that the live music scene in

Melbourne has faced, resulting in at first a gradual and then (with the lockout laws) a more abrupt erosion of music activity in the city:

> Sydney used to have a massive music scene, but it got squandered. It got crushed. Primarily, that's around the pressures of land use and the expectation of what you can use – who takes – what's more important. They've not protected their night-time economy like we have.
>
> (Perring 2017)

> I think the Melbourne scene has changed but we're still so incredibly lucky with the amount of venues, and venues have disappeared – some of my favourite venues no longer exist – but they've been replaced, and so I don't think it's like Sydney, where poker machines came along and ruined the scene, and also in Sydney where Double J became Triple J and then going national, so they kind of lost their local station. I think that really impacted on Sydney. I think in Melbourne we've been incredibly lucky to have great community radio. That's continued. Triple R and PBS are still really vibrant. Street press still exists.
>
> (Jenkins 2018)

> Sydney's gone – at this moment in time, has gone to some sort of weird – okay, if Melbourne is going to go in that direction, we're going to go totally the opposite. We're basically going to shut this city at 6 o'clock at night and unless you work in one of those weird – you're a weirdo, works in the service industries, you should be at home with your wife and kids and in bed by 9:00 and ready for bed at 8 o'clock in the morning. It's like – this is like a science fiction show.
>
> (Milne 2017)

In these quotes, land use, loss of venues and local music media, and lockout laws are presented as problems that Sydney has failed to overcome, unlike Melbourne. The final quote from Bruce Milne connects this failure, in a tongue-in-cheek way, to the ongoing rivalry, with his suggestion that Melbourne's success has led Sydney to deliberately go in the other direction. For broadcaster Jane Gazzo, the tendency for people in Melbourne to react strongly to events happening in their music scene has been important, and different to Sydney:

> What had happened in Sydney, too, The Hopetoun (which was a real mecca for live music in the 90s) closed without a whimper. It closed, and I think it still remains closed to this day, it just remains boarded up. No one held a placard, no one kind of did anything about it. And to see that dichotomy between Melbourne and Sydney, that was actually heartbreaking.
>
> (Gazzo 2018)

Gazzo's final statement, that this is 'heartbreaking', points to a changing dynamic in the Melbourne/Sydney relationship. Rather than needing to reiterate claims that Melbourne leads Sydney on the live music front, some interviewees shifted to a narrative of Melbourne needing to support Sydney. For example, Quincy McLean (2017) points out the problems with being too celebratory about Melbourne's apparent supremacy over Sydney in the live music stakes: 'by Sydney not being strong, like it was in the '80s, for example, there's a break in the chain for the touring circuit. So all of this Melbourne/Sydney rivalry is a load of crap, in our opinion'. This is echoed by Bruce Milne:

> I think Melbourne has got to be really careful – and this is specifically about Melbourne, so – we've definitely got a second-city chip on our shoulder. That is, we feel the need to keep going, 'Hey, Sydney, look at us', which is silly. You've got to ignore that. Or a smirkiness. 'Hey, we've got this and you don't' ... The fact is that we – there's no venues to play in Sydney and there's no venues to play along the road in Sydney and that's not working for anyone. We've only got a few cities – we need to have a healthy music community in each one of them.
>
> (Milne 2017)

This suggests that currently Melbourne's dominance in music is so clear that pity or sympathy can be extended towards an apparently defeated rival. This notion of Melbourne's music victory can also be seen in materials suggesting Sydney's plans to revive their live music ecology based on a 2019 inquiry are largely based on copying Melbourne's way of doing things. The ability of Melbourne to market itself as a *global* music city, and establish overseas cities such as Austin as the main point of comparison (Baker 2019) can arguably be seen as partly connected to the declining force of the Sydney rivalry.

Success as selling out

The authenticity narratives discussed above, and the strict adherence to ideas about what behaviour and music is or is not authentic, must by its nature result in exclusionary behaviour. Some interviewees described situations where perceptions that they had achieved the wrong type of success – in particular where they made decisions that others in the Melbourne scene interpreted as being about money rather than artistic integrity – led to them being openly criticized or made to feel unwelcome in various ways that show the problematic aspects of the way Melbourne music has been framed. For example, Caroline Kennedy describes the response to her leaving her indie-rock band the Plums to work with an older man from the commercially successful Melbourne band, Hunters and Collectors. She describes how 'some of my original fans became angry and hissed *sellout* at me as I walked down Brunswick Street … any gravitas I had gained through my own performances and hard-fought artistic integrity in The Plums was quickly questioned and mocked as I attempted a change' (Kennedy 2019: 77). In our interview, she elaborates on how her new venture was treated in the Melbourne music media:

> The way I was positioned in the media was that I was a sellout by journalists like Anthony Carew, who put like a dollar sign instead of an S, Deadstar with a dollar sign. So, there was a bit of that. I understood it. I wasn't pleased about it and I remember leaving an interview that we were doing where he sort of was like 'so you're kind of like a put together sort of super group, kind of put together to make commercial music', or something like that in the interview and I remember just sort of saying 'fuck you' and walking out of the room … I think there was a sense that we were a constructed band and I was sort of horrified by this. I was kind of like, well, how did this kind of happen? [But] the concerns that were really like a hot bed of concern in Melbourne were absolutely of no consequence anywhere else in the world.

These types of 'divisions and politics', as Kennedy describes it, are also discussed by Jane Gazzo, whose position within the music media at RRR and later Triple J gave her an opportunity to observe how bands were treated at different stages of their careers:

> Q: How do you think [RRR] negotiated that line that you were just talking about between bands – so if bands sort of get too big in a particular scene it's seen as being a bit of a sell-out or too commercial or whatever?
> A: Yeah. They would have dropped them, they would have stopped playing them, and all the DJs would have stopped playing them. So I know Frente!, for a fact, wasn't played after they released *Marvin the Album* (certainly not on Triple R); on Triple J, yes. I think once you really made that sell-out – and sell-out was everywhere back in the 90s – once you sold out you were kind of forgotten about. But that was good, because it just meant that Triple R would foster more new, emerging talent.
> Q: So it was really, then, wanting to sort of keep the cred or whatever it was that they were associated with.
> A: Yeah, and the indie-ness, you know?

This was confirmed by Angie Hart, who also discussed the way Frente! were given the cold shoulder when they unexpectedly became successful nationally. Gazzo notes that while the 1990s was a time when concerns about 'selling out' were particularly heightened (this was also when Deadstar were being assessed as 'sellouts'), these divisions reappear periodically:

> I think the backlash to success with bands that we've kind of seen with Killing Time and Frente! in the early 90s, I don't think that really started again, from memory, until Jet got signed and became international. I remember there was a lot of bitterness in the Melbourne music scene because they were regular guys who had played the Tote constantly, you know, the Duke of Windsor in Prahran, they were regular knock around guys and they had a lot of friends in the scene, and then when *Get Born* was released and it went gangbusters for them, there was a lot of noses out of joint in the Melbourne musician scene. And it was just a case of sour grapes.

Gazzo also describes how she herself was affected by the tendency in parts of the Melbourne scene to be dismissive of people who have gained success outside this milieu. Her move from RRR to Triple J elicited a reaction from peers in Melbourne not dissimilar to that experienced by Kennedy:

> I didn't change, but everyone's perception of me changed because it's like 'she's on Triple J now so she's high and mighty'. Certainly my relationships at Triple R were really, really messy. I lost a lot of friends when I took the plunge to Triple J, and there were so many people who had always said to me 'oh, if Triple J came calling I'd definitely take it'. Well, when it came for me, they couldn't have sent me out packing quick enough, and I lost a lot of good friends, and that really hurt at the time.

These types of stories are in no way unique to Melbourne: wherever culture exists, claims are constantly being made for certain ways of creating, using and profiting from that culture being more or less proper than others. Gazzo and Kennedy are relaying stories of being denied the cultural capital most valued within the Melbourne music community, while at the same time gaining economic capital and a different type of cultural capital that has more resonance on a national scale (i.e. the cultural capital that comes from having a hit single or being on a radio show broadcast nationally). This can, however, be considered as part of the processes by which the distinctions between 'Melbourne' and 'not-Melbourne' are maintained, insofar as intellectualism, anti-commercialism and 'authenticity' have been established as the narratives by which Melbourne distinguishes itself from Sydney in particular and other cities more generally. Establishing and policing boundaries in this way helps to establish 'correct' behaviour that is reinforced by those who adhere to this being more likely to gain access to a place in the ongoing collective story of 'what 'makes Melbourne music'. However, at times such policing goes well beyond notions of success or authenticity, and in the following chapter we will examine how more deep-seated prejudices can make being a part of the Melbourne music scene much harder for some groups of people than others. As will be shown, it is probably no coincidence that the interviewees who most strongly reported being criticized for their success were women.

7

The divided city

Introduction

Although the discourses described in the previous chapter are some of the ways in which a common idea of what 'Melbourne' is in relation to music has been developed, it is also important to note the fractures and divisions that exist within this. A failure to attend to these risks missing the ways music scenes can be built on conflict and exclusion as much as shared ideas and cooperation. Melbourne's scenes in 2020, before the COVID lockdown, could be described as almost radically inclusive in some regards, with various strategies being implemented by the State government, industry bodies and grassroots organizations to improve the representation of oppressed and marginalized groups in music-making. The 2019 documentary on Melbourne music, *Now Sound*, makes a clear statement of this, with the variety of different types of people featured a stark contrast to the more monochrome and male-centric celebrations of music from previous decades. While this book has made a point of ensuring that different types of voices have been included throughout, it is still important to spend time drawing attention to the way that the diversity of Melbourne's current popular music activity, and its celebration, has only come about because of significant struggle on the part of those on its fringes.

In this chapter we will look at how many groups have needed to spend decades creating their own pathways into rock and pop, often against significant barriers, many of which have by no means been completely overcome. Here, we will focus on women, First Nations people, and to a lesser extent, the queer community. These are also not the only lines of division that have existed within Melbourne scenes – similar stories could be told about class, migrant communities or people living with disabilities – but these are offered as important case studies in how silencing and exclusion are maintained, but also the strategies that are used to counteract these. It should be noted that the clean division offered in this chapter between experience based on gender and that based on Indigeneity is artificial, and that for First Nations women in particular, the way these exclusions are compounded cannot be understated.

'A bit of a pain in the arse to the patriarchal music scene': Gender and Melbourne music

One place where these processes of exclusion have clearly played out is around gender. Certain themes emerge in the materials collected for this project that echo those found more widely in studies of gender inequality in music-making, and often in the creative industries more broadly (see Strong and Raine 2019; Glitsos 2017, 2018). These include women performers being policed and belittled (particularly in relation to their technical abilities and know-how), and at times abused in various ways by men in music-making spaces, pressures on women to conform to certain types of roles and ways of performing and a reduction of women to their gender in a variety of ways. Despite this, women have played an important role in Melbourne's music scenes from the outset. They were foundational to the pop and rock and roll eras of the 1950s and 1960s, although generally allowed access to only certain highly gendered roles. They used fringe and underground music scenes to maintain a presence, and eventually reinsert themselves into mainstream rock after this became a highly masculine genre in the late 1960s and 1970s.

This has resulted in music scenes where women are no longer regarded as quite the novelty that they were during the 1970s, and that is also becoming more intersectional in its debates about diversity, but that is, nonetheless, often still strongly experienced as exclusionary by women entering the scene. As such, the story of women's place in Melbourne's popular music history is not a linear one, where women inexorably make further gains in participation until one day the sought-after equality is achieved. It is, rather, a story of slow visible increments that do not fully represent what women are actually doing, and a consistent sense of outsiderdom partly created by the failure of Australian music histories and collective memories to capture or celebrate the contributions of women in the same way as men's.

Of fundamental importance to this discussion is the way in which women have always been present in Melbourne music. Older interviewees noted the importance of women in the formation of Melbourne's rock 'n' roll scene in the

1950s. For example, Ian Allen recalled that 'Bev[erly Dick] was on the first rock and roll album recorded in Australia in '58 on Planet Records, called Rock and Roll Party, and it's with the Henri Bource All Stars', and also discussed the role of Marion Grossman in the original line-up of the Thunderbirds. By the time Melbourne's influential music- and youth culture-focussed publication *Go-Set* launched, at a time when 'pop' was the key genre covered, women were under-represented compared to men, but still featured prominently and regularly in the publication. This was, however, in ways that were highly gendered. Coverage of women artists almost invariably focused on their looks, clothes, boyfriends or heteronormative life plans. For example, an article on Marcie Jones and Yvonne Barrett in 1967 followed them on a shopping trip (Meldrum 1967), and a feature on Lynne Randell in 1968 described her getting her hair done but said little about her music ('Lynne has gone curly' 1968). This type of coverage was in some ways simply part of the content of the magazine that was aimed at teenage girls, and which also incorporated fashion and romance advice (Kent 2002). This came, though, with a strong emphasis on gender norms and stereotypes: there were also numerous articles focusing on women singers' relationships and/or plans for marriage and family rather than their careers, or other articles where girl fans are denounced as hysterical and problematic. This could have negative consequences for women singers (women instrumentalists, though present, were few and far between in *Go-Set*). Marcie Jones (2017) describes how:

> … mainly the audience were girls and they bought the boys' records. I had a lot of tomatoes and eggs thrown at me because I was on tour … we were on the road the whole time and, of course, the girls hated me, you know. I was up there with all the boys. And then as soon as Norm[ie Rowe] and I became boyfriend and girlfriend, oh, I was the worst person in the world.

The press' emphasis on these artists' position as objects of gossip may have encouraged antagonistic relationships with the audience, but evidence also emerges from *Go-Set* of male audience members contributing to the problem of violence at gigs:

> Apart from the obvious problems of travelling alone late at night, and having boys waiting for you after the show ('Some of them are really nice, but you can't really tell, and you're usually alone' [Dianna Bailey]), there are many other difficulties – *all the girls have been dragged off the stage at one time or another,*

and have had to rely solely on the bouncers to help them, and when the dance only provides one bouncer – boy, can you be in trouble!

(Brett 1966, emphasis in original)

So women artists in the 1960s were both framed as role models and threats (as competition for their objects of desire) to teenage girls and were themselves put in threatening situations. However, as mentioned above, *Go-Set* did include women regularly in its early days, and is also recognized for giving women opportunities as contributors to the publication in various ways. According to Kent (2002: 1), '*Go-Set* was the first music newspaper to give female writers a prominent place as rock and pop music journalists'. This included writers such as Lily Brett, Jean Gollan and Wendy Saddington, and the magazine also had a woman, Vera Kass-Jager, as a primary photographer for some years. The place that *Go-Set* held was between serious music publication and gossip mag (made clearer by later speculation from key figures in the magazine that it mutated into *Dolly* magazine, a publication with teen girls as its main readership (Kent 2002)) at a time when rock and roll and pop were being marketed to families and housewives in Australia as much as to exclusive youth audiences (Giuffre 2016), as these genres sought to consolidate where they sat in the Australian market. There is, however, a very clear shift in tone towards the end of the 1960s. 'Rock' (or blues, or rhythm and blues, as it is also referred to during this time of genre formation) started to become the dominant genre in the Melbourne music scene, and as a result, the coverage of women in the magazine drops off dramatically. As one indicator of this, in its first four years *Go-Set* features women on its front cover on the magazines sampled about one-third of the time; during the 1970s, this drops off to closer to one-tenth. Indeed, an online repository of *Go-Set* covers for the entirety of 1972 shows that no women at all were included on the cover in this year.[1] It is worth noting, however, the continued strong coverage of women artists by Molly Meldrum in his weekly column, an inclusive trend he continued throughout his career.

The exclusion of women in the late 1960s and early 1970s is unsurprising, as it demonstrates the coming together of a number of well-understood factors relating to genre, gender and authenticity that played out across popular music at this point in time (Railton 2001; Coates 2003), and that took a particular form in Australian culture (see Glitsos 2017, for how this played out in Perth in a similar manner). The emergence of music journalism that took its subject seriously coincided with the separation of 'rock' from 'rock and roll' or 'pop' as certain artists began to produce work that was experimental and virtuosic in a way that enabled music journalists to call upon tropes associated with 'serious' music to make a case for the value of rock (Gendron 2002). This meant that certain types of popular music could be framed as 'important' as opposed to a disposable novelty of interest only to young people. This also necessarily involved contrasting rock with pop in a way that downplayed the value of not only pop as a genre, but its artists and audience, both more likely to be women and girls than the audience for rock. This gendered divide was particularly the case in Australia, where the specific tradition of Australian pub rock that emerged in the early 1970s was embedded in spaces ('the pub') that were strongly marked as masculine (Homan 2000; Hawkings 2014). Women had only been granted access to the front bars of pubs in 1965, and the process of gaining full acceptance in these fortresses of male sociality was a slow one, involving sometimes violent conflicts between women activists, male pub clientele and publicans, and the police (Kirkby 2003). It was therefore rare for women to be a part of mainstream rock bands in Australia at this time; and the corollary of this was that pop, the genre where women could still gain access to the music industry, was delegitimized.

This is borne out in the accounts of interviewees. While women in the industry in the 1950s and 1960s by no means had an easy time entering the industry, there were certain pathways. For Wendy Stapleton, this was through the connections between education and entertainment institutions:

> Mum sent me into a dancing school. Right in the centre of Melbourne, there were two dance schools if you were very serious about being involved in entertainment. One was called May Downs Dancing School in Bourke Street and the other was called Olive Wallace, and that was in Elizabeth Street, and they were the only two feeder dance schools that all the children would go into the theatre: Her Majesty's, the Princess, the Comedy, Tivoli. For some reason, that was just where all of the producers would source their kids from. So consequently, from my school, going back: Patti Newton, Patti McGrath as she was, Denise Drysdale, heaps. Heaps and heaps of people from both those dance schools went on to become TV stars or theatre stars.
>
> (Stapleton 2017)

Marcie Jones, after gaining skills through singing lessons, used formal audition processes to gain access to gigs, and later the television shows that greatly increased performers' profiles. Press accounts and interviewees suggest that until the late 1960s, women's presence was normalized in the Melbourne music scene.

However, it was a slow process for women to find a place in the dominant new rock paradigm, and for those venturing into the pub rock world in the 1970s and into the 1980s, post the rock boom, they were encountering a situation where they felt, and were treated, like a novelty. Chris Scheri from Sweet Jayne and Sue World from the Wet Ones both describe how, in the late 1970s and mid-1980s respectively, they were able to get gigs at times purely because an all-woman band was so unusual that it was considered a drawcard in its own right. Scheri, describing Sweet Jayne's experience winning the Battle of the Bands in 1978, states:

> We went to the heats and I've never seen anything like it, because there were no other girls there. They were all guys, all guy bands. We're talking '77 so there was just no girl bands around. They come running from everywhere. We started to play and there was just – whoosh – it reminded me – on a much smaller scale of course – but you know at the Super Bowl where all the people from the crowd come running up to the stage that's usually in the centre of the oval at half time. It was like that. And I thought wow, hey, they love us. This is great.
>
> (Scheri 2017)

While the band's musicianship was unquestionably very high, Scheri saw the fact that all-women bands – and women musicians in general – were such an unusual feature in the rock world as important in initially capturing audiences' attention. Sue World also notes how this novelty factor could be an advantage, but also describes the less positive reactions that could accompany this:

> I remember at 17 there were very few other women. There would be occasionally one woman, like a bass player or something in a band here and there but there was very few all-female bands, so we were always a novelty. I was aware straight away it's a double-edged sword, so we were – so like, 'Oh, there's these four schoolgirls from Warrandyte who can play. They'll be fun. Book them a gig, you know. We all want to see that'. So we'd get gigs because we were a novelty, so you'd think great, and people would go, 'Oh, we've been trying to get a gig there for two years, you know. Because you're girls you got a gig'. We're going, 'I guess so'. But then again we were never taken seriously. Look, there was some nasty stuff happened when we very first started playing. Some roadies and sound guys were quite hostile. They seemed to be like they were jealous that their band couldn't play there or something and they were quite rude.
>
> (World 2017)

Both Scheri and World discussed how they lacked women as role models to draw inspiration from as they established their careers, and it is noteworthy that another interviewee, Caroline Kennedy, describes seeing the Wet Ones as an important moment in her own musical development, offering her new ways of understanding how women could express themselves. Scheri and World also both discuss being pressured at various points to portray themselves in more conventionally 'sexy' ways to appeal to a male audience, and needing to develop strategies to resist this.

However, the 'no women' scenario that Scheri and World were encountering in places like the Battle of the Bands and the beer barns of the suburbs where they both often played was not entirely reflected in other areas. For example, the slow insertion of women into mainstream and commercial rock in Melbourne was accelerated somewhat by the more inclusive attitudes in the Melbourne punk and post-punk scenes which reflected the global manifestations of the punk movement (Reddington 2007). Sue World noted that 'there were far more women in the St Kilda scene, just people going to see bands. Yeah, it seemed to be almost 50/50 I'd say. But also just the atmosphere was far more relaxed'. Musicians like Marie Hoy, Denise Rosenberg and Penny Ikinger were prominent members of these scenes, helping to (re)normalize women's presence and reconfigure the boundaries of what was considered acceptable behaviour for women. This should not be overstated though; at the 2017 panel discussion 'Why Punk',[2] Penny Ikinger noted that:

> There was still a lot of resistance, a lot of sexism. It was just better than what had preceded it. It's not like it suddenly disappeared. It's just that considering what had come before when women didn't have any of these sorts of opportunities, when their roles in rock and roll were possibly as groupies or muses or something … so at least it opened a lot of doors, but it didn't solve all the problems.

Starting somewhat earlier than the punk scene, in the early 1970s, and overlapping with it into the 1980s, there was also a thriving women's music scene across Australia that involved over a hundred bands that were all or almost-all women, with more than thirty in Melbourne (including some of the bands that interviewees for this project performed in, such as the Wet Ones, Toxic Shock and Sweet Jayne). This scene has been documented thoroughly by Kathy Sport (2015), but otherwise the majority of these bands, and the circuits they moved in, remain largely overlooked in either historical accounts or contemporaneous media. This is partly because few of these bands recorded their material, existing through live performances that make them harder to include in music histories that privilege recorded music. In addition, many of these bands had explicitly feminist and lesbian politics, and performed in spaces created by women, for women, such as feminist rallies and women's dances, meaning they were overlooked by most music press. Some deliberately avoided the pub and hotel circuits because of their associations with patriarchal and masculine cultures (Sport 2015: 90), but a number of pubs in Melbourne were known for staging nights for these bands, including the Tote, the Kingston Hotel and the Burnley Tavern (Sport 2015: 93). Helen Smart, who participated in this scene as part of Toxic Shock, described the band in the following way:

> It was an overtly feminist band, although it wasn't separatist. We had me – I was heterosexual, and Eve Glenn, the guitarist, was heterosexual and in a relationship, et cetera, so it wasn't a radfem band. It did have radfems in it, but it did have a whole spectrum, but it was overtly all-female and it was overtly singing about women's issues and being a bit of a pain in the arse to the patriarchal music scene.
>
> (Smart 2018)

Despite these fertile training grounds, and headway being made into the pub rock scene by artists such as Chrissy Amphlett, Stiletto and Cheetah, by the mid-80s, guitarist Fiona Lee Maynard recalls that:

Figure 13 Toxic Shock, 1982. Source: Ruth Maddison Collection.

... in terms of bands, it was rare to see girls in bands. There were some great examples. Do Re Me, I'm Talking, Essendon Airport, Weddings, Parties Anything had a female bass player who also played for the Saints sometimes. There were pockets of it. It was Jenny Morris and Meo 245, there was Annalise Morrow from the Numbers, there were some really great examples, but in terms of every day going into the pub to play, there would often be like four bands and I would be the only female on the bill and it's still likely to happen now.

(Maynard 2019)

In other words, despite the presence of many all-woman bands in the women's music scene, the perception of the 'novelty' of Sweet Jayne and the Wet Ones in being all-women bands did not noticeably wane through this period. To the contrary, Claire Moore (2018) notes that 'There was a real lull in [women in bands] after the Seaview Ballroom time. Every band had a least one female in them. After that, it sort of petered out and a lot of the ones that who were playing stopped playing'.

In the 1990s there was increasing recognition of the exclusion of women in combination and a wider acceptance (or at least visibility) of the feminist politics that had been fostered in fringe scenes in the 1970s and 1980s (see Strong and Rogers, 2016). This led to a trend for the establishment of women friendly spaces in the Melbourne music scene, including training focused on women, in particular the Rock 'n' Roll High School in Collingwood, and women friendly events and collectives emerging during the early 1990s, and continuing sporadically until the present day. These included residencies at various venues for women only events such as Sisters in Song in 1994–5 (McArdle 1994) and Femrock, which ran throughout the 1990s and eventually diversified into also running music business workshops ('Hot Talk' 1998). Other initiatives included Laura McFarlane's 'Decibels' program designed to get women behind the mixing desks at gigs, and producer Siiri Metsar curating and recording compilations of women performers called 'Girl Zone', and organizing the launch of the second volume of this with an all-women crew (Simpson 1996). Moving into the 2000s, small-scale women-focused festivals held in the city over a number of years culminated in a Melbourne iteration of the global Ladyfest event in November 2004 (Sheridan 2004), and International Women's Day had become a fixture in the calendar where women-centric gigs were held throughout the city and local broadcasters gave more time to women presenters and artists. Youth-focused music organization The Push also implemented programs supporting young women performers. In 2009, a Melbourne record label HerStory was releasing work by women artists, in a precedent to the LISTEN label of the mid- to late 2010s. These activities represent only a section of the labour that women were putting in to claiming space for themselves and amplifying the voices of other women across this time period.

For Laila Costa, this moment emerged out of a confluence of events, including the success of a few key Australian rock bands such as Spiderbait and Magic Dirt that featured women who served as role models for aspiring musicians, and a collective consciousness of the need for a more explicitly feminist approach to music-making informed partly by global information flows, particularly Riot Grrrl:

> It might have been people like – I'm thinking Janet from Spiderbait. Snark – all of Snark, they were all females. Adalita was just starting in Magic Dirt. Nadia Markovic was in Christbait. There were a lot of bands with one female in them and I think I just started going, 'I can do this'. And then, I was listening – also, this was the time of that whole Riot Grrrl scene. And so, that was filtering in as well and listening to that via mixtapes.
> **Q:** How did you hear about that?
> **A:** I'm not exactly sure. I think it might have been Bikini Kill. You know what? […] I think it was just likeminded ladies that liked music that would start saying, 'Hey, have you heard this? Do you know this? Do you know this? Do you know this?'. First, it would be the music and then it would be more about the politics, 'Did you see what they were wearing? Did you see what they were saying?', passing VHS tapes onto each other (Costa 2017).

This later translated into women-focused events designed to give emerging artists a place to perform. Costa notes that 'there was a lot of I guess people who were getting on-board with this who were trying to have the Ladyfests and the Femfests and CD recordings, trying to have female-only bills or majority female'. Costa's band Mace was part of a wave of punk- and Riot Grrrl-influenced bands made up mainly of young (sometimes school age) women playing in Melbourne in the early 1990s that benefited from and often helped to organize these initiatives. She also points to the influence of managers such as Fiona Duncan who worked to change the masculine culture behind the scenes of the industry. The increasing presence of women in other roles, such as Sage Forrest and Chris Scheri as engineers in recording studios, and actions by allies such as Bruce Milne who worked to make the Tote a more accessible venue for women punters and performers when he took over the venue, added to a shift in what was seen as possible. Caroline Kennedy describes how:

> It was sort of like a concentration of possibility and then by 2000 it wasn't outrageous for women to be in bands and [discrimination] wasn't really acceptable because there was a third wave of feminism and we were part of it in the Melbourne music scene. The Plums and all of that were part of that. I mean, my songs were about gender precisely, performances were about gender and sexuality and about these issues, so there was a lot of correcting going on then and it sort of opened the scene up, I think, to it being permissible to play and not be disenfranchised. I kind of engaged in a mode of discourse that aims to open things up even more and that's as it should be, in my view, and that's what young people always do and it's the right thing.
>
> (Kennedy 2017)

Kennedy also recounted instances of being subjected to gender-based abuse during her career, and it is noteworthy that, after all this work being done to claim space for women and normalize their presence in the industry, as a young woman starting a band in the 2010s, Grace Kindellan's experiences were in some ways almost the same as Sue World or Chris Scheri's in the 1970s and 1980s. She describes her experience of being asked to play at an event as follows:

> [It was] like really macho, rough, dude-heavy bands who were all very, very trendy. And I was like, 'Let's do this gig. It will be really good. It's at the Northcote Social Club'. And we were added to the event. And on the Facebook event, it actually listed all of the male bands, and then Wet Lips (girls), Girl Crazy (girls). And there was like this post – oh, that's right, and we were booked because someone had posted in the event saying, 'There's no women on this line-up'. So we were a total afterthought, totally token women.
>
> (Kindellan 2019)

Kindellan's sense that women-centric activities in a scene she describes as 'very male dominated, quite macho' are something she sees emerging as though for the first time was also apparent in the establishment of the grassroots feminist music collective LISTEN in Melbourne in 2009. Starting with a Facebook post by musician Evelyn Morris noting the poor representation of women in a book on the Australian underground scene, LISTEN quickly grew into a collective that incorporated many of the activities noted above, including releasing music by women and gender non-conforming artists, putting on events such as gigs, panel

Figure 14 Wet Lips, 2016. Source: Zo Damage Collection.

discussions and even a multi-day conference and using social media and the LISTEN website to intervene in public discourse. This task was made somewhat easier by the increasing presence of women such as Helen Marcou and Kirsty Rivers in important policy and advocacy roles in Melbourne.

However, interviewees note places where advances have been clear to them, and in particular the increasingly intersectional nature of the discussion around inclusion. Grace Kindellan describes how:

> ... when we went on tour with Wet Lips in 2017, we went to Hobart and Brisbane and Sydney, and Canberra and Wollongong, and we were definitely like, 'Oh, there are people doing what we're doing in every one of these cities'. And I think there is much more of a movement in all those cities being like women, 'We need more representation of women', and 'Girl power'. But if you look a little bit deeper and look at like really amazing pioneering gender non-binary artists, like Habits and Friendship, and trans and gender non-binary artists, like Callan and Simona [Castricum], and lots more people who I can't name, there's a bit more of – like Evelyn Ida Morris. I think the conversation in Melbourne is much more complex and nuanced and is starting to recognise that the conversation is much more broader than just 'Girl Power'. It's actually, no, there's space for people who are non-binary, who don't fit into our outdated binary understand

of gender. There are really amazing trans artists who are pushing boundaries sonically, and who have this incredibly rich scene, that I think probably only exists in Melbourne.

(Kindellan 2019)

Another element of this inclusiveness is the ability for people re-entering the music scene as older performers to find space and acceptance within the community. A number of women interviewees commented on this, describing the reestablishment of their performing careers, albeit generally on a more low-key, local level, after taking time away from the scene as primary carers for children. These changes represent improvements for women since, in particular, the extremely masculine environment of the early days of pub rock; but the continued disparity and the persistence of certain types of discriminatory practices have resulted in the continuing re-emergence of gender as an unsolved issue in Melbourne music.

Creating their own venues: First Nations artists

It is almost impossible for any understanding of music in Australia to be divorced from the colonial background of the country. There is a history of music-making in the place now called Melbourne that spans over tens of thousands of years, which cannot be covered in a project that was designed to only examine the period from the 1950s, but which should still be acknowledged, as should the destruction of much of that musical culture. The performance of rock and pop in Melbourne involves the adaptation of imported genres and styles played on stolen land, with the inescapable legacy of violence, dispossession and brutality as a largely unacknowledged but always-present accompaniment to the music. While women have needed to struggle to claim space in Melbourne's music scenes, this has been as much about claiming greater legitimacy and being able to move beyond the circumscribed roles that were available to them, and policed by others in the industry, as being able to make music at all. For Indigenous musicians in Melbourne, this policing has been much more explicit and literal, and directly connected to the tools that the state has used to enact the broader oppression directed at them. First Nations participation in rock and pop has been more a fight to be given any space at all; but also a story of resourcefulness and resilience where music making has often been, by necessity, tied to a broader political struggle for equality. As such, music-making has been more tightly connected to both grassroots groups and government-funded institutions that have acted as hubs for Indigenous communities in inner city Melbourne than was the case for women's musical activism described above. In this section of the chapter, the voices of our First Nations interviewees – Grant Hansen, Lou Bennett and Robert Bundle – will be foregrounded so as much of this story as possible is told in their own words.

While Indigenous adoption and adaptation of various musical styles imported by invaders – particularly country music – have been well researched (Walker 2000; Martin 2015), King (2017: 132) has noted that:

> ... there were very few popular Indigenous singers and performers in 1950s and 1960s Australia. Though Aboriginal participation in local festivals, touring vaudeville shows and community gatherings was well documented before the 1950s ... there were very few opportunities for Aboriginal participation in more mainstream venues or media.

By the 1970s, when our interviewees were starting to be involved in music-making in Melbourne to varying degrees, a strong community of musicians and bands existed in Melbourne that was mainly based around Fitzroy, where a large Indigenous population had lived since the end of the Second World War (*Snapshots of Aboriginal Fitzroy*, 2004). Grant Hansen describes this community as follows:

> So yeah, so the first band I played in was an Aboriginal band called Interaction, which became a very popular community band in the aboriginal community in Fitzroy ... This was a music industry scene within an industry. If you go back to the early days in Fitzroy, there were performers like Harry Williams and Wilga Williams, who had a very famous outfit called the Country Outcasts and very well-known basically around Australia but, in particular, New South Wales and Melbourne. So they were very well known. And then you had the band called Hard Times and also, you had Herb Patten and the famous gumleaf player, that was one of those music shows a couple of years ago, Carol Fraser, Buster Thomas. So those were the bands that were in around at the time. Then you had a band called Koori Connection which Archie Roach played with. And Archie and Ruby would play with that band.
>
> And then they had another band called Altogether with their nephew, David Arden. Then my band came along, Interaction, which had Richard Frankland in it, who went on to form his band Djaambi. Then out of Djaambi became Tiddas. And out of Interaction, I formed the band, Blackfire, which was another

big Victorian Indigenous music act. So we had an industry within an industry because we were able to play to our own mob out at community functions and events. But some of the hotels that were Koori-friendly in those days were hotels like the Eastern Hill. I can remember playing with Interaction on the Thursday night and most of the time I'd have my guitar about here and someone standing right in front of you.

There were what we used to call blackouts, where you couldn't actually move. The place was just full of Aboriginal people from all around Melbourne. So that was a good venue. And we also played at the Baden Powell Hotel, which one of my bands, the Mercury Blues, played there regularly and that became a very well-known venue for our Indigenous Koori bands in Melbourne. The Royal Derby Hotel was very popular. Blackfire played there many, many times. The John Curtin Hotel in Lygon Street in Carlton there, which is just opposite the Trades Hall – the Trades Hall was another venue that we played at quite often. So we had the Aboriginals Advancement League and we had some other venues in and around Melbourne that were Aboriginal owned. And the community was a very big community in those days, something like 25,000 people living in around metropolitan Melbourne. So we were lucky that in one way, in one sense, we were able to play to our own mob, so an industry within an industry because the doors weren't always open to indigenous acts to engage to play in the wider mainstream music industry (Hansen 2020).

The need to create 'an industry within an industry' stemmed from difficulties in getting access to music-making spaces freely available to white people, which was noted by all interviewees. Lou Bennett, for instance, noted that 'there were environments that we would never step into because of our beliefs and understanding of our history and knowing where we sat and they were our choices, but then there were a lot of choices that were taken away from us because of what we were standing for.' Similarly, McKinnon (2010: 225) describes how:

> In the late 1970s in the inner city suburbs of Melbourne, such as Fitzroy, Carlton and Richmond, Indigenous peoples often had problems getting into local pubs, bars, general nightlife and music venues. As Uncle Alf Bamblett states: "we finished off being barred from all the places around, purely on the base of race".

This meant that the few venues that were more welcoming became central to the activities of Melbourne Indigenous musicians and those that were touring from other parts of the country. The downside to this was that these venues could then become the focus of police attention. In 1980, activist Gary Foley – at this time the coordinator of the State's Aboriginal Health Service – approached the press about being harassed by an officer at the Grace Darling Hotel, and described:

> ... a 'Gestapo-like raid' on the Builder's Arms Hotel in Gertrude Street, Fitzroy. 'Police blocked off all exits from the pub then arrested several people for drunkenness,' he said. 'There were white people in the hotel who were just as inebriated but were not even looked at,' he said. (Robinson 1980: 5)

The discriminatory attitudes of the police, and the ways in which places like the Builder's Arms could become a focal point for these, were evident in other media coverage. In particular, a notorious 1983 article on policing in Fitzroy described how the officer being shadowed by a journalist:

> ... pointed out the Builders Arms Hotel. Walk through there in a blue uniform, she said, and you'll find out how the [racist expletive] feel about police. The coppers never went in there alone; there had to be at least four of them going in together (Gawenda 1983: 3).

The outcry over the explicit racism in this article led to 'the placement of trainee police with Aboriginal health and legal services as part of their preparation for transfer to Fitzroy' (*Snapshots of Aboriginal Fitzroy* 2004, 38). Progress was very slow on this issue however, with the State government again having to acknowledge in the early 1990s that discrimination on the basis of race was still common in hotels and nightclubs, after a high profile case of a bar in St Kilda refusing to serve Mandawuy Yunupingu from Yothu Yindi (Kelly 1992: 1). Grant Hansen elaborated on how this type of exclusion, and the negative stereotypes of Indigenous people that it stemmed from, had consequences for access to other parts of the music industries, particularly because of the importance of pubs and hotels to establishing careers in rock and pop in Australia:

> Well, I think there was always a problem with record companies about promoting Indigenous bands and all the associated perceived problems they had with Indigenous audiences going to hotels and large numbers of Indigenous people being in live venues. I think a lot of the publicans were loath to have Indigenous acts for all those types of reasons. They thought we couldn't behave ourselves or something. But I think the record companies – if you look at the history of Australian music, Jimmy Little was the first one to have a golden record in 1967, then Lionel Rose in 1970 with a golden record, 'I Thank You', penned by Johnny Young. And then it wasn't until something around about '96, '98, before YothuYindi came along.

> So there was a 25-year gap in between where there was no Indigenous music recorded on a major record label in Australia. So that's dumbfounding when you think about how many Indigenous acts were actually floating around, how many good bands there were at the time. So a lot of the record companies were, I think, scared. And music was always pigeonholed in those days, whether it was rock music or pop music and whether they could actually have a market to sell the music and all that sort of stuff. And I think Indigenous music, at the time, was thought to be – sometimes you'd see it in a 'world' category in music shops. It wasn't in the mainstream section of the record shop. So if you wanted to go and buy a Coloured Stone album or a Warumpi album or one of those like Scrap Metal, you'd have to go to the 'world music' section.
>
> So they always found it difficult, for some reason, to really relate to where indigenous music should be promoted. And a lot of the A & R people haven't gone out to go and see a lot of the great Aboriginal bands that were performing in that time. So there was probably one or two decades of great Indigenous music that was lost, that a lot of people didn't get to hear.
>
> (Hansen 2020)

This notion of exclusion from the mainstream was also noted by Lou Bennett, for whom the barriers put in place by the Indigenous identities of herself and others in Tiddas were compounded by their unconventional expressions of femininity:

> There is a part of the industry definitely that has excluded us, and it's the popular, or the mainstream is what a lot of people refer to. So the commercial radio stations never played us, and we know very well it wasn't anything to do with our craft and our skill. We know we could sing. We could hear what we could do production-wise in our albums and our song compositions, but I don't think – we didn't fit their little boxes and we were three girls that were not size 10 and wore make-up and shaved under our arms, so we broke those conventions and we broke – in a way we broke their understanding of what a woman singer was supposed to be. So yeah, there were times where it was really frustrating because we knew that we could bring something quite beautiful and, if people had a chance to listen to us, we knew very well that we would be able to bring them in as part of our musical family, our musical punters – musical lover punters.
>
> (Bennett 2019)

Lack of access meant that the pubs that did support Indigenous musicians were vital, whether these were formal venues that ran paying gigs, or places that supported the type of community music-making similar to that described as taking place in public places by interviewees. However, there was recognition among interviewees that creating one's own venues or gigging in the limited number of pubs that were accessible did not go far enough in providing the extra support Indigenous people needed to fully participate in music-making in the city. Bennett describes how her band Tiddas actively pushed to find different types of venues (such as the Continental) as a way of 'adding value' to what they were doing. In a similar vein, Grant Hansen describes the processes through which the Koori Music Club, and then Songlines, organizations designed to fill the gap in support, were created:

> Well, I was, as I said, playing with a band called Interaction, and we used to rehearse at a place called Koori College in Cambridge Street in Collingwood. And it was a Koori health workers' training course programme that was run out of there. And I had this idea that we needed to have people involved in the music industry, not just in front of the microphone, so to speak, but behind the scenes. There were a lot of people interested in being roadies, sound engineers, lighting and all that stuff. So I had this idea that we should form an organisation to help people get into the music industry, besides just playing. So I formed the Koori Music Club and we had all these aims and objectives about what we would do. We had a working party committee and that sort of stuff.
>
> And then about a year later, that sort of stalled and Songlines came into fruition with a couple of other people that formed Songlines but basically used the same principles as what the Koori Music Club was about. And I came on to their board. And after that, basically, as I said, I became the CEO. But the idea of Songlines Music, at the time, was to do exactly the same thing as the Koori Music Club. But also, my idea was to become like a Motown music label here in Australia – was to have our own record label and have our own Koori infrastructures and all that sort of stuff. So once again, I had this idea about building an industry within an industry because not all the doors are open to us and to have a major record label that we could use to promote our aboriginal acts.
>
> (Hansen 2020)

For Robbie Bundle, who was also involved in the establishment of Songlines, the idea of the organization was 'to be able to encourage singer-songwriters, give them the opportunity that they wouldn't normally get and they had the backing if there was any problems with getting gigs, which there usually were, because you'd get knocked back from the pub' (Bundle 2019).

Music-making also intersected with activities in other areas, particularly including Indigenous well-being and politics. Ryan (1994) described what she called the 'Koori Musical Network' as it existed in the late 1980s and early 1990s, whereby music-making was supported in various ways by diverse institutions such as the Aboriginal Advancement League, the Aboriginal Health Service and

ATSIC, as well as more obviously music-focused organizations such as 3CR (and later 3KND) and the Koori Music Club. Robert Bundle describes how, as one example, the Aboriginal Health Service was at the centre of political activism, using music to promote awareness of inequalities and also inspiring musicians to be more political:

> I was always politically motivated because, I mean, I went to Koori College in Victoria, in the Aboriginal Health Service in Fitzroy when the whole movement started in Australia. You had people like Mohammed Ali that people would call into the area, into the health service and then because they'd be catching up with the local mob. We had [Gary] Foley go, Foley and Bruce McGuinness, who are predominantly the two iconic figures, along with all the others, the Elders like the Sir Doug Nicholls and Faith Bandlers of the world, and so many others. But they were all based in Fitzroy, so when we'd do the politics of health, we would study health and we would get on the bus, almost like the Freedom Rides with Charlie Perkins, your Uncle Charlie. We'd get on a bus and we'd go to Uluru, and we'd go to all these communities and we'd see things like leprosy and we'd see such horrific conditions. We thought we were living bad in humpies and in tin shacks, but the mob out there had nothing. It was just on the ground, a little humpy. So music was kind of like the thing that was going to take you to the next level, just so you can give people a voice. That was the most important thing for me, and it still is today.
> **Q:** Was there much music that emerged out of the centre?
> **A:** Absolutely, I was surrounded by it. Because you had No Fixed Address coming to town at the time; and Us Mob and local bands – Hard Times and stuff – they'd set up the Rock Against Racism concerts. You'd have all these other people, like the Oils and whoever else, they'd rock along … It was all just amazing things that were going on. They'd all come to the health service to see it because they'd hear all these things that were happening in our world, in Australia, concerning Aboriginal people and their health conditions. It was kind of 'out of sight, out of mind', but the political element was that music was attached together and became one, then it just exploded. And we're still doing that today which is great. You've got young performers like Briggs and, of course, Archie and still the No Fixed [Address] boys, they're still going. It's a wonderful thing.
>
> (Bundle 2019)

Bundle also discussed the ways in which bands would use their music to benefit the community in various ways – for example, No Fixed Address would do free gigs, and Hard Times would do benefit shows for a community funeral fund. Lou Bennett described how at times there were intersections between a variety of political issues, and how musicians from different marginalized groups supported each other:

> Here in Melbourne we were so spoilt for choice, and so I would go out one week with the girls, and I mean with my girlfriends, and we'd go and see other girl bands, gay bands. So there was that scene and then there was the blackfella scene. (…)
>
> **Q:** So were there particular venues associated with, say, the lesbian scene or the … ?
>
> **A:** Well yeah, some of them did, and they would change too. So, for instance, Empress of India was a great place for both the lesbian scene and the blackfella scene. So there were combined venues that we would frequent and always seem to run into the same like-minded people. Sydney Road was another area where there were venues along that way. Builders Arms, I think, was one of the pubs that sort of has still continued as well to have live music. The Cornish Arms. That sort of came a bit later. But up and down. I do remember going up and down Sydney Road and in areas around Brunswick where, if there were blackfellas, you'd often find lesbians. If there were lesbians, you'd often find blackfellas. And I think it was because maybe the music scene brought those mobs together, or the cause or the theme or the event, because a lot of the times we done – because we done so many charity or non-paying gigs, fund raisers for all kinds of good charities, whether it be about deaths in custody, whether it be about Reclaim the Night. Reclaim the Night was a huge one for us to be involved in. Not only just to be involved in to sing but also to enjoy being a punter.
>
> (Bennett 2019)

Making connections like these across groups and in particular finding ways to engage allies was of key importance to Robbie Bundle, who discussed the role that musicians such as Midnight Oil, Paul Hester and Paul Kelly have played in helping to amplify the work of organizations such as Songlines and introduce First Nations artists to new audiences. He described the annual Share the Spirit festival, which had been held just before his interview, in very hopeful terms:

> As time went by, it just became more and more open and then it's just like at Share the Spirit. Last Saturday was mind altering, it's the biggest one I've ever been to. We had the [Invasion Day] march from Parliament House and we came down and we walked into Treasury gardens, and this massive throng of people came in. We got it all on film, we filmed the whole concert. To hear people like Mojo Juju now, they just come through. You sit back and see all these young ones

come through and you go, 'Man, this is where it's at'. Because of that interaction. You look in the audience, which is massive – the crowd – and they're all black and white people and people of all colours, and that's what you love. That's what you love.

(Bundle 2019)

All interviewees reflected positively on the current strength and visibility of Indigenous music making – particularly, as Grant Hansen noted, in hip-hop.

Conclusion

While women (and increasingly gender-diverse and non-binary persons) and First Nations artists are currently lauded as important parts of the Melbourne rock and pop scenes, it has taken decades of work to arrive at this point, and ensuring they have full access to music-making is still very much an incomplete project. The advances that have been made have been overwhelmingly due to the efforts of people within these groups, who have created communities, opportunities and structures for themselves when denied access to conventional routes to participation and success. The goal of this chapter has been to highlight this work and provide examples of the struggles experienced by marginalized groups in the Melbourne scene, not all of which could be explored here.

8

The branded city

Introduction

In February 2015, after a sustained campaign by journalists, academics and the general public, a small lane at the rear of the former Palace nightclub in Bourke Street in central Melbourne was officially renamed Amphlett Lane in tribute to the late singer Chrissy Amphlett. After achieving national and international fame with the band the Divinyls in the 1980s and 1990s, Amphlett had died of breast cancer, aged only fifty-three, two years earlier (Northover 2015). The renaming of this lane from the starkly utilitarian Corporation Lane 1639 and its decoration with iconic imagery of the singer are considered groundbreaking by many for not only commemorating a woman performer as an important musician and artist worthy of formal recognition amongst the pantheon of Melbourne and Australian musical history, but also because it celebrates an artist whose music and performance openly challenged one of the dominant stereotypes of Australian music, namely that women's music is pop, while that of men is rock (Strong 2014). Many of those who advocated for the name change ('Team Chrissy') were women, who saw the commemoration of Amphlett in the physical fabric of Melbourne as both a singular tribute to the artist herself, but also as a way of broadening the history and memory of the previously male-dominated Australian pub rock era of the 1970s and 1980s to include the role of strong, confident and pioneering women. In doing so they also hoped to ensure that the voices and experiences of women become more central to the story of rock music in Melbourne, Australia more generally.

Part of an increasing trend in music cities across the globe to officially recognize sites of musical heritage as urban landmarks (Roberts and Cohen 2014; Strong, Cannizzo and Rogers 2017), a program of renaming Melbourne streets and lanes after musicians and performers began in the early 2000s with the renaming of Corporation Lane in the CBD, home to iconic live music venue

Cherry Bar, to AC/DC Lane. As in Amphlett Lane, AC/DC Lane features artwork celebrating the band, most notably its late original lead singer, Scottish-born Bon Scott. Scott's cameo playing the bagpipes atop a flatbed truck in the video for the song 'Long Way to the Top' which was filmed in Melbourne's Swanston Street in early 1976 has become an iconic image of the 1970s pub rock era in Australia. So too the naming in 2005 of a canal-side path in suburban Elwood as Paul Hester Walk in memory of the late Crowded House drummer; and the 2015 renaming of a lane in beachside St Kilda after the Boys Next Door's Rowland S. Howard cemented in physical form the role that that Melbourne neighbourhood played in post and post-punk experimentation (Strong 2015).

The renaming of these lanes and walks reflects the popular embrace of Melbourne's twentieth-century musical and cultural heritage not only by fans, musicians and music historians but also by important urban political and economic players who are increasingly seeking to extract economic value from the city's musical heritage. Part of an ongoing strategy to reinvent the previously rather drab and dour manufacturing city as a culturally inclusive, vibrant post-industrial metropolis, the renaming of streets and lanes after musicians reflects a growing recognition in Melbourne and around the world that heritage tourism, and specifically music heritage tourism, has the potential to be a vital part of a city's twenty-first century cultural 'brand' and tourism 'offer'. This desire to commercialize and draw economic benefit from Melbourne's musical heritage was specifically addressed by the then Lord Mayor, conservative Robert Doyle, in his opening remarks about Amphlett Lane, which he said would take 'its place in the panoply among the laneways of Melbourne. I think this will become, as the laneways of Melbourne are, a destination for music lovers from our state, nation and the world and remember a wonderful contributor to world music' (Northover 2015). The use of Chrissy Amphlett's and other musicians' stories in this way raises important questions about the use and abuse of rock and music history more generally for city 'branding' purposes.

Drawing on methods derived from urban history and urban sociology, cultural and heritage studies and utilizing sources including oral history interviews, policy papers and field observation and research, this chapter seeks to answer these questions by investigating the ways in which Melbourne's music history and the stories of these select musicians and music scenes have been embedded into both the tourism 'branding' of the city and into its physical and cultural fabric in recent decades. We begin with a brief overview of changes in the economic and social structure of the inner city in the 1970s and 1980s which saw the decline of manufacturing employment and rapid falls in population, which when combined not only gave rise to a narrative of urban 'crisis' but also, as in other cities around the world, freed up space for musical and other artistic experimentation. The chapter then discusses planning policy changes in the 1980s, 1990s and beyond that radically altered the culture, ambience and built form of the inner city, sometimes creating tensions between newer and more established land uses and residents. A discussion then follows about how these economic shifts have, in the 2000s, seen Melbourne's long history of musical experimentation being increasingly used by governments and policy-makers as key features of the city's official cultural 'brand' and tourism 'offer'. The final section of the chapter then both documents examples of these cultural tourism and heritage practices and asks questions about whose stories and which histories are told in these official government and municipal cultural tourism programs. In doing so, we explore how these inclusions and exclusions expose some problematic issues about the nature of contemporary music history and music city heritage policies in Melbourne and elsewhere around the world.

Economic restructuring

Life in Australia: Melbourne is a 1966 documentary-cum-commercial made by the Australian Government's Commonwealth Film Unit. One of a series of films featuring each of the major capitals and aimed at attracting tourists, investors and new migrants to the country, the film focuses on the lifestyle and economic and cultural opportunities the city offered visitors and residents by following a 'day in the life' of an unidentified young couple as they worked, socialized, window-shopped and prepared for their new married life together. Along the way we see glimpses of Melbourne's urban landmarks, including the Melbourne Cricket Ground, the Yarra River, the CBD skyline and the Queen Victoria Market, where people of multiple European ethnicities shop, trade and mingle. The previously dour city's growing youth cultural offerings are displayed when, in the evening after work, the young couple visit a city nightclub and drink European-style coffee and dance to the latest sounds.

While clearly working- or lower middle-class, in the affluent growing economy of the mid-1960s the young couple have access to a range of consumer goods and opportunities unimaginable to their parents' generation. Both have full-time jobs, she as a shop assistant in a CBD 'variety' store while he is a manual worker, employed on the assembly line making engines at the General Motors-Holden factory in Port Melbourne. As such their lives and jobs are presented as typical of those of young people in Melbourne at the time, and in many ways they were. At a time when about one-third of all men were employed in manufacturing and young women typically had 'white' or 'pink' collar jobs between leaving school in their mid-teens and getting married in the early twenties, and when most were expected to leave the workforce to become full-time housewives and mothers, the young couple reflect the experiences of the hundreds of thousands of Melbourne baby boomers who reached adulthood in the decades after the Second World War.

Many of these experiences and opportunities, and the economic and social assumptions that underpinned them, were to dramatically change over the next two decades, however. Feminism and equal pay legislation meant that employment opportunities for many women expanded dramatically in the 1970s when resignation from the workforce upon marriage became a choice rather than an expectation. Sadly, the same was not true for motherhood until attitudes and access to affordable childcare began to become more common in the 1980s. These were major social changes, but equally dramatic economic ones were to have more profound impacts on 'life in Australia', especially working life, in the last decades of the twentieth century and beyond. Economic restructuring and the growth of car-based suburbia forced the closure of major department stores in the CBD and inner suburbs in the 1970s, dramatically cutting the numbers of jobs available to young women like the one featured in the documentary. At the same time the early stages of competition from Asian manufacturers brought the closure or rapid scaling back of employment numbers in many inner city factories such as GMH at Port Melbourne (where the fiancée worked in the 1966 Commonwealth film), decimating job opportunities for men, young and old. While some former retail jobs moved to the new drive-in shopping malls such as Chadstone, Northland and Westfield Doncaster then proliferating in the suburbs, others simply disappeared (Dingle and O'Hanlon 2009; Bailey 2020). Similarly, some (men and women's) manufacturing jobs migrated to new factories in the outer suburbs; many more, especially those in the inner city-based and women-dominated clothing, textile and footwear industries, went overseas to the rapidly industrializing countries of Asia.

As the economic structure of Melbourne began to change in the 1970s – a process that rapidly accelerated from the early-1980s onwards – so too did its demographic profile. While gentrification saw some wealthier and social liberals begin to move to and renovate old houses in some inner areas such as Carlton and East Melbourne, as the economy turned down in the later-1970s, economic restructuring more often meant a loss of jobs and population, rather than increasing wealth, giving the city's inner region an increasingly down-at-heel, abandoned feel. A growing sense of crisis about the current state and future prospects of inner Melbourne began to develop, with a number of government and semi-government reports presenting an increasingly pessimistic prognosis about the future of the region. One report from 1977 went so far as to predict the possibility of European or North American-style urban decay and violence if something was not done to arrest the decline of the inner city economy (MMBW 1977; Urban Economic Consultants 1977; O'Hanlon 2009). Proffered solutions ranged from re-populating the inner suburbs through urban renewal projects, increased government protection and financial support for struggling manufacturing and other businesses, and a scaling-up of the community sector through education and social welfare initiatives.

Perhaps most contentious and important for our purposes, however, was the suggestion that there be a clear recognition by government that the industrial era was coming to an end in Melbourne (and the West more generally) and that rather than continuing to support fading industries, public policy should instead facilitate a move towards what was increasingly being referred to as a 'post-industrial' urban economic future based on services, new technologies, education, culture and tourism. While most of these ideas were initially dismissed as heartless and politically unfeasible, from the late-1970s federal, state and local governments of various political persuasions have essentially implemented them by reducing tariff protection, encouraging foreign investment in new industries, especially in financial services, technology and tourism, and promoting education and research, along with culture as key sectors of the inner urban economy. Inner Melbourne's economy today is essentially post-industrial; at the time of the 1971 Census, about 40 per cent of all jobs in inner Melbourne were described as 'blue collar' (i.e. manufacturing and the production of tangible things); the most recent count in 2016 has seen that number drop to below 10 per cent (MMBW 1977: 33; Australian Bureau of Statistics Census 2016). Even then many of those jobs are about consumption as much as production as they centre around artisanal food and drink consumed in the hospitality sector. The demographic structure of the population has also changed: while in the mid-1970s just under 30 per cent of the population of the inner city worked in manufacturing, by 2016 that figure had declined to around 5 per cent, with more than half of all workers in the inner city now employed in the professions and the finance and business services sector (MMBW 1977; Australian Bureau of Statistics 2016).

Planning the 'new' inner city

The major response to the crisis of the inner city was to reorient economic policies and rewrite planning rules in order to revitalize the rundown region economically, culturally and morphologically. The former involved the reinvention of major sporting fixtures such as the AFL and Melbourne Cup racing carnival as major tourism 'events', inventing or rebranding popular and ethnic festivals as 'spectacles' and the marketing of them as national and local tourist attractions as a way to draw visitors back to the city (O'Hanlon 2009: 32–4). The latter involved governments overriding planning laws (and often the concerns of residents) to facilitate the refurbishment of older, economically redundant neighbourhoods and strategically located sites. Government-funded cultural facilities such as those found on Southbank or Federation Square were often used as a means of seeding the regeneration of these often abandoned and redundant former industrial zones (O'Hanlon 2018: 174–5). More broadly, harnessing the tourism potential of the inner city to replace lost manufacturing jobs became a key element of urban economic strategy after the recessions of the 1970s and 1980s.

Most of the major cultural infrastructure projects undertaken by both Labor and Coalition (conservative Liberal-National Party) governments since the 1980s have been publicly funded and mostly restricted to the sporting and cultural sectors. Perhaps the most important method adopted to achieve the restructure of the inner urban economy in recent decades was the easing of planning restrictions on the private sector, dramatically liberalizing what could be built and where it could be built. Whereas for much of the twentieth century urban planning ideas had revolved around the desire to separate industrial, commercial, entertainment and residential land uses, and thus to avoid the often squalid and unhealthy urban environments of the nineteenth century, from the 1980s these ideas were abandoned, especially in inner city areas, in favour of what were called 'mixed use' developments in which office space, retail, cultural and leisure and entertainment facilities were co-located, often on sites formerly occupied by factories, warehouses and similar structures. Examples of such developments from this period included Melbourne Central (advertised at the time as the 'Life of the city' and featuring a branch of the Japanese department store Diamaru) which was built above a new underground railway station in the CBD; Southgate, an overtly cultural, leisure and tourism-oriented development on the south bank of the Yarra River; and the 'Como' and 'Jam Factory' projects which both replaced former factories with retail, fashion and tourist facilities on the increasingly fashionable Chapel Street in South Yarra. In each of these cases the Victorian state government created Major Projects Victoria in the mid-1980s to expedite and facilitate urban renewal; it was legislatively empowered to override normal planning rules, and was the major driving force behind these developments (O'Hanlon 2009).

Repopulating the inner city

Such commercial and entertainment-oriented development and an increasing emphasis on developing an economy based on tourism, leisure and culture succeeded in bringing some 'life' back to the inner city in the 1980s. Yet the CBD and some adjacent neighbourhoods remained largely devoid of people, especially after dark when the office workers and shoppers went home. Unlike in the 1950s, the city centre no longer emptied out at 5 p.m. on week days and after the shops shut at noon on Saturday; the CBD and the inner city generally remained largely empty after business hours. This became a major public policy issue in the 1970s and 1980s when the area began to not only lose jobs and economic importance, but also population. Where up until the early-1970s the population of the area that encompassed the CBD and the seven municipalities that surrounded it was about 300,000, by 1986 that number had dropped to less than 230,000, representing less than 7.5 per cent of the metropolitan total. Thirty years earlier, at the end of the Second World War, that number had been over 375,000, or about a quarter of the metro total (MMBW 1977: 5).

As such, there was an increasing fear in planning and policy circles that Melbourne might follow the fate of a number of older manufacturing cities in the United States and become what was known as a 'donut city': thriving on the periphery, but empty at the core (O'Hanlon 2009). A city that had previously been important politically, economically and culturally, not only in Victoria but nationally, was by the 1980s increasingly empty and economically and socially marginal. This was especially true for certain neighbourhoods such as

Collingwood, a suburb and municipality that had once been central to Australian politics and culture as one of the birthplaces of the Australian Labor Party and home to a nationally famous football team. By the time of the 1986 Census it was practically empty, with a population of just 13,340 people, down by a third since 1971 and more than 50 per cent below its post-war high. The adjacent suburb of Richmond, which again had been a similarly important site of politics and sport housed only 23,275 residents in 1986, down from 28,300 fifteen years earlier and less than 60 per cent of its mid-century total (MMBW 1977: 5; Dingle and O'Hanlon 2009: 54).

Stuart Grant of the Primitive Calculators recalls the emptiness and abandonment of much of the inner northern suburbs at this time; when he and his bandmates moved to Fitzroy in the late-1970s, it was 'just a blasted dead inner city industrial zone. Brunswick Street was completely boarded up. There was half a dozen shops that were open and the rest of it was just dead' (Grant 2017). But while this emptiness and abandonment were a problem in many ways, especially for those who had lost their jobs in the factory closures, for young people, including musicians and particular music scenes, it was a positive. With limited demand for accommodation and so few residents wanting to live in the inner city, not only were rents low, but night-time noise from live music venues was not much of an issue. This is one of the reasons why inner north venues such as the Champion Hotel in Fitzroy, the Club and the Tote in Collingwood and the Corner Hotel and the Tiger Room in Richmond could offer live music multiple nights per week without worrying too much about disturbing their neighbours. That many of the few remaining local residents were, like Stuart and his housemates and neighbours, young musicians and thus likely patrons of the venues, also aided the development of the scene. Population decline in other inner city neighbourhoods such as Carlton, North Melbourne and Prahran similarly helped to build their reputations for night-time activity and music at this time.

Another major site of popular live and recorded music venues, the CBD, was also essentially resident-free, again meaning that late-night noise from pubs, clubs and other live music venues was not really an issue. However, this began to change in the 1990s as government policy sought to reverse population loss and rapidly repopulate the inner city. 'Urban consolidation', as these policies were known, sought to do a number of things using a variety of planning tools and economic incentives: the first was to rezone and reuse redundant industrial land for high density residential development, as in Southbank, the Docklands and Port Melbourne where land was rezoned and sold off to developers for residential use, sometimes at below market rates and with promises of state-supplied or supported infrastructure development. Secondly, former industrial spaces such as factories and warehouses were rezoned for conversion to residential use, as seen in places such as Richmond, Collingwood and Fitzroy. Changes to planning regulations to encourage residential development around public transport nodes and tram routes also brought residents back to inner city high streets such as Brunswick and Smith Streets, which, as we have seen, were in Stuart Grant's days either abandoned or dominated by day time retail uses. Few people, other than the dwindling number of shopkeepers who still lived above their businesses, resided in these streets.

These areas were, like the CBD itself, essentially empty after dark and at weekends. As a result of these policies, the contemporary population of the 'inner core' area has grown from just over 230,000 in 1991 to almost 500,000 today (ABS 2021: Table 2). Perhaps the most visible manifestation of the success of these repopulation policies was in the CBD itself, where the encouragement of the diversification of its functions and the revitalization of its economy through residential development have seen its population skyrocket since the 1990s. This was mainly achieved through the conversion of redundant former office and other buildings, and the encouragement of residential development into areas that were previously zoned commercial. And while changes in planning laws to facilitate these changes were a State government responsibility, local government also played an active role, such as in 1992 when the Melbourne City Council explicitly endorsed CBD revitalization through its Postcode 3000 strategy which offered incentives to owners and developers to convert empty or redundant office and other commercial space to housing. An empty Council-owned property opposite the Town Hall was offered as a demonstration project for the campaign, which also offered rental subsidies to tenants who wished to move to what at that stage was largely a place of daytime business and retail and tourism and night-time entertainment, (Dovey, Adams and Jones 2018). Postcode 3000 and subsequent policies to encourage city living have seen the CBD population rise from under 5,000 in 1991 to more than 50,000 today (City of Melbourne 2021). Before the depressive effects of COVID-19, Melbourne's CBD was one of the fastest growing urban areas in the country throughout the 2010s.

Selling the new inner city

As the economic, social and cultural structure of the inner city changed in the post-industrial era and its residential and tourism population began to grow in the 1990s, so too did the imagery and language used to advertise Melbourne to both tourists and locals radically change. While in 1966 *Life in Australia: Melbourne* had focused on jobs in factories and departments stores, and the 'Australian Dream' of a house in suburbia, contemporary advertising increasingly favours the inner city as a place of urban heritage or fun, leisure and entertainment. While sport, shopping and fashion remain a fixture of the city's 'brand', since the 1980s advertising campaigns have become increasingly dominated by images of the city's cosmopolitanism, cultural facilities and nightlife offerings. A 1987 film produced by Osborne Video Productions and simply called *Melbourne, Australia* and aimed at international investors and tourists offers an example of this shift. While continuing the tradition of presenting sport in the form of the AFL football grand final and the Melbourne Cup as major features of Melbourne life, the film's focus on the Cup is less about horse racing and more about fashion. Melbourne's role as Australia's most overtly fashion-conscious city was not only evident; the film also displayed the city as the country's leading shopping destination and home to much of its textile, clothing and footwear industries. This was a link that a newly elected Cain State Labor Government had made in a 1984 plan for the future urban economy, where it overtly linked the 'Melbourne Cup and Melbourne's leadership in the Australian fashion industry' (Government of Victoria 1984: 171; O'Hanlon 2009). The built heritage of the inner city and the diverse and important night-time economy were also central to the Melbourne presented in the film, especially the restaurants and nightclubs of the CBD, Carlton and South Yarra. While live music was only a minor component of the entertainment focus – which mostly emphasized the numerous and at that stage rapidly expanding nightclubs in King St and elsewhere in the CBD – one nightclub, Inflation, which was known to feature live music several nights per week, was depicted as a central component of the city's increasingly 'cosmopolitan' vibe.

As the urban economy was restructured in the 1980s and 1990s, and as the construction of new and refurbished sporting and cultural facilities saw an increasing emphasis on shopping fun and leisure, improving the city's nightlife 'offer' became central to the process of reinventing Melbourne as an attractive cultural tourism destination. This included the deregulation of liquor licensing laws and the encouragement of small bars and a diversity of venues (see Chapter 3). At the same time there developed a strong recognition that as many residents of the inner city were artists, musicians, writers and cultural practitioners, their art, music and lifestyles (lived out in the pubs, cafes, galleries, venues, etc.) offered opportunities that could be harnessed and sold into what was increasingly being called 'experiential tourism', capable of appealing to visitors from outer suburban Melbourne, Australia and internationally. As urban sociologist Sharon Zukin has shown, this was an idea that emerged in New York's SoHo in the 1970s and quickly went global, becoming the basis of what has since become known as a 'creative city' strategy (Zukin 1982; Landry and Bianchini 1995; Florida 2002). Whether intentionally or not, the 1984 urban economic strategy document developed by the new Cain Labor Government, which emphasized the role of fashion and retail in the city's 'brand', similarly recognized that inner Melbourne's cultural ambience and its cultural economy were a competitive strength that could and should be developed for economic purposes, including tourism.

As the city sought to develop these ideas and began to gain a reputation as Australia's coolest, most cultured and most alternative city in the 1990s and 2000s, and as the determination of civic leaders to cash in on this growing reputation developed, advertising and the city's projection of itself increasingly exploited this new cultural ambience. One outcome was that tourism advertising campaigns for Melbourne become increasingly self-consciously 'arty'. Rather than only focus on sport, let alone jobs in factories, in the 2000s, the emphasis in these advertising campaigns became increasingly quirky and whimsical. A focus on women – as both producers and consumers – also became distinctly pronounced. For example, a 2006 tourism advertisement featured a young female model pushing a ball of red wool through iconic Melbourne locations, including its newly refurbished laneways. Accompanied by a soundtrack featuring US singer-songwriter Joanne Newson performing 'The sprout and the bean', the ball of wool was designed to prevent the young woman from becoming lost amongst the city's myriad (and presumably safe) lanes and cultural offerings (Tourism Victoria 2006). A later commercial from 2014 entitled 'Play Melbourne', backed by American singer, Sarah Jaffe singing 'Perfect Plan', further developed the idea that Melbourne was hidden, quirky and safe. The burgeoning CBD 'laneway culture' with its growing numbers of bars, cafes and clubs again featured in this commercial; so too did live music in the form of a laneway music festival (Tourism Victoria 2014).

This emphasis on Melbourne's live music scene has become an increasingly important part of the city's urban brand. While live music and pub rock had long been an aspect of the city's culture that had appealed to younger people, a sanitized version of this subculture has been important at least since the 1960s, as a largely underground drawcard for new settlers and tourists from the rest of Australia (O'Hanlon 2005: 46). Since the 1980s, live rock and pop have been formally recognized and harnessed as key economic assets, central to the idea of the 'new' Melbourne. The social democratic Labor Government of the 1980s was the first to recognize this potential in developing The Push which, as we shall see below, was a government-funded program designed to support and enhance Melbourne (and Victoria's) youth music scenes and encourage young people to pursue music as a career.

From the 1990s, popular music and the local music industries became more integrated into the city's official 'brand'. 1993 saw the launch of the Melbourne Music Festival, supported by Arts Victoria and the City of Melbourne and sponsored by corporate donors such as Manchester Unity and the *Herald and Weekly Times*. Described by Director Michele Tayler as 'the largest contemporary music event in Australia', the festival was said to be 'about music – playing it, listening to it, learning about it – enjoying it' (MU Music Festival 1993). In the new century, streets and lanes were renamed in honour of musicians and in 2010 Melbourne Music Week, a nine-day celebration supported by the City of Melbourne, was launched, designed according to founding director Elise Peyronnet as a way of 'partnering with local industry' to 'increase opportunities' for it 'to stage its own events' (*Beat* 2011). In the same period, both the State Government (through its Victoria Rocks program) and the City of Melbourne's Music Strategy argued that 'Melbourne is a city where music matters' and 'makes a huge contribution to the social, cultural and economic fabric of the city'. This strategy culminated in a commitment to pursue an agenda and provide support so that Melbourne could 'take its rightful place alongside some of the great music cities of the world' (City of Melbourne 2014: 6; Strong et al 2017).

Heritage

In Melbourne, as elsewhere, the idea of rock and pop as an aspect of the heritage of the city has emerged slowly, becoming fully embedded into the discourses about what value music brings to the city only since the turn of the century. The more official manifestations of pop music as a form of heritage have been tied to the attempts to brand Melbourne as a 'music city', and these have sometimes embraced and sometimes been at odds with heritage-making activities by participants in music scenes. In this section, we will explore how heritage has become an aspect of Melbourne's claims to be a leader in music, and the relationship between different types of heritage in this area.

Heritage is somewhat of a contested term, but generally refers to aspects of the past that are used to give meaning and a sense of identity to a nation or community. When considering it in relation to music, Branderello et al. (2014: 224) define heritage in the following way:

> Heritage is both a source of identity and a receptor of value attributed to it by communities, institutions and people. It encompasses a sense of time, providing a sense of one's own past ... while at the same time becoming a 'resource for the present' (Graham 2002: 1004). Insofar as understandings of heritage are necessarily embedded in time and space ... heritage is in itself a manifestation of culture, better understood in its representational sense, that is to say, in the meaning given to it.

Heritage is therefore not just about knowledge of the past, but the selective use of it to understand and guide action in the present. Roberts and Cohen (2014: 230) have noted that music heritage can be official, where it has been 'formally legitimized ... using structures of authority recognized and agreed on within a society'; 'self-authorised', where it emerges from within local communities and music scenes, but usually through the authority of taste-makers (such as journalists) and interested commercial entities (such as tourism operators); and 'unauthorised', where it emerges through the practices and memories of musicians and audiences. As will be shown here, the recent official uses of music heritage have their roots in decades of self-authorized and unauthorized heritage making in Melbourne music scenes.

Establishing the value of rock and pop histories and heritage

Pop and rock are, of course, relatively young forms of culture, so it is unsurprising that claims for their heritage status were not being made in Melbourne in the 1950s, 1960s or even 1970s. A certain amount of time is generally needed for something to be thought of as having a history, and in the case of popular music it has taken decades for it to be considered worth taking seriously as an art form, let alone one that could be seen as being vital to understanding the character of a city or community. This was mainly because of pop and rock's association with consumer culture, and with youth; however, as the youthful audiences of the first waves of these music forms grew up and began to take on positions where their tastes became influential, this began to shift. In Melbourne, a process where those associated with popular music began to professionalize (for example, through the formation of The Push and the Victorian Rock Foundation (1987–95), a precursor to Music Victoria) alongside increasing interactions and collaborations between popular music and the formal institutions of art and culture (such as the appointment of Michael Gudinski to the Arts Centre Trust (Eliezar 1995)) evidenced this slow legitimization during the 1980s and 1990s. As rock and pop's economic contributions also became more widely recognized and the advantages of being able to brand Melbourne as a 'music city' became more apparent to institutions such as local and State governments, claims that Melbourne has a strong historical legacy of musical activity were recognized as a vital component of this branding exercise.

However, as the literature on heritage and music has established (Cohen 2013; Roberts and Cohen 2014), our understanding of what constitutes 'heritage' is never completely shaped by the types of official heritage that are pursued by governments in attempts to gain music city status. The recent acknowledgment of the importance of rock and pop as aspects of official heritage was preceded and enabled by a slow increase in unauthorized and self-authorized heritage-making by musicians, audiences and journalists from the earliest days of rock and pop. As far back as the early 1970s, even *Go Set* engaged in early forms of historicization, producing retrospectives on the best of Australian music (for example, see Wood 1973). These types of articles serve a number of purposes, claiming space for the idea that Australian popular music is worth celebrating and commemorating, but also shoring up the position of journalists as tastemakers and gatekeepers in this regard. They set the scene for the incorporation of music into official heritage discourses, but in doing so also helped to establish limitations on who or what might be included in these.

This increasing focus on history and heritage was particularly apparent in the late 1990s and into the 2000s, in the lead-up to the SLAM rally and subsequent Music Accord, when there was an increase in the marking of anniversaries and the use of historical framing in articles in the street press. These were particularly focused on venues, or on physical locations in the city, rather than artists or bands, and the historicizing that was present in these articles was often used to explicitly critique contemporary events in the music scene. For example, an article on the Esplanade Hotel presents what is described as an 'oral history' of the venue and a variety of figures involved with it. This is accompanied by a cartoon by St Kilda musician and personality Fred Negro, which covers points in the venue's history dating back to the 1800s. 'Pubs come and go, the music scene ebbs and wanes, yuppies renovate and developers raze, but the Espy remains' (Best 2000: 24), the article declares. Similarly, coverage of the Winter 2C festival, which incorporated events at venues in the Fitzroy and Collingwood areas, discusses the criminal history of the area before noting that:

> Winter 2C takes on a greater significance this year, in light of the ongoing Live Music Vs Noise Pollution legal battle. [It] is highlighting the dark, criminal history of this inner hotbed, whilst celebrating its present and future. The official theme is: "No longer Australia's crime capital, this is live music central!" although it could just as easily be "Live Music is not a Crime".
>
> (Sheridan 2003: 66)

At a point in time where venues were seen to be at considerable risk in the face of multiple threats, including noise complaints, gentrification and increasing policy and compliance pressure from government, these articles can be interpreted as performing a number of functions. They help to incorporate the venues into the broader history of Melbourne, claiming space for them to be considered as an important part of the city's story in the same way that 1800s parliamentarian James Orkney (referenced in Negro's cartoon) or Melbourne's gangland tales might be. They also engage in history-building for these venues, framing them as having worth beyond utilitarian spaces for the provision of entertainment, but as having unique characters and communities.

This type of history-building and self-authorized heritage-making can also be observed in relation to the closure of venues. For example, the last week of the Punters Club in Fitzroy in 2002 was covered extensively in *Beat*, which declared that 'The Punters wasn't ever pretty but it was *real*, and played a real and vital role in Melbourne's live music culture, reflecting and boosting the diversity of the scene … we miss the Punters already, and we fear the wasteland that Brunswick Street may now become' (Best and Scott 2002: 13). This tribute is accompanied by two pages of stories from prominent punters on their experiences in the establishment. There are also documentaries produced during this time that focus on closing or threatened venues – for example, 'Last

Drinks' covers what was thought to be the last days of the Prince of Wales in St Kilda, and 'Persecution Blues' performs a similar role for the Tote, although both venues were subsequently reopened. Venues also undertook other activities that were forms of self-heritagization. For example, in 2005 the Corner Hotel asked punters to bring in any memorabilia they had of the venue, with the intention of making a souvenir magazine to celebrate their tenth anniversary (Eliezer 2005: 32); and in 2010, an event to commemorate the Punters Club was held at the Corner Hotel (Eliezer 2010: 72). These types of celebrations of venues perform a mythologizing function, preserving the image of these places at a moment of change and elevating them to a level beyond the normal ebbs and flows of constantly changing music scenes. They also capture and help shape the collective memories of the communities associated with these venues. This strong focus on venue closures, and venues under threat, during the 1990s and 2000s, would also have served a political purpose in highlighting the danger to Melbourne of rapid economic change, gentrification and endless venue closures.

The way this type of heritage construction is initiated from within the music community means that these types of histories are often created by the people within those communities with the most motivation and resources to undertake such activities. These will be people who have an interest in how the history of music in Melbourne is constructed, and who may wish to claim space there. For example, in his interview, 1950s/60s musician Ian Allen noted preservationist activities he had undertaken:

> So those interviews (that he had done with Stan Rofe) – because we recorded them in coffee shops – they're probably in the Performing Arts Museum, or the National Film and Sound Archives. Because I've made a habit of putting stuff into those places, so when guys like you come along there's a fair chance you can get to some real stuff.
>
> (Allen 2017)

The willingness of participants in music scenes to do these types of things shapes the heritage discourse. For instance, The Australian Music Vault draws heavily on the archives of the Performing Arts Centre for its exhibitions, and these archives have been reliant on donations for the bulk of their materials, meaning the perspectives and interests of those who are motivated to preserve something about music history are best represented. The extensive Nick Cave archives in the Performing Arts Centre are a case in point – the willingness of the artist to hand over personal items en masse has enabled exhibitions dedicated to his work, thereby raising his profile and helping to consolidate his place in music history. This type of self-authorized heritage has also been undertaken by Mushroom Records, with a 2011 exhibition 'Melbourne, Music and Me', where a partnership with RMIT University saw a variety of objects from the label's history displayed at a campus art gallery as a celebration of the label's fortieth anniversary.

This raises issues around cultural capital and who has the ability to engage with historical and heritage discourses to embed venues and scenes in Melbourne's collective musical memory. For example, divisions between the inner city and the suburbs, and the dismissal of the audiences in suburban beer barns using descriptors like 'block-jawed, stiff-lipped, inebriated amateur football players' (Jennings 2001: 60) meant that rather than effusive multi-page write-ups of their final nights in the street press, or documentarians creating lasting records of experiences inside their walls, these venues and the cultural experiences they represented could come and go without being documented or remembered, let alone included in heritage discourses. Songlines founder Robbie Bundle (2019) also noted that he and others:

> ... originally started off as going out into communities and recording people and stuff, and they suddenly got a backlog of different things, so it's about getting all that material together and housing it, so hence the conversation of the archives has come up. Just of late I've heard so much more (...) because it's a very real and tangible thing that all of this information that we have is very important and precious to us, so we want to be able to preserve it and conserve it as best we can.

Bundle suggests that there is still considerable work to be done in ensuring a range of voices and stories are included from Indigenous communities, and there is a need to acknowledge the biases that a music heritage constructed for a long time by scenes in an ad hoc manner may have left a variety of gaps. As Baker (2017) has noted, these can sometimes be filled by DIY archives run by community members. In Melbourne, organizations such as the Australian Gay and Lesbian Archives have documented parts of music scenes that may be underrepresented elsewhere. However, as we turn to a consideration of how pop and rock heritage have been used officially in Melbourne for marketing purposes, it is important to note that these practices may put the histories of marginalized groups whose story is not seen as fitting in with the Melbourne story and branding at further risk of being lost.

The music city and heritage

As the concept of the 'music city' has become more recognized as a potentially desirable designation, and one that cities can strategically work towards (see IFPI/Music Canada 2015), the need to draw on aspects of music heritage to achieve this has been frequently highlighted. This has been generally mentioned in relation to two specific ends. First, music heritage is seen as being an aspect of music tourism, with cities that can claim rich musical histories being a tourist drawcard in and of themselves, and sites of musical history or commemoration providing specific possibilities for tourist activities. Second, heritage policies can be used to protect sites associated with music, which in some cases may be again mainly related to tourism (e.g. preserving the house a famous musician lived in), but in other cases can be used strategically to protect venues and other sites of current music-making, particularly against gentrification processes (IFPI/Music Canada 2015: 37).

In Melbourne, both of these uses of heritage have emerged in policy, although sometimes in contradictory ways. For example, City of Melbourne music strategies have, from their first iteration in 2010, always included aspects related to heritage. These are, however, relatively minor elements of the overall strategy. For example, the 2013 City of Melbourne *Music Strategy* (p. 45) includes 'improved information relating to music heritage and tourism for city residents, national and international visitors' in the recommendations, but the Council strategy mentions only the possibility of developing a music history walk in relation to this. This walking tour was established by the time the 2018–21 *Music Strategy* was released, and this included plans to 'collaborate with industry and other partners on a comprehensive heritage study of Melbourne's music venues to determine their heritage significance, with the aim of achieving greater protection under the Planning Scheme' as one of its key goals in relation to 'Regulation, urban growth and infrastructure' (City of Melbourne 2018: 17).

While this planned work has not yet taken place, the idea that the concept of heritage can be used to help preserve music scenes (thereby protecting or enhancing claims to 'music city' status) has emerged in Melbourne in other ways, and not only as an official strategy. For example, from 2012 to 2016, activists fought against the redevelopment of the Palace Theatre in the CBD (Bourke Street), which was due to be demolished to make way for a hotel. Among the strategies used by opponents to the redevelopment, an attempt was made to have the building heritage-listed based on its physical features, as well as its decades of use as an entertainment hub. While this ultimately failed, with only the facade being given protection, it called to attention some of the competing uses of heritage. In this case, the City of Melbourne and the Andrews State Government that make prominent uses of popular music and the concept of the 'music city' as a marketing tool had heritage processes deployed against them by a community group acting to save a venue. This clearly highlighted the gap between a 'pro-music' rhetoric and the realities of managing the uses of space in a gentrifying commercial property market. Another venue, Festival Hall, was put on the market in 2018, but with a different outcome: in this instance, heritage status was granted to the building, partly on the grounds of its importance to the music community in Melbourne (and partly because of its connection to boxing).[1] Unlike the Palace, this heritage application was backed by the Victorian Government.

The self-authorized activities by venues and participants in the different music scenes described above (which have of course continued to the present day) started to be matched by official activities by State and local governments from the mid-2000s. When opening the Paul Hester Walk mentioned at the start of this chapter, the Mayor of Port Phillip called it the 'first high-profile rock or contemporary music example' of historical commemoration in the area (Barry 2005: 4); but it has been swiftly followed by not just the dedication of Amphlett and Rowland S. Howard Lanes, but other more conventional commemorative activities, such as the inclusion of a bronze statue of Bon Scott in AC/DC Lane and the dedication of a statue of broadcaster Molly Meldrum near the Corner Hotel, with further plans for the creation of a statue in honour of INXS singer/songwriter Michael Hutchence. This increase in official heritage activities related to rock and pop signifies the complete incorporation of popular music into overarching conventions in Australia about what properly constitutes heritage, and has culminated in the establishment of a dedicated institution within the Arts Centre focused entirely on celebrating the history of popular music, the Australian Music Vault.

Not all of these official manifestations of pop heritage have been successful or established without criticism. A series of statues of musicians such as John Farnham and Kylie Minogue erected in Docklands in 2007 were removed to make way for further development and have yet to be re-homed (Baker 2019: 254). The incongruity of some of the artists chosen to be commemorated has

Figure 15 Statue of Molly Meldrum looking on to the Corner hotel, Richmond and mural celebrating live music. Source: Catherine Strong.

also been noted at times. In arguing against the idea of a statue for Michael Hutchence (a Sydneysider), Paul Cashmere (2018) discussed how:

> Melbourne has made some strange decisions with dedications for artists not related directly to the city while ignoring those who are. It's like we just adopt people first so no-one else can have them. Chrissy Amphlett Lane and AC/DC Lane both honor acts not related directly to the city. Chrissy hailed from Geelong and Divinyls formed in Sydney. AC/DC spent 18 months in Melbourne but originated in Sydney.

This critique points to tensions between the use of music heritage as a branding and marketing tool in a way that connects to global flows of both music and tourists, whereby a monument to the biggest name artist will serve the purposes of both associating the city with a general idea of music and attract visitors, as opposed to the commemoration of more local and less well-known artists in a way that helps consolidate the identity of Melbourne music scenes (see Strong, Cannizzo and Rogers 2017 for a further discussion of this).

Conclusion

Seeking to integrate music into the official brand of the post-industrial city also brings to the surface other tensions. Beyond the equity issue of mostly only giving prominence to musicians who are already well-established and successful, it also means that there is a danger that a city's music story is inherently nostalgic, celebrating the past rather than supporting the present and the future. As argued by historian David Lowenthal (1998), this is an inherent problem with heritage. In contrast with 'history', which is about the processes and drivers of change, heritage can seek to preserve one version of the past rather than multiple and competing ones, usually the one most amenable to powerful contemporary interest groups. These 'acceptable' histories are also often presented in teleological terms, positing the present as the inevitable outcome of past decisions or practices. In the past, heritage practices have reflected older and outdated models of history that privileged the stories of the 'heroic' and 'great men' of the past, in this case mostly male musicians, producers and promoters. The example of Chrissy Amphlett Lane, as well as the inclusive practices of institutions such as the Music Vault, which foregrounds women, Indigenous performers and a variety of genres, not just rock and pop, suggests these ideas have shifted. Increasingly, more inclusive and democratic approaches to music heritage are ensuring lesser-known artists, especially those who never achieved national or international fame, are not left out of the story.

Rock music is almost by definition about change, about updating and adapting to new ideas and new circumstances. From the time of its emergence in the 1950s, it has at least in theory sought to challenge accepted social and musical norms and open up spaces to the voices and experiences of new individuals and groups and their sounds. Central to our study of the story of rock in Melbourne has been a determination to include the voices of Indigenous people, of women, of newly arrived immigrants, and of the multiple waves of young people who over more than six decades now have sought to differentiate themselves and their music from earlier generations and practitioners. We have deliberately sought to include these peoples' stories not as adjuncts to the mainstream history of rock and roll in the city but as central to it. These stories and the importance of less well-known and less commercially successful musicians to Melbourne's rock history and heritage may not appeal to a mass tourism market, nor perhaps even to a niche music heritage one. But they more accurately reflect the history and fragile contemporary reality of the Melbourne music scene for most artists and their fans. A music heritage strategy that recognizes and celebrates multiple pasts and presents, combined with a public policy agenda that seeks to ensure that live music sites remain alive and viable in an increasingly economically stratified city, will guarantee that the city's musical heritage is about the future as well as the past and the present. However, this must also work towards keeping the residential and social spaces of the city economically accessible to younger, poorer, marginalized and emerging artists and fans. Such a strategy is also likely to mean that the city's music industries will remain viable well beyond the lifecycles and KPIs of contemporary political gatekeepers and cultural administrators. As in the 1970s and 1980s, these musicians, their fans and their contributions to Melbourne's cultural ambience may well provide the undergirding that will facilitate the revival of the city in the post-COVID-19 era.

9

Conclusion

This book has not attempted to provide a definitive and all-encompassing account of Melbourne's emergence as a music city. As a *history*, rather than an encyclopedia, we have sought to offer an impressionistic narrative that focuses on key signposts and turning points, and underlying structures and cultures (and not singular genres, stars) in Melbourne's emergence as a music city. In this sense we have sought to constantly place pop/rock activity in the wider social and cultural life of the city. The structure, tone and style of the book have also sought to actively reflect the cross-disciplinary and collaborative make-up of the research team, which has brought together sociologists, historians, cultural theorists and popular music and media studies specialists. The methods and sources of these disciplines, as well as the interests and expertise of the various project researchers/authors, have influenced the style and content of individual chapters which were led by a particular researcher. This led to interesting discussions about specific emphases in different chapters; yet the book as a whole is the product of all four researchers. This approach has meant that there has not been room to explore or sometimes even to mention every important artist, venue, entrepreneur or decision-maker that played a part in making Melbourne what it is (this would be a hard, if not impossible, task for one book to undertake). In particular, the focus of this project only encompassed rock and pop. There is still much story-telling to take place to understand the development of other genres, and to fill in all the nooks and crannies that remain empty in our story. We hope to see other researchers (particularly those who have been part of creating this story) taking up this challenge.

Throughout, we have attempted to situate this city as not only typical of other cities, as a jumble of urban structures, ideas and lived practices; 'Melbourne' as an evolving idea is also central to this history. The city's sense of itself has at least partly been constructed against the country's foundational city of Sydney, which also claimed for itself the original headquarters of

Australian rock and roll. Melbourne's role as Australia's 'second city', and especially its declining economic importance in the post-industrial era, is also an important part of this story. While in the early post-war years the city's commercial and strengths meant that it was a magnet for immigrants and international investment, as the Western world's economic structure moved towards services, Sydney emerged as not only Australia's 'gateway' city for immigrants and tourists, but also for inward investment in finance and technology. It also consolidated its traditional role as the national headquarters of the media and recording industries and the Australian home of the major international record labels. While this was problematic for Melbourne artists (particularly in the 1950s and 1960s), it was to some extent offset by industries' and government needs for innovation caused by the loss of manufacturing industries. The figurative free spaces created by the absence of the need to achieve short-term commercial success meant that Melbourne artists had the time and freedom to hone their skills and experiment with their sounds. And as Sydney globalized in the 1980s and 1990s, its increasingly expensive real estate and general cost of living led to Melbourne becoming an attractive destination for musicians looking to relocate from the smaller capitals and rural and regional Australia.

Perhaps ironically given the recent strong commitment of the City of Melbourne and the Victorian state government to supporting the music industry, in many ways it was politicians' and bureaucrats' ignorance and almost total lack of interest that allowed it to flourish in the 1960s and 1970s. This was especially true at a time when interest in popular and youth culture was seen to be beneath the dignity of conservative political and business interests, and when, for the most part, governments saw young people and their public and private culture (including their music, fashions and social and sexual behaviour) as things to suppress and control rather encourage or exploit for economic purposes. Changes in liquor licensing laws in the 1960s, and again in the 1980s, helped to free up spaces for musical and artistic experimentation, but this was as much an unintended by-product of attempts to modernize the city's 'wowserish' reputation and thus make it attractive to older and wealthier tourists, as an attempt to support the music and cultural industries.

Instead of government support, it was the rapid population growth and widespread affluence of the 1960s and 1970s that fed a growing market for youth-oriented products and services, especially in inner city areas, which in turn underpinned the strength of the emerging music industries. So too, an increasing number of outmoded and redundant spaces freed up room in these areas and beyond to provide the locations where youthful desires could be served. In the face of government neglect and indifference, a number of young entrepreneurs stepped into this economic and social void to create their own local music economies by taking over and adapting church halls and town halls, movie theatres, hotel dining rooms and former industrial and warehouse spaces for use as live music venues and nightclubs (both licensed and unlicensed). Similarly, cheap restaurants, coffee shops and clothing and record stores which catered for young people with cash to spare brought new life and vitality to often rundown and semi-abandoned inner urban high streets. The role of young entrepreneurs in creating not only the spaces where musicians could perform and develop, but also the urban milieus where young people could meet informally and develop new ideas and new ways of living, is an important part of Melbourne's story that has until now been relatively neglected by writers more interested in specific artists and genres than their urban social contexts.

As we have charted pop/rock from accidental industry to the forefront of city policy and marketing, the changing city and the evolving fortunes of some of its neighbourhoods have been consciously presented as 'characters' in this story, as have many of the venues which allowed the industry to thrive. Too many of these are sadly no longer with us, sometimes falling victim to changing music tastes or new forms of leisure and entertainment. More often, their disappearance is due to the changing economic fortunes of neighbourhoods that have moved from rundown, affordable and experimental to the gentrified, expensive and somewhat bland, rendering them economically non-viable as live venues.

Our study on how media has sustained Melbourne as a music city challenges the functional view of media as simply marketing or there for the promotion of music industry interests and product sales. We suggest that when media is viewed historically, its dynamic impact on music and city cultures becomes clearer. As platforms shift over time and fans assume more control over production and distribution, spaces emerged that provided for innovative formats, expanded musical knowledge and built strong affective relationships with the city's music industry workers. Zines (online or printed), community radio broadcasters and dedicated music journalists who worked for free music newspapers, have contributed significantly to local music cultures beyond narrow commercial considerations.

As we have seen throughout this book, Melbourne's emergence as an innovative and culturally diverse city from the 1960s onwards was in part a response to government initiatives – driven in the 1970s and 1980s by an imperative to reinvent the economy after the shock of deindustrialization and the decline of traditional strengths in manufacturing – but also because it was a comparatively cheap place to live and where people could be themselves while they pursued their cultural ambitions. While economic prosperity and rapid population growth in the 2000s was broadly welcomed in Melbourne, as in other successful post-industrial and 'super-gentrified' (Butler and Lees 2006) cities, geographic and economic divergence in access to the city's cultural offerings between those at the top of the wealth pyramid and those at the bottom did have the potential to undermine the role of popular culture in this success. Increasing tensions between the desires of the newer and mostly older and wealthier inhabitants of now-gentrified inner-city neighbourhoods for domestic peace and quiet, and the desires of young people, musicians and cultural entrepreneurs to enjoy the attractions of the city in noisy venues in increasingly crowded and contested urban spaces, were beginning to threaten the sustainability of an urban economic model built on twenty-four-hour access to consumption. Legislative machinery such as the Agent of Change principle has gone some way to recognizing and addressing these tensions, even as venue owners are finding that there are deviations and considerable bureaucracy in practice.

In seeking to document and interpret key moments in the city's music history, we have drawn on the stories and experiences of individuals and groups to illuminate broader aspects of the evolution and changes in the city's demography, including the documentation of social and cultural mores over more than five decades. Conscious that previous iterations of rock and pop history, both in Melbourne and elsewhere, have marginalized or suppressed the stories of women, Indigenous people and other oppressed groups, we have actively sought to integrate these into our narrative. While we have had some success in doing so, we remain acutely aware that more needs to be done on this issue. A number of these people and their stories have featured in this book, but the need remains for more work on the contributions of women, Indigenous people and post-1970s non-European immigrant groups in the creation and nurturing of the music city in the 1990s and 2000s. Too many of the voices here (and in histories of rock and pop more generally) are those of white Australian-born, or long-term English-speaking immigrant, males. Uncovering and documenting more of the stories of women, gender-diverse, and Indigenous musicians and audiences and of people of colour is an urgent task for future historical research.

COVID-19 effects

This book was mostly written in 2020 and 2021 in the shadow of the COVID-19 pandemic. While the Australian experience was not as severe as elsewhere in the world, the pandemic impacted upon Melbourne far more than other Australian cities. Major lockdowns, including an extended four-month period from early July to late October 2020, disproportionately affected the city's hospitality industries, especially live music, whose lifeblood relies on bringing people together in often small and enclosed venues where social distancing was all but impossible. As such gatherings were restricted and then banned in 2020, venues were forced to close their doors, dramatically curtailing the incomes of not only musicians but also of those involved in the broader music, cultural and hospitality infrastructure of the city. Gradual reopening and flexible responses to the provision of outdoor dining and drinking have alleviated these problems somewhat. However, noise regulations and social distancing rules, including ongoing restrictions on crowd sizes, mean that the small- and medium-sized venues that became such a feature of Melbourne after the licensing reforms of the 1980s and 1990s still find themselves facing challenging economic circumstances at the time of writing in mid-2021.

As in other music cities across the globe, the musicians most affected by COVID-19 restrictions were the young and not yet established, whose incomes relied on performance fees rather than royalties from recording. The Victorian State Government had at the time of writing provided almost $25 million in pandemic-related assistance, including funding for shuttered venues and support for related businesses (Arts Hub 2021). The City of Melbourne (2021a) had also provided support through a $2.5 million program across the creative industries. The Morrison Coalition Government provided several (and controversial) pathways of federal support, principally through its RISE (Restart Investment to Sustain and Expand) program, with $125 million marked for artist, touring and festival support; and a further $10 million provided for Support Act, a charity organization established by Lindy Morrison (former Go-Betweens drummer) that assists industry workers with financial and mental health issues. However, while established businesses and long-term employees were eligible for the federal wage subsidy program, Jobkeeper, strong criticism emerged that many within the music industries did not fit the criteria, especially the stipulation that applicants demonstrate employment with the same employer for twelve months (Australia Council 2020; Morrow and Long 2020). The music/creative industries were carved out of this targeted support as the Federal Government resorted to its preferred workforce of 'tradies'; many believed that the slow roll-out of the RISE assistance, coupled with the comparatively higher support for other sectors, revealed how low music and the creative/cultural industries are placed in hierarchical value within the federal Government (Caust 2021).

This essentially meant that young people and those precariously employed in the sector were forced to rely on unemployment and similar welfare benefits for survival. One outcome of this was that many younger people and new arrivals to the city were forced to move home. Whether they can and will return to the city post-Covid remains to be seen. As COVID-19 regulations forced venues to close and strict night-time curfews were imposed on the city, the once bustling de facto music precincts of Fitzroy, Brunswick, St Kilda and the CBD took on an eerie, empty feel. As venues fell silent, the night-time economy that had become so central to Melbourne's contemporary sense of itself, and the 'brand' it presents to the world, took a major economic hit. A City of Melbourne report does not provide specific statistics for the music industries but does indicate a loss of 5,300 jobs and $756 million in economic output of the arts and recreation services (City of Melbourne 2021b: 3). A survey of COVID-19 impacts upon the live music sector in Victoria revealed that 58 per cent of respondents were considering leaving the industry; 57 per cent were concerned about paying for basics like rent and food; 44 per cent of respondents lost all their music-related work during the pandemic; and those in full-time employment dropped from 34 per cent to just 7 per cent (Strong and Cannizzo 2021). The pandemic thus exposed the fragility of Melbourne's new post-industrial economy, especially the night-time and cultural sectors that underpin local economies across the inner city. It also exposed the precarious economic situation of those at the bottom of the music industries hierarchy, and some deeper underlying problems of a city that was perhaps in danger of becoming too reliant on a narrow range of industries, but also somewhat complacent about its status as a music and cultural hub.

Final thoughts

In the sweep of history presented here, the initial 1950s fears of the city as a cultural desert have been well and truly buried: in the 2000s, Melbourne has taken its place as the proverbial vibrant music city. In the last century, much of what was good and interesting about pop and rock in the city occurred beyond

Figure 16 You Am I's Russell Hopkinson and Tim Rogers at the Forum, 23 October 1999. Source: Shellie Tonkin Collection/Performing Arts Collection/Arts Centre, Melbourne.

the view of local and State governments, when enthusiasts were left to their own devices. The particular 'authenticities' of Melbourne sounds and nightlife were initially grounded in the lack of infrastructure available to youth. At the same time, a series of regulatory, commercial and community quirks – from licensing to laneways, Mushroom to *Countdown*, Italian ballroom pop to pub rock, community radio activism to SLAM – have featured as a series of very localized contributions to a wider national pop and rock heritage.

The more recent story of Melbourne success also lies in part with the receding capacity and interest of Federal governments in the popular music sphere (and in cultural policy more generally). Local and State governments have taken up much of the slack in funding local/regional activities, and 'connecting the dots' between sectors (including export strategies). With the exception of the work of the federally funded Live Music Office, it is no surprise, then, that Australian popular music policy is currently dominated by the efforts of the larger cities, who have realized that the next national cultural policy, where city strengths might be properly harnessed to a wider cultural plan, is in the far distance politically. In relation, it is no accident that those most passionate about governmental reform have been able to revise tactics and egos in the past ten years. The collective policy ensemble evident in the city has reaped rewards in providing an increasingly united front to governments and achieving mastery of both the politics and policy complexities.

If history is able to inform the present, it is in the ideas and activities of the music industries that occur unplanned, and not part of a music strategy (useful as these might be). Melbourne gained a reputation for Australia's most 'authentic' music city with a distinct set of scenes and sounds. It is ironic, but not surprising, that it was able to exploit this for commercial gain in the era of city 'branding' in the new century. To return to our nod to Will Straw's theme of 'underground incubators' briefly discussed in Chapter 5, a central challenge for the city lies in the less observed and promoted. The more marginal components of popular music activity – the recording label run out of a bedroom, the hole-in-the-wall bar, the sub-sub-genre, the fashion shop by day-venue by night enterprise – must be encouraged and provided with regulatory breathing space. And, as ideas of the suburban entertainment/cultural 'precinct' take hold, then they must serve as spaces of experimentation as much as touristic designations of venues, studios and genres. As Melbourne enjoys its reputation as a 'music city', protection of the less shiny and obvious aspects is essential in proving to industries and fans that 'strategies' do not simply hollow out to mean more promotion and branding, but to recognize that innovation is also part of the city's popular music heritage.

Notes

Chapter 3

1. In the same month, the newspaper reported that an East German newspaper accused Americans of 'using boogie woogie for their colonization work in Germany' (*The Sun* 1950b).
2. The owner of Sebastian's, Anthony Knight, cites Annabel's club in London as a model of what was desired (Knight 2017).
3. Lawrence was married to Ceresoli until the early 1980s.
4. Manuelle's father emigrated to Melbourne in 1955; Sam, his mother and brother followed in 1958.
5. Two or three course dinners would be served, with the band playing to dancers between courses.
6. Domenico Modugno won the San Remo Song festival in Italy in 1957 with 'Volaro' which became an international hit. He toured Australia in 1959, playing at Festival Hall in Melbourne on 12 December (Whiteoak 2007: 245).
7. In NSW, the Cahill Labor Government introduced 10 p.m. hotel closing in February 1955 after a review and referendum process. Hotels were to observe a 'dinner' break from 6.30 to 7.30 p.m. (Homan 2000: 25–9).
8. Speaking to concerns about youth drinking, the Royal Commissioner believed that later hotel trading would allow youth to drink at properly supervised sites rather than drinking in cars or public spaces (*The Age* 1964). In relation, the 1968 change of the Licenses Reduction Board to its new title of the Liquor Control Commission implied a shift in looking at the types of drinking environments, rather than fears of an overall increase in consumption.
9. 1970s parliamentary debates raised these (mainly) suburban hotels in the context of under-age drinking, excessive consumption *and* live rock.
10. In the publican's (partial) defence, fifteen categories of liquor licence were on the books in Victoria in the mid-1970s.
11. The pub was the site for several live recordings, including albums by the Dingoes, Dutch Tilders and Saltbush.
12. Before this, the *Sunday Entertainment Act 1967* allowed the Chief Secretary to grant permits for Sunday trading with entertainment; and its amendment in 1968 allowed Saturday trading to conclude at 1 a.m. on Sunday with a permit.
13. Licence fees were calculated on liquor turnover.

14 Prior to this, Maas had been a co-founder of the cabaret act the Busby Berkeleys in 1974, performing at venues such as the Flying Trapeze in Brunswick Street (owned by John Pinder, who operated the TF Much Ballroom in the 1960s). He also ran a venue, Hoagies, in Waverley Road, East Malvern, for a short time (Maas 2020).

15 Artist Kate Ceberano worked for a period at the Black Cat: 'One of my favourite cafes … I thought it would be cool to work there … It was all about the atmosphere, and Henry thought I had the right look' (Ceberano 2014: 46).

16 Maas's involvement in the ten-piece Bachelors from Prague was arguably the culmination of earlier constructions of other performative alter egos, such as his Buddy Lovestein character who sang 'punk jazz', drawing on comedian Jerry Lewis's Buddy Love character in *The Nutty Professor* (1963) (Maas 2020).

17 Goldsmith joked that 'TC' stood for Trainee Customers (Goldsmith 2019).

18 Established by the managers of Icehouse (Ray Hearn), Cold Chisel (Rod Willis) and the Angels (John Woodruff) in 1978.

19 Frente!'s first album, *Marvin the Album*, has sold more than 1.2 million copies worldwide (The Harbour Agency 2021).

Chapter 4

1 For a discussion of the dynamic between consumption, alienation and authenticity with regards to music in Melbourne, see Tebbutt (2020).

2 The use of the Myer Music Bowl for youth-oriented concerts continued to be a point of contention. The Melbourne-based *Juke* magazine later took up the issue with some success and in 1973, local bands once again staged well-attended concerts at the venue.

Chapter 5

1 In 1974 the buildings were sold to *The Age* newspaper group, and the company became known as Armstrong Audio Video (AVV).

2 This has never entirely disappeared as an issue. In 2001, the Federation of Australian Broadcasters lamented the 'massive reverse subsidy to the recording industry by radio… The amount of "free" commercial airtime for Australian music on FARB's 235 member licencees [sic] resulting from these quotas would run into the hundreds of millions of dollars a year' (FARB 2001: 10). In 2010, the CEO of Commercial Radio Australia, Joan Warner, complained that adherence to local radio airplay quotas could amount to 'forced supply from a particular group of music companies' (cited in Sexton 2010).

3   On these parameters, Ron Tudor's Fable Records was an independent that also reflected the need for some integration: Tudor did a P&D (production and distribution) deal with Phillips/Phonogram.
4   The Flying Lizards' version of 'Money' charted at no. 11 in Australia, no. 5 in the UK and no. 50 in the US in July 1979.
5   Distribution problems were resolved for a time by an agreement with Sydney's Powderworks label, who had their own pressing plant; and later with CBS Records.
6   One of the authors, Shane Homan, attended a two-day NY:LON seminar in London in 2018 where leading UK industry figures discussed technological and business changes. The Managing Director of Abbey Road Studios, Isabel Garvey, noted the studio's equal emphasis in the 2000s on partnering technological innovation with relevant ideas and businesses.

Chapter 6

1   In Helen Marcou's estimation, '126 venues either reduced or ended their live music programs' (Marcou interview).
2   The drummer Dempster is referring to is Harold Frith, who began his career with the Thunderbirds in the 1950s. This is part of Dempster's speech at the SLAM rally.
3   Helen Marcou and Quincy McLean credit Kirsty Rivers with assembling the list of industry demands of the future, including Agent of Change legislation, the protection of all age performances, provision of regular data on the contribution of live music to the State, licensing changes and the need for a peak body acting for the live music and other sectors.
4   Arriving at Parliament for the speeches, marchers were confronted by Opposition Liberal Party members on the steps with placards proclaiming their (new found) love of live music. The discourse of seeing venues as small businesses has been prominent at both State and Federal levels of government-industry debates.
5   A Deloitte Access Economics report was released in June 2011, stating that the live music sector provided $501 million GSP (Gross State Product) to the State economy, employing approximately 17,200 people (Arts Victoria 2011: ii).

Chapter 7

1   *Go-Set* covers: http://www.poparchives.com.au/gosetcharts/jpgs/covers1972.html
2   'Why punk?' seminar, Bakehouse Studios, Richmond, 18 November 2017: https://www.facebook.com/watch/live/?v=1619147538096644&ref=watch_permalink.

Chapter 8

1 However, its subsequent purchase by the Hillsong church has caused some consternation as to what this might mean for music in the venue in the future.

References

3KND (2006), South East Indigenous Media Association, Submission to the Standing Committee on Communication, Information, Technology and the Arts, July.

ABC Radio (2013), 'Rare Collections: The Studios of Bill Armstrong', Interview with Jordie and David Kilby, 16 August. Available online: https://www.abc.net.au/local/audio/2013/08/16/3827266.htm?site=canberra (accessed 15 April 2021).

Adams, D. (1994), 'Music in Melbourne, Sound Cheques in Sydney', *The Age Entertainment Guide*, 13 May: 3.

Allen, I.B. (2017), Interview with Shane Homan, 10 July.

'Archie "n" Jugheads' (1971), [Television series episode], *GTK*, Melbourne, Australian Broadcasting Commission. Available online: https://www.youtube.com/watch?v=4xIT393oiVo&fbclid=IwAR2gJhWxeT2Ti3N1Ad1Xd64NMeEWiDXk_qJron6KlDqlVpWm0IA4VDD87zM (accessed 16 April 2021).

Armstrong, B. (2018a), Interview with Shane Homan, 22 February.

Armstrong, B. (2018b), Interview with Lilith Lane.

Arrow, M. (2009), *Friday on Our Minds: Australian Popular Culture in Australia since 1945*, Sydney: University of New South Wales Press.

Arrow, M. (2019), *The Seventies: The Personal, the Political and the Making of Modern Australia*, Sydney: New South.

Arts Centre Melbourne (2019), 'Melbourne Music Bus Tour'. Available online: https://www.artscentremelbourne.com.au/whats-on/2020/contemporary-music/melbourne-music-bus-tour (accessed 15 April 2021).

Arts Hub (2021), '$8m in Government Support Flows to Victoria's Music Industry', *Arts Hub*, 15 January. Available online: https://www.google.com/search?q=Victorian+Government+pandemic+assistance+to+music+industry&oq=victorian+government+pandemic+assistance+to+music+industry&aqs=chrome.0.69i59.6102j0j7&sourceid=chrome¡UTF-8 (accessed 9 November 2020).

Arts Victoria (2011), *The Economic, Social and Cultural Contribution of Venue-based Live Music in Victoria*, Deloitte Access Economics, June.

Australia Council (2020), 'Jobkeeper and the Cultural and Creative Industries', Briefing Paper, 13 May. Available online: https://www.australiacouncil.gov.au/workspace/uploads/files/briefing-paper-jobkeeper-and-5ebcc73109bea.pdf?fbclid=IwAR1Lr9vmw9q12NePiD8fE7HsBj-lavMAY58IH364eH9pIk14FF_z3KxVf8Q (accessed 10 May 2021).

Australian Bureau of Statistics (2007), 'Births', *Yearbook Australia 2007*, Catalogue no. 1301.0. https://www.abs.gov.au/ausstats/abs@.nsf/2f762f95845417aeca25706c00834efa/C5F935614146DE94CA2572360000E3D4?opendocument (accessed 20 August 2020).

Australian Bureau of Statistics 1947–2016, *Census*, Canberra.

Australian Music Vault (2021), 'Explore the Exhibition', Arts Centre of Melbourne. Available online: https://www.australianmusicvault.com.au/exhibition (accessed 15 April 2021).

Bader, I. and Scharenberg, A. (2010), 'The Sound of Berlin: Subculture and the Global Music Industry', *International Journal of Urban and Regional Research*, 34 (1): 76–91.

Bailey, M. (2020), *Managing the Marketplace: Reinventing Shopping Centres in Postwar Australia*, Basingstoke: Routledge.

Baker, A. (2019), *The Great Music City: Exploring Music, Space and Identity*, New York: Springer.

Baker, G.A. (1981a), 'Aussie Missing Link Label Retains Quirky Image', *Billboard*, 10 October.

Baker, G.A. (1981b), 'The Australian Record Buyer', in P. Beilby and M. Roberts (eds), *Australian Music Directory*, 480–3, Melbourne: AMD.

Baker, G.A. (1990), 'CBS Records Australia Looks South for Stars', *Billboard*, 3 November.

Baker, S. (2017), *Community Custodians of Popular Music's Past: A DIY Approach to Heritage*, London: Routledge.

Barber, J. (2017), Interview with Lilith Lane.

Barry, E. (2005), 'Hester Part First Modern Memorial', *MX*, 6 July: 4.

Bennett, A. (2009), '"Heritage Rock": Rock Music, Representation and Heritage Discourse', *Poetics*, 37: 474–89.

Bennett, L. (2019), Interview with Catherine Strong, 20 June.

Bessant, J. (1991), 'Described, Measured and Labelled: Eugenics, Youth Policy and Moral Panic in Victoria in the 1950s', *Journal of Australian Studies*, 15 (31): 8–28.

Best, S. (2000), 'Tall Tales from the Esplanade Hotel', *Beat*, 1 November: 24–5.

Best, S. and T. Scott (2002), 'All Bets Are Off', *Beat*, 1 February: 13.

Bianchini, F. (1995), 'Night Cultures, Night Economies', *Planning Practice & Research*, 10 (2): 121–6.

Bianchini, F., M. Fisher, J. Montgomery. and K. Worpole (1988), *City Centres, City Cultures*, London: CLES.

Blainey, G. (2013), *A History of Victoria*, Cambridge: Cambridge University Press.

Blair, D. (2016), *Life in a Padded Cell: A Biography of Tony Cohen, Australian Sound Engineer*, Dale Blair website. Available online: http://www.daleblair.com.au/wp-content/uploads/2019/08/tony-cohen-life-in-a-padded-cell-free-ebook-dale-blair.pdf (accessed 14 April 2021).

Blake, W. (1975), Supervisor of Licensed Premises Letter to Station Hotel Prahran, 22 August, Public Records Office Victoria, VPRS 7712/P/0002, Liquor Control Commission correspondence, Unit 000212.

'Bodgies Jived a Protest' (1952), *The Argus*, Monday 28 July: 5.
Bongiorno, F. (2014), *The Sex Lives of Australians: A History*, Melbourne: Black Inc.
'Boogie-woogie Menace, German Reds Warn' (1950), *The Sun*, 11 January: 4.
Brady, M. (2018), Interview with Shane Homan, 13 November.
Brandellero, A. and S. Janssen (2014), 'Popular Music as Cultural Heritage: Scoping Out the Field of Practice', *International Journal of Heritage Studies*, 20 (3): 224–40.
Brett, L. (1966), 'The Problems Facing Girls on the Pop Scene', *Go-Set*, 3 August: 5.
Bright, B. (2008), Interview with Geoff King, 27 September.
Bruce-Rosser, K. (2009), 'Sour Note Setback', *Stonnington Leader*, 29 September.
Bundle, R. (2019), Interview with Catherine Strong, 6 February.
Butler, T. and L. Lees (2006), 'Super-gentrification in Barnsbury, London: Globalization and Gentrifying Global Elites at the Neighbourhood Level', *Transactions of the Institute of British Geographers*, 36: 467–87.
Bye, S. (2008), '*Sydney Tonight* versus *In Melbourne Tonight*: Television, Taste and Identity', *Media International Australia*, 128: 18–30.
'Cabaret Theatre Brightens City' (1950), *The Age*, 31 October: 7.
Camillieri, J. (no date), 'Joe Camillieri – A Life in Music', *The Black Sorrows: Roots Soaked Blues Rock*. Available online: https://www.theblacksorrows.com.au/ (accessed 4 March 2021).
Carroll, C., B. King Mott, T., McDougall, W. and Overall, A. (1991), *Still Noise; Australian Rock Photography*, Sydney: ABC Books.
Cashmere, P. (2018), 'Michael Hutchence Statue Set for Melbourne – the Question Is Why?', *Noise11*, 6 December. Available online: http://www.noise11.com/news/michael-hutchence-statue-set-for-melbourne-the-question-is-why-20181206 (accessed 4 February 2019).
'Catcher Owner Gets Year Bond' (1967), *The Sun*, 13 July: np.
Caust, J. (2021), 'How the Arts in Australia Suffered (but Survived) in 2020', *The Conversation*, 6 January. Available online: https://www.artshub.com.au/news-article/features/covid-19/the-conversation/how-the-arts-in-australia-suffered-but-survived-in-2020-261690 (accessed 10 May 2021).
Ceberano, K. (2014), *I'm Talking: My Life, My Words, My Music*, Sydney: Hatchette.
Chandler, R.S.E. (1967), Letter from Truth Newspaper Editor to Victorian Police Commissioner, 28 June. Public Records Office Victoria, The Catcher, General Health Branch, VPRS 7882/P/0001, Unit 001179.
Chester, J. (2008), Interview with Geoff King, 10 November.
'Children Can't See This' (1955), *The Argus*, 25 June: 39.
City of Melbourne (2010), *Melbourne Music Strategy 2010*, Melbourne: City of Melbourne.
City of Melbourne (2014), *City of Melbourne Music Strategy: Supporting and Growing the City's Music Industry 2014–17*, Melbourne: City of Melbourne.

City of Melbourne (2018), *Melbourne Music Plan 2018–21: Supporting, Growing and Promoting the City's Diverse Music Industry*, Melbourne: City of Melbourne.

City of Melbourne (2021a), *Melbourne Facts and Figures*, Melbourne: City of Melbourne. Available online: https://www.melbourne.vic.gov.au/about-melbourne/melbourne-profile/Pages/facts-about-melbourne.aspx (accessed 18 March 2021).

City of Melbourne (2021b), *Economic Impacts of COVID-19 on the City of Melbourne*, Melbourne: City of Melbourne. Available online: https//www.melbourne.vic.gov.au/sitecollectiondocuments/economic-impacts-covid-19-summary.pdf (accessed 10 May 2021).

City of Melbourne (2021c), 'Assistance for Creatives during COVID-19', *City of Melbourne* web site. Available online: https://www.melbourne.vic.gov.au/arts-and-culture/strategies-support/funding/Pages/assistance-creatives-covid-19.aspx (accessed 10 May 2021).

City of Toronto (2018), *Night-time Economy – Stakeholder Consultation Results and Next Steps*, Toronto: Economic Development and Culture.

Coates, N. (2003), 'Teenyboppers, Groupies, and Other Grotesques: Girls and Women and Rock Culture in the 1960s and Early 1970s', *Journal of Popular Music Studies*, 15 (1): 65–94.

Cohen S. (1991), 'Popular Music and Urban Regeneration: The Music Industries of Merseyside', *Cultural Studies*, 5 (3): 332–46.

Cohen, S. (2007), *Decline, Renewal and the City in Popular Music Culture: Beyond the Beatles*, Farnham, Surrey: Ashgate.

Cohen, S. (2013), 'Musical Memory, Heritage and Local Identity: Remembering the Popular Music Past in a European Capital of Culture', *International Journal of Cultural Policy*, 19 (5): 576–94.

'Cold Chisel' (gig review) (1979), *Juke*, 6 January: 16.

Connell, J. and C. Gibson (2003), *Sound Tracks: Popular Music, Identity and Place*, New York: Routledge.

Corr, C. (2017), Interview with Lilith Lane.

Correia, A. and T. Denham (2016), *Winning from Second: What Geelong Can Learn from International Second Cities*, Geelong: Committee for Geelong.

Costa, L. (2017), Interview with Catherine Strong, 28 January.

Coupe, S. (2015), *Gudinski: The Godfather of Australian Rock 'n' Roll*, Sydney: Hachette Australia.

Crabshaw, P.B. (1976), 'Tamam Shud: Recollections of Australia's Surf Songsters', *Juke*, 6 November: 17.

Crawford, R. (2015), 'A Tale of Two Advertising Cities: Sydney Suits v. Melbourne Creatives', *Journal of Australian Studies*, 39 (2): 235–51.

Creative Victoria (2016), *Creative State: Victoria's First Creative Industries Strategy 2016–2020*, Economic Development, Jobs, Transport and Resources, Melbourne.

Dahlstrom, K. (2017), Interview with Lilith Lane.

Daley, P. (2014), 'Australian Anthems: Cold Chisel – Khe Sanh', *Guardian Australia*, 28 January. Available online: https://www.smh.com.au/entertainment/music/dancing-to-the-music-of-the-banned-20040709-gdjawi.html (accessed 15 March 2021).

'Dancing to the Music of the Banned' (2004), *Sydney Morning Herald*, 9 July. Available online: https://www.smh.com.au/entertainment/music/dancing-to-the-music-of-the-banned-20040709-gdjawi.html (accessed 18 March 2021).

'Dangers in Liquor Bill' (1953), *The Age*, 27 November: 2.

Davey, P. (2005), *When Hollywood Came to Melbourne: The Story of the Making of Stanley Kramer's on the Beach*, Melbourne: P.R. Davey.

Davino, B. (2018), 'Melbourne Is Now Officially the Live Music Capital of the World', *The Industry Observer*, 12 April. Available online: https://theindustryobserver.thebrag.com/melbourne-officially-the-live-music-capital-of-the-world/ (accessed 15 April 2021).

Davison, G. (1997), 'Welcoming the World: The 1956 Olympic Games and the Re-presentation of Melbourne', *Australian Historical Studies*, 28 (109): 64–76.

Davison, G. (2001), 'The European city in Australia', *Journal of Urban History*, 27 (6): 779–793.

Davison, G. (2002), 'The Imaginary Grandstand', *Meanjin*, 61 (3): 4–18.

Dawkins, J. (1986), 'Export of Australian Rock Music', press release, Minister for Trade, 26 November.

Denver Arts and Venues (2018), *2018 Denver Music Strategy*, Denver Arts and Venues.

Diggin' Melbourne (2020), Diggin' Melbourne: Vinyl Lovers Tour Guide. Available online: https://digginmelbourne.com/ accessed (15 April 2021).

Dingle, T. and S. O'Hanlon (2009), 'From Manufacturing Zone to Lifestyle Precinct: Economic Restructuring and Social Change in Inner Melbourne, 1971–2001', *Australian Economic History Review*, 49 (1): 52–69.

'Disco Owner Resigns as Headmaster' (1967), *The Age*, 29 June: 3.

'Discotheques Need control' (1967), *Melbourne Herald*, 28 June: np.

Dix, A. and Committee of Review of the Australian Broadcasting Commission (1981), Submissions/Committee of Review of the Australian Broadcasting Commission, Sydney: The Committee.

Dixon, R. (nd), 'Be Home before Midnight ! … … … … Rae Dixon Interview', *Fantastic Mess Records*. Available online: http://www.fantasticmessrecords.com/independent-music-articles.html (accessed 11 February 2021).

Dogs in Space (1986), [Film], Dir. Richard Lowenstein, Australia: Central Park Films.

Dovey, K., R. Adams and R. Jones (2018), 'How a Three-Decade Remaking of the City Revived the Buzz of "Marvellous Melbourne"', *The Conversation*, 26 February. Available online: https://theconversation.com/how-a-three-decade-remaking-of-the-city-revived-the-buzz-of-marvellous-melbourne-91481 (accessed 18 March 2021).

Duffy, T. (1994), 'Melbourne Rises Up from Down Under', *Billboard*, 12 November, 1: 24.

Du Noyer, P. (2002), *Liverpool Wondrous Place: From the Cavern to the Capital of Culture*, Virgin: London.

Eliezer, C. (1982), 'The Models for Sale', *Juke*, 4 September: 15.
Eliezer, C. (1995), 'Industrial Strength Music News', *Beat*, 2 August: 31.
Eliezer, C. (2005), 'Industrial Strength Music News', *Beat*, 5 October: 32.
Eliezer, C. (2010), 'Industrial Strength Music News', *Beat*, 29 September: 72.
FARB (2001), Final Submission by Federation of Australian Broadcasters Limited to House of Representatives Standing Committee on Communications, Transport and the Arts, Inquiry into the Adequacy of Regional Radio, 23 May. Available online: http://203.63.5.202/files/uploaded/file/Regulation/Broadcasting/010523%20Final%20Submission%20on%20the%20Regional%20Radio%20Inquiry.pdf (accessed 15 April 2021).
Fleckney, P. (2018), *Techno Shuffle: Rave Culture and the Melbourne Underground*, Melbourne: Melbourne Books.
Florida, R. (2002), *The Rise of the Creative Class: And How It's Transforming Work, Leisure, Community, and Everyday Life*, New York: Basic Books.
Florida, R. (2005), *Cities and the Creative Class*, Abingdon: Routledge.
Florida, R. and S. Jackson (2010), 'Sonic City: The Evolving Economic Geography of the Music Industry', *Journal of Planning Education and Research*, 29 (3): 310–21.
Florida, R., C. Mellander, and K. Stolarick (2010), 'Music Scenes to Music Clusters: The Economic Geography of Music in the US, 1970–2000', *Environment and Planning A*, 42: 785–804.
'From "society" to … YOU!' (1966), *Go-Set*, 2 February: 4.
Garner, H. (1977), *Monkey Grip*, Melbourne: McPhee Gribble.
Gawenda, M. (1983), 'Only Good Coppers Survive in Fitzroy', *The Age*, 15 October: 1, 3.
Gazzo, J. (2015), *John Farnham: The Untold Story*, Sydney: Penguin Random House.
Gazzo, J. (2018), Interview with Catherine Strong, 5 November.
Geddes, G. (2018), Interview with Shane Homan, 10 July.
Gendron, B. (2002), *Between Montmartre and the Mudd Club: Popular Music and the Avant-Garde*, Chicago: University of Chicago Press.
Gibson, C. (2005), 'Recording Studios: Relational Spaces of Creativity in the City', *Built Environment*, 31 (3): 197–207.
Giuffre, L. (2016), 'Not Just Boys and Rock "n" Roll: Rediscovering Women on Early Australian Music Television', *Journal of World Popular Music*, 3 (1): 17–37.
Glass, K. (1994), Interview with Geoff King, 5 July.
Glitsos, L. (2018), 'Nice Girls Don't Jive: The Rise and Fade of Women in Perth Music from the Late 1950s to the Early 1970s', *Continuum*, 31 (2): 200–15.
Glitsos, L. (2019), 'Ebbs and Flows: Women as Musicians in Perth Popular Music, 1980s–1990s', *Perfect Beat*, 19 (2): 142–60.
Global Victoria (2020), 'World's 2nd Most Liveable City', State Government of Victoria. Available online: https://global.vic.gov.au/victorias-capabilities/why-melbourne/worlds-2nd-most-liveable-city (accessed 5 April 2021).
Globe International Limited (2021), 'History', https://globecorporate.com/history/ (accessed 15 February 2021).

'Go-Go Where?' (1966), [Television series episode] *Four Corners* program, Melbourne, Australian Broadcasting Commission. Available online: https://www.youtube.com/watch?v=xkcXeUPQZrM (accessed 15 April 2021).

Goldsmith, B. (2019), Interview with Shane Homan, 31 October.

Government of Victoria (1984), *Victoria: The Next Step: Economic Initiatives and Opportunities for the 1980s*, Melbourne: Government Printer.

Graham, D. and A. Markus (2018), *Gen 17: Australian Jewish Community Survey. Preliminary Findings*, Melbourne: ACJC Monash and Jewish Communal Appeal.

Grant, S. (2017), Interview with Seamus O'Hanlon, 25 May.

Grodach, C. and D. Silver (eds) (2012), *The Politics of Urban Cultural Policy: Global Perspectives*, London and New York: Routledge.

Giulliatt, R. (1983), 'Clubs Stage Daring Rescue Bid on Melbourne Nightlife', *The Age*, 21 October: np.

Guilliatt, R. (1985), 'Where to Rage All Night', *The Age*, 3 January: 30.

Hall, P. (1998), *Cities in Civilization*, Michigan: Pantheon.

Hall, S. (1976), *Supertoy: Twenty Years of Australian Television*, Melbourne: Sun Books.

Hanson, G. (2020), Interview with Catherine Strong, 6 July.

The Harbour Agency (2021), 'Frente-Biography', *Mushroom Group website*. Available online: https://theharbouragency.com/artist/frente/ (accessed 15 April 2021).

Harden, M. (2009), *Melbourne: The Making of a Drinking and Eating Capital*, Prahran: Hardie Grant.

Harrison, S. (2005), 'Jean Shrimpton, the "Four Inch Furore" and Perceptions of Melbourne Identity in the 1960s', in S. O'Hanlon and T. Luckins (eds), *Go!: Melbourne in the Sixties*, 72–86, Melbourne: Melbourne Publishing Group.

Hart, A. (2020), Interview with Shane Homan, 9 July.

Haslem, D. (2000), *Manchester, England: The Story of the Pop Cult City*, New York: HarperCollins.

Hawkings, R. (2014), '"Sheilas and Pooftas": Hyper-Heteromasculinity in 1970s Australian Popular Music Cultures', *Limina*, 20 (2): 1–14.

Healey, T. (1966), 'The Go! Show at the Myer Music Bowl', *Go Set*, 22 March: 10.

'"Hepcats" Go Wild at Town Hall Concert' (1953), *The Herald*, 13 February: 5.

Herd, N. (2006), '"The Weaker Sisters": The First Decade of ATV-0 Melbourne and TEN-10 Sydney, 1964–1975', *Media International Australia*, 121: 119–35.

Hesmondhalgh, D. (1999), 'Indie: The Institutional Politics and Aesthetics of a Popular Music Genre', *Cultural Studies*, 13 (1): 34–61.

Hesmondhalgh, D. and A. Pratt (2005), 'Cultural Industries and Cultural Policy', *International Journal of Cultural Policy*, 11 (1): 1–13.

Holden, J. (2015), *The Ecology of Culture*, Swindon: Arts and Humanities Research Council.

Holt, F. and C. Wergin (2013), 'Introduction: Musical Performances and the Changing City', in F. Holt and C. Wergin (eds), *Musical Performance and the Changing*

City: Post-industrial Contexts in Europe and the United States, 1–26. New York and London: Routledge.

Homan, S. (2016), 'SLAM: The Music City and Cultural Activism', *Law, Social Justice and Global Development*, 1: 1–12.

Homan, S. (2000), 'Losing the Local: Sydney and the Oz Rock Tradition', *Popular Music*, 19 (1): 31–49.

Homan, S. (2010), 'Governmental as Anything: Live Music and Law and Order in Melbourne', *Perfect Beat*, 11 (2): 101–16.

Homan, S. (2011), '"I Tote and I Vote": Australian Live Music and Cultural Policy', *Arts Marketing: An International Journal*, 1 (2): 96–107.

Horne, C. (2019), *Roots: How Melbourne Became The Live Music Capital Of The World*, Melbourne: Melbourne Books.

Horsfall B. (1993), Interview with Denzil Howson. Oral History, 'Once Upon a Wireless', National Film and Sound Archive, Canberra.

'Hot Talk' (1998), *Beat*, 1 July: 14.

Houston, C. (2008), 'Rush of Clubs Try to Evade Lockout'. *The Age*, 3 June: 1.

'How to Succeed in Rock'n'Roll' (1995), *Form Guide*, September: 3.

Howe, R. (ed.) (1988), *New Houses for Old: Fifty Years of Public Housing in Victoria*, Melbourne: Department of Housing and Construction.

Hyde, M. (2010), *All along the Watchtower: Memoir of a Sixties Revolutionary*, Carlton North: Vulgar Press.

'The Iconic Melbourne Bands Who Rose during the MySpace Era' (2020), *Beat*, 20 August. Available online: https://www.beat.com.au/the-iconic-melbourne-bandswho-rose-during-the-myspace-era/ (accessed 11 February 2021).

IFPI/Music Canada (2015), *The Mastering of a Music City: Key Elements, Effective Strategies and Why It's Worth Pursuing*, London: IFPI and Music Canada with MIDEM.

International Federation of the Phonographic Industry (2018), *Global Music Report 2018: Annual State of the Industry*, Switzerland: IFPI.

It's Easy to Lose Yourself in Melbourne (2006), [Film], Melbourne: Tourism Victoria.

Jenkins, J. (2018), Interview with Catherine Strong, 9 November.

Jennings, J. (2001), 'The Fauves', *Beat*, 5 September: 60.

Johnston, C. (2012), 'The Razor gang', *The Melbourne Magazine*, 30 March: 46–8.

Johnston, D. (2010), *The Music Goes around in My Head: Australian Pop Music 1964–69*, Melbourne: Independent Publications.

Johnstone, D. (1991), 'Johnny Chester, Shaking All Over, the Chess Story', in D. McLean (ed), *Collected Stories on Australian Rock'n'Roll*, 153–65, Potts Point, N.S.W: Canetoad Press.

Jones, M. (2017), Interview with Shane Homan, 12 July.

Kaji-O'Grady, S. (2006), 'Melbourne versus Sydney', *Architectural Theory Review*, 11 (1): 60–72.

Keays, J. (1999), *His Master's Voice*, Sydney: Allen and Unwin.
Kelly, H. (1992), 'Crackdown on Racism', *The Age*, 7 November: 1.
Kennedy, C. (2017), Interview with Catherine Strong, 8 February.
Kennedy, C. (2019), 'The Plums, *Gun* (1994); Deadstar, *Deadstar* (1996); *Milk* (1996); *Over the Radio* (1999)', in J. Stratton and J. Dale with T. Mitchell (eds), *An Anthology of Australian Albums*, 67–82, New York: Bloomsbury.
Kent, D. (2002), *The Place of Go-Set in Rock and Pop Music Culture in Australia, 1966 to 1974*, Masters Thesis, University of Canberra.
Kindellan, G. (2019), Interview with Catherine Strong, 6 February.
King, A. (2017), 'From Moomba to the Dreaming: Indigenous Australia, Popular Music and Reconciliation', in S. Harrington (ed.), *Entertainment Values: How Do We Assess Entertainment and Why Does It Matter?*, 132–41, London: Palgrave Macmillan.
King, A.D. (1990), *Global Cities: Post-Imperialism and the Internationalization of London*, London and New York: Routledge.
Kirkby, D. (2003), '"Beer, Glorious Beer": Gender Politics and Australian Popular Culture', *Journal of Popular Culture*, 37 (2): 244–56.
Kirkby, D, T. Luckins and C. McConville (2010), *The Australian Pub*, Sydney: New South.
Knight, A. (2017), Interview with Seamus O'Hanlon, 15 December.
Kruger, D. (2005a), 'Melbourne for a Song', *Melbourne Weekly Magazine*, 3–9 August.
Kruger, D. (2005b), *Songwriters Speak: Conversations about Creating Music*, Balmain NSW: Limelight Press.
La Greca, J. (2020), Interview with Shane Homan, 11 June.
Laing, D. (2004), Copyright, Politics and the International Music Industry in *Music and Copyright*, L. Marshall and S. Frith (eds), 70–88, New York: Routledge.
Laird, R. (1999), *Sound Beginnings: The Early Record Industry in Australia*, Sydney: Currency Press.
Landry, C. (2008), *The Creative City: A Toolkit for Urban Innovators*, Abingdon: Earthscan.
Landry, C and F. Bianchini (1995), *The Creative City*, London: Demos.
'Late Hours Not Olympic Spirit' (1952), *The Age*, 24 October: 4.
Lawrence, J. (2020), Interview with Jen Rose, 16 April.
Leone, M. (2014), 'Melbourne versus Sydney: Semiotic Reflections on First and Second Cities', *Glocalism: Journal of Culture, Politics and Innovation*, 3: 1–20.
Leonard, M. (2007), 'Constructing histories through material culture: popular music, museums and collecting', *Popular Music History*, 2 (2): 147–167.
'Letter to the Editor' (1967), *Go Set*, 6 September: 7.
Leyshon, A. (2009), 'The Software Slump?: Digital Music, the Democratisation of Technology, and the Decline of the Recording Studio Sector within the Musical Economy', *Environment and Planning A*, 41: 1309–31.
Life in Australia: Melbourne (1966), [Film], Dir. Douglas White, Australia: Commonwealth Film Unit. Available online through the National Film and Sound

Archive, https://www.youtube.com/watch?v=TC7D5T_m_-k (accessed 18 March 2021).
Lowenethal, D. (1998), *The Heritage Crusade and the Spoils of History*, Cambridge: Cambridge University Press.
Luckins, T. (2007), 'Competing for Cultural Honours: Cosmopolitanism, Food, Drink and the 1956 Olympics, Melbourne', in D. Kirkby and T. Luckins (eds), *Dining on Turtles: Food Feasts and Drinking in History*, 82–100, Basingstoke: Palgrave Macmillan.
'Lynne has gone curly' (1968), *Go-Set*, 6 March: 10.
Maas, H. (2020), Interview with Shane Homan, 1 June.
MacLean, S. (1971), 'Winds of Change on the Melbourne Rock Scene', *Go-Set*, 26 June: 18–19.
Malcolm A. and C. Doucouliagos (2003), 'The Changing Structure of Higher Education in Australia 1949–2003', SWP 2003/07, *School Working Papers – Series 2003*, School of Accounting and Management, Melbourne: Deakin University.
Manchester Unity Melbourne Music Festival Program (1993), Melbourne: *In Press*.
Manuelle, S. (2020), Interview with Shane Homan, 11 June.
Marcou, H. (2017), Interview with Shane Homan, 2 September.
Markusen, A. (2014), 'Creative Cities: A 10-Year Research Agenda', *Journal of Urban Affairs: Double Special Issue*, 36(s2): 567–89.
Markusen, A. and A. Gadwa (2010), 'Arts and Culture in Urban or Regional Planning: A Review and Research Agenda', *Journal of Planning Education and Research*, 29 (3): 379–91.
Martin, T. (2015), *Yodelling Boundary Riders: Country Music in Australia since the 1920s*, Sydney: Allen & Unwin.
Masterton, A. (1998), 'Canned Lyrics', *The Age*, 24 April: 50.
Maynard, F.L. (2019), Interview with Catherine Strong, 6 February.
McArdle, M. (1994), 'Sisters Underground', *Beat*, 5 October: 24.
McKinnon, C. (2010), 'Indigenous Music as a Space of Resistance', in T. Banivanua Mar and P. Edmonds (eds), *Making Settler Colonial Space: Perspectives on Race, Place and Identity*, 255–72, New York: Palgrave Macmillan.
McLean, Q. (2017), Interview with Shane Homan, 2 September.
Mean, M. and C. Tims (2005), *In Concert: Growing NewcastleGateshead as a Music City*, Demos, 16 May.
Melbourne, Australia (1987), [Film], Australia: Osborne Productions. Available online: https://www.youtube.com/watch?v=jkW3XilJ7KQ (accessed 18 March 2021).
Melbourne and Metropolitan Board of Works (MMBW) (1977), *Melbourne's Inner Area: A Position Statement*, Melbourne: MMBW.
'Melbourne Music Week' (2011), *Beat*. Available online: https://www.beat.com.au/melbourne-music-week (accessed 9 February 2021).
Meldrum, M. (1967), 'A Day in the Life of Yvonne Barrett and Marcie Jones', *Go-Set*, 4 October: 12.

Mihelakos, M. (1999), 'Liner Notes', *Stuck on the 90s; Sound as Ever Australian Indie 1990–1999*. Available online: https://soundaseveraustralianindie90-99.com/ (accessed 11 February 2021).

Milne, B. (2017), Interview with Shane Homan, 7 November.

Moore, C. (2018), Interview with Catherine Strong, 18 November.

Morris, B. and D. Verhoeven (2004), 'Performing Urban Rivalry: The Cultural Politics of First and Second Cities', in B. Morris and D. Verhoeven (eds), *The Passionate City: An International Symposium*, 27–35, Melbourne: RMIT University, School of Applied Communication.

Morris, E. (2014), 'Noise in My Head'. Available online: http://www.listenlistenlisten.org/noise-head/ (accessed 18 August 2020).

Morrow, G. and B. Long (2020), 'The Government Says Artists Should Be Able to access JobKeeper Payments. It's Not That Simple', *The Conversation*, 26 May. Available online: https://theconversation.com/the-government-says-artists-should-be-able-to-access-jobkeeper-payments-its-not-that-simple-138530 (accessed 10 May 2021).

Mullins, P. (2020), *The Trials of Portnoy: How Penguin Brought down Australia's Censorship System*, Melbourne: Scribe.

Munsen, C. (1970), 'The Radio Record Ban: Bang Go Our British Sounds', *The Canberra Times* 16 May: 17.

Music Canada (2015), *The Mastering of a Music City*, industry report, Toronto: Music Canada. Available online: https://musiccanada.com/resources/research/the-mastering-of-a-music-city/ (accessed 15 April 2021).

Music Victoria (2014), *Position and Priorities*, March, Melbourne: Music Victoria. Available online: https://livemusicoffice.com.au/policies/music-victoria-2014-white-paper-positions-and-priorities/ (accessed 5 May 2021).

Music Victoria (2015), *Women in the Victorian Contemporary Music Industry*, Melbourne: Music Victoria. Available online: https://www.musicvictoria.com.au/assets/Women%20in%20the%20Victorian%20Contemporary%20Music%20Industry.pdf (accessed 12 September 2018).

National Gallery of Victoria (2021), 'Meet the Artist: Toni Miticevski', *Melbourne Now*. Available online: https://www.ngv.vic.gov.au/melbournenow/artists/toni-maticevski.html (accessed 14 February 2021).

Newton, D. and R. Coyle-Hayward (2018), *Melbourne Live Music Census 2017 Report*, Melbourne: Music Victoria.

NFSA Online (2021), Community Radio: Background Information. Available online: https://dl.nfsa.gov.au/module/89/ (accessed 5 January 2021).

Nichols, D. (2016), *Dig: Australian Rock and Pop Music, 1960–85*, Oregon: Verse Chorus Press.

Nichols, D. and S. Perillo (eds) (2020), *Urban Australia and Post-punk: Exploring Dogs in Space*, Basingstoke: Palgrave Macmillan.

Nieuwenhuysen, J. (1986a), *Review of the Liquor Control Act 1968*, Melbourne: Government Printer, Volume 1: Report.

Nieuwenhuysen, J. (1986b), *Review of the Liquor Control Act 1968*, Melbourne: Government Printer, Volume 2: Report.
Nieuwenhuysen, J. (2008), 'Peace in Small Places'. *The Age*, 21 September: 21.
Nieuwenhuysen, J. (2018), Interview with Shane Homan, 17 July.
'Night Life, 1966' (1966), *The Herald*, 24 January: 5.
Nimervoll, E. (1970), 'Talking Aztec Blues', *Go-Set*, 5 September: 9.
'No Cuddling on Dance Floors' (1950), *The Sun*, 5 January: 13.
'No Late Drinks for the Games' (1956), *The Argus*, 26 March: 1.
Northover, K. (2015), 'Melbourne Puts Rock Icon Chrissy Amphlett on the Map', *The Age*, 18 February. Available online: https://www.smh.com.au/entertainment/music/melbourne-puts-rock-icon-chrissy-amphlett-on-the-map-20150218-13i9jv.html (accessed 18 March 2021).
Now Sound: Melbourne's Listening (2018), [Film], Dir. Tobias Willis, Kewl Productions, Melbourne.
O'Hanlon, S. (2004), 'From Rooming Houses to Share Houses: Tenants', in P. Yule (ed), *Carlton: A History*, 111–21, Melbourne: MUP.
O'Hanlon, S. (2005), 'Where All the Action Is Man: Youth Culture in 1960s Melbourne', in S. O'Hanlon and T. Luckins (eds), *Go! Melbourne: Melbourne in the Sixties*, 45–57, Beaconsfield: Melbourne Publishing Group Pty Ltd.
O'Hanlon, S. (2009), 'The Events City: Sport, Culture, and the Transformation of Inner Melbourne, 1977–2006', *Urban History Review/Revue d'Histoire Urbaine*, 37 (2): 30–9.
O'Hanlon, S. (2015), 'A Victorian Community Overseas Transformed: Demographic and Morphological Change in Suburban Melbourne, 1947–1981', *Urban History*, 42 (3): 463–82.
O'Hanlon, S. (2018), *City Life: The New Urban Australia*, Sydney: New South.
O'Hanlon, S. (2019), 'New People, New Ideas and New Attitudes: Melbourne's Long Sixties', *Victorian Historical Journal*, 90 (1): 19–29.
O'Hanlon, S. and A.E. Dingle (2010), *Melbourne Remade: The Inner City since the Seventies*, Melbourne: Arcade Publications.
O'Hanlon, S. and R. Stevens (2017), 'A Nation of Immigrants or a Nation of Immigrant Cities? The Urban Context of Australian Multiculturalism, 1947–2011', *Australian Journal of Politics and History*, 63 (4): 556–71.
O'Hanlon, S. and S. Sharpe (2009), 'Becoming Post-industrial: Victoria Street, Fitzroy, c1970 to Now', *Urban Policy and Research*, 27 (3): 289–300.
Oram, J. (1966), *The Business of Pop*, Sydney: Horwitz.
O'Shea, J. (1951), 'And They Call It Music; Life among the Hepcats', *The Herald*, 5 May: 9.
'Our Changing Recreations' (1953), *The Age*, 28 March: 2.
Overell, R. (2010), 'Emo Online: Networks of Sociality/Networks of Exclusion', *Perfect Beat*, 11 (2); 141–62.
Overell, R. (2019), '"I Think Sydney's Pretty Shit": Melbourne Grindcore Fans and Their Others', in C. Hoad (ed), *Australian Metal Music: Identities, Scenes and Cultures*, 73–90, New York: Emerald.

Padula, M. (2016), 'Melbourne's 2 AM lockout (A)', ANZOG [Australia and New Zealand School of Government] web site. Available online: https://www.anzsog.edu.au/resource-library/case-library/melbourne-s-2am-lockout-a-2016-93-1 (accessed 17 July 2021).

Parliament of Victoria (2010), 'Questions without Notice'. Legislative Assembly, 25 February. Available online: http://tinyurl.com/2uuahjf (accessed 15 April 2021).

Paine, C. (2018), Interview with John Tebbutt, 15 November.

PBS-FM (2006), Mick Geyer Musical guru, Transcript, documentary #4 First broadcast on Thursday 13 April, 7–8 pm. Available online: https://www.pbsfm.org.au/mick-geyer-music-guru (accessed 26 August 2019).

Pennell H. (2007), (nee Pennell), Interview with Ken Berryman. Oral History, National Film and Sound Archive, Canberra.

Pennell, H. (2020), Interview with John Tebbutt, 19 November.

Perring, J. (2017), Interview with Catherine Strong, 13 February.

Perring, J. (2020), Interview with Shane Homan, 29 January.

Planet Records Finale (2017), 'Planet Records Finale: PR Stunts, Red Indian Spirits … and Eartha Kitt', 8 January. Available online: https://holy-gogo-boots-batman.blogspot.com/2017/01/the-star-crossed-story-of-planet.html (accessed 15 April 2021).

Play Melbourne (2014), [Film], Publicis Mojo for Tourism Victoria. Available online at: https://www.youtube.com/watch?v=iYgz5ylq0Po (accessed 18 March 2021).

'Police Declare War on Bodgies' (1951), *The Herald*, 4 December: 8.

'Police Hunt Bodgies and Widgies from City Store' (1956), *The Argus*, 12 June: 3.

Price, M. and L. Benton-Short (2007), *Counting Immigrants in Cities across the Globe*, Washington, DC: Migration Policy Institute. Available online: https://www.migrationpolicy.org/article/counting-immigrants-cities-across-globe (accessed 28 August 2020).

'Q.C. – Late Hours May Lift Conduct' (1964), *The Age*, 14 March: np.

'The Quiet Aboriginal: The Greatest Fight Is for His People' (1959), *Australian Women's Weekly*, 30 September: 7.

Quite a Party: The Story of Melbourne Rock & Roll (2017), [Documentary] Dir. Tim Rivers, Melbourne: Channel 31. Available online: https://www.youtube.com/watch?v=_ovYMMSaBP4 (accessed 16 April 2021).

Railton, D. (2001), 'The Gendered Carnival of Pop', *Popular Music*, 20 (3): 321–31.

Rayner, J.F. (1977), Acting Secretary, Commission of Public Health, letter to Station Hotel, 14 November, Public Records Office Victoria, VPRS 7712/P/0002, Liquor Control Commission correspondence, Unit 000212.

Reddington, H. (2007), *The Lost Women of Rock Music: Female Musicians of the Punk Era*, Abingdon: Ashgate.

Redlich, A. (2020), 'Neon Sunset: Ollie Olsen Remembers The '70s Melbourne Music Scene and Reveals Why Whirlywirld Broke Up', *Neon Sunset* program, RRR, 15 August. Available online: https://www.rrr.org.au/on-demand/segments/neon-sunset-ollie-olsen-remembers-the-70s-melbourne-music-scene-and-reveals-why-whirlywirld-broke-up (accessed 15 April 2021).

'Reverend Black Loses His Cool' (1968), *Go-Set*, 4 September: 6.

Rickard, J. (2005), 'The Melbourne Theatre Scene: A Personal Perspective', in S. O'Hanlon and T. Luckins (eds), *Go!: Melbourne in the Sixties*, 17–30, Melbourne: Melbourne Publishing Group.

Roberts, L. and S. Cohen (2014), 'Unauthorising Popular Music Heritage: Outline of a Critical Framework', *International Journal of Heritage Studies*, 20 (3): 241–61.

Robinson, P. (1980), 'Police Out to Get Us, Say Blacks', *The Age*, 16 February: 5.

Rofe, S. (1970), 'Stan Rofe's Tonic', *Go-Set*, 1 January: 17.

Rofe, S, (1980), transcript, Greig Pickhaver interview, Pickhaver sound recordings, 1975–1989, MLOH429, Tapes 1–5, Sydney: NSW State Library.

Rogers, B. and D. O'Brien, (1975), *Rock 'n' Roll Australia: The Australian Pop Scene, 1954–1964*, Stanmore, N.S.W: Cassell Australia.

Rogers, J. (2013), *The Death and Life of the Music Industry*, New York: Bloomsbury.

Roodhouse, S. (2010), *Cultural Quarters Principles and Practice* (2nd ed.), Bristol: Intellect.

Rudd, M. (2017), Interview with Shane Homan, 10 July.

Rushton, M. (2002), 'Political Oversight of Arts Councils: A Comparison of Canada and the United States', *International Journal of Cultural Policy*, 8: 153–65.

Ryan, R. (1994), 'Tracing the Urban Songlines: Contemporary Koori Music in Melbourne', *Perfect Beat*, 2 (1): 20–37.

San Miguel, D. (2011), *The Ballroom: The Melbourne Punk and Post-Punk Scene*, Melbourne: Melbourne Books.

Schauble, T. (1966), 'A Message from the President of the Go Set', *Go-Set*, 14 February: 2.

Scheri, C. (2017), Interview with Catherine Strong, 12 February.

Schutt, S. (2017), Interview with Catherine Strong, 21 November.

Searle, G. and K. O'Connor (2013), 'Why Has Melbourne Closed the Gap on Sydney since 2000?', SOAC 2013: 6th State of Australian Cities Conference, Sydney, NSW, Australia, 26–29 November. Hobart: State of Australian Cities Research Network.

Sexton, E. (2010), 'Sound and Fury over Copyright Act Cap', *The Examiner*, 13 October. Available online: http://www.examiner.com.au/news/national/national/general/sound-and-fury-over-copyright-act-cap/1967126.aspx?storypage=1 (accessed 5 December 2011).

Shaw, K. (2005), 'The Place of Alternative Culture and the Politics of Its Protection in Berlin, Amsterdam and Melbourne', *Planning Theory & Practice*, 6 (2): 149–69.

Shaw, K. (2009), 'The Melbourne Indie Music Scene and the Inner City Blues', in L. Porter and K. Shaw (eds), *Whose Urban Renaissance? An International Comparison of Urban Regeneration Strategies*, 366–85, London: Routledge.

Shaw, K. (2013), 'Independent Creative Subcultures and Why They Matter', *International Journal of Cultural Policy*, 19 (3): 333–52.

Shaw, K. (2014), 'Melbourne's Creative Spaces Program: Reclaiming the "Creative City" (If Not Quite the Rest of It)', *City, Culture and Society*, 5 (3): 139–47.

Sheridan, M. (2003), 'Winter 2C', *Beat*, 6 August: 66.

Sheridan, M. (2004), 'What Is Ladyfest?', *Beat*, 19 November: 49

Shorrock, G. (2018), *Now Where Was I? My Career with the Twilights, Axiom and Little River Band and Back Again*, Sydney: New Holland.

Shrok, J. (2008), 'Sureshock', *Beat*, 2 August: 50.

Simpson, K. (1996), 'Girl Power', *Beat*, 17 April: 27.

Smart, H. (2018), Interview with Catherine Strong, 20 July.

Smith, D. (2019), Interview with John Tebbutt, 31 March.

Sound Diplomacy (2019), *This Must Be the Place: The Role of Music and Cultural Infrastructure in Creating Better Future Cities for All of Us*, London: Sound Diplomacy.

'Special Squad Watches "Go-Go"' (1966), *Melbourne Herald*, 10 October: 7.

Sport, K. (2015), *Women's Music in Australia: Space, Place, Bodies, Performance*, PhD Thesis, Sydney: Macquarie University.

Spry, G. (2009), Interview with Geoff King, 26 August.

Stafford, A. (2021), 'Michael Gudinski: Record Industry Mogul Who Lived and Breathed Australian Music until the End', *Guardian Australia*, 3 March. Available online: https://www.theguardian.com/music/2021/mar/03/michael-gudinski-record-industry-mogul-who-lived-and-breathed-australian-music-until-the-end (accessed 4 March 2021).

Stapleton, W. (2010), Interview with Ron Tudor and Ernie Ball, *Wrockdown Australia*, 21 May. Available online: https://www.youtube.com/watch?v=-OU-8xUCZMg (accessed 4 April 2021).

Stapleton, W. (2017), Interview with Seamus O'Hanlon, 20 November.

Stevens, L. (1994), *Nature Strip*, Adelaide: Wakefield Press.

Stratton, J. (1984), 'Bodgies and Widgies – Youth Cultures in the 1950s', *Journal of Australian Studies*, 8 (15): 10–24.

Stratton, J. (1992), *The Young Ones: Working-class Culture, Consumption and the Category of Youth*, Perth: Black Swan Press.

Straw, W. (2015), 'Some Things a Scene Might Be', *Cultural Studies*, 29 (3): 476–84.

Strong, C. (2015), 'Laneways of the Dead: Memorialising Musicians in Melbourne' in Strong, C. and Lebrun, B. (eds), *Death and the Rock Star*, 103–18, Aldershot: Ashgate.

Strong, C. (2018), 'Popular Music and Heritage Making in Melbourne' in S. Brunt and G. Stahl (eds), *Made in Australia and Aoteoroa/New Zealand*, 76–85, New York: Routledge.

Strong, C. and E. Morris (2016), '"Spark and Cultivate: LISTEN and Grassroots Feminist Activism in the Melbourne Music Scene', *Journal of World Popular Music*, 3 (1): 108–24.

Strong, C. and F. Cannizzo (2017), *Australian Women Screen Composers: Career Barriers and Pathways*, Melbourne: RMIT University.

Strong, C. and F. Cannizzo (2021), *Understanding the Challenges to the Victorian Music Industry during COVID-19*. Victorian Music Development Office/RMIT, December. Available online: https://static1.squarespace.com/static/5b88e39855b02ce9bc082fcf/t/6025f440368a713f9ba08f6a/1613100101425/Understanding+Challenges+to+the+Victorian+Music+Industry+During+COVID-19+-+Research.pdf (accessed 10 May 2021).

Strong, C., F. Cannizzo and I. Rogers (2017), 'Aesthetic Cosmopolitan, National and Local Popular Music Heritage in Melbourne's Music Laneways', *International Journal of Heritage Studies*, 23 (2): 83–96.

Strong, C. and I. Rogers (2016), 'She-Riffs: Gender and the Australian Experience of Alternative Rock and Riot Grrrl in the 1990s', *Journal of World Popular Music*, 3 (1): 38–53.

Strong, C., S. Homan, S. O'Hanlon and J. Tebbutt (2017), 'Uneasy Alliances: Popular Music and Cultural in the "Music City"', in V. Durrer, T. Miller and D. O'Brien (eds), *Routledge Handbook of Global Cultural Policy*, 468–81, New York: Routledge.

Strong, C. and S. Raine (eds) (2019), *Towards Gender Equality in the Music Industry: Education, Practice and Strategies for Change*, New York: Bloomsbury.

Strong, C. and Whiting, S. (2018), '"We Love the Bands and We Want to Keep Them on the Walls": Gig Posters as Heritage-as-praxis in Music Venues', *Continuum*, 32 (2): 151–61.

'Sydney Lockout Laws to Be Scrapped Almost Entirely from 14 January' (2019), *The Guardian Australia*, 28 November. Available online: https://www.theguardian.com/australia-news/2019/nov/28/sydney-lockout-laws-to-be-scrapped-almost-entirely-from-14-january, (accessed 10 July 2020).

Tan, S-L. (2016), 'Melbourne Recording Studio Hits the Note at $4 Million', *Australian Financial Review*, 10 February. Available online: https://www.afr.com/property/melbourne-recording-studio-hits-the-note-at-4-million-20160209-gmps2q (accessed 15 April 2021).

Tavan, G. (2005), *The Long, Slow Death of White Australia*, Melbourne: Scribe.

Taylor, J. (2020), 'Everyone Was Interchangeable', in D. Nicholls and S. Perillo (eds), *Urban Australia and Post-Punk*, 67–72, Singapore: Palgrave Macmillan.

Tebbutt, J. (2007), 'Hanging Her Laundry in Public: Talkback Radio, Governmentality and the Housewife, 1967–73', *Media International Australia*, 122: 108–21.

Tebbutt, J. (2020), 'Hidden Technicians; Music and Radio-making at 3PBS in the Prince of Wales', *Media International Australia*, 176: 107–19.

'A Third Programme of Serious Music' (1968), Wayback Machine Internet Archive. Available online: https://web.archive.org/web/20070828221508/http://3mbs.org.au/TheAgearticle.jpg (accessed 26 April 2021).

Thorpe, B. (1998), *Most People I Know (Think That I'm Crazy)*, Sydney: Pan Macmillan.

Turnbull, L. (1955), 'He'll Sing Here', *The Sun*, 6 January: 6.

Tweedie, N. (2020), Interview with Shane Homan, 8 May.

United Nations (2008), *Creative Economy Report*, UNCTAD.

Urban Economic Consultants (1977), *Socio-Economic Implications of Urban Development*, Melbourne: MMBW.

'Valentines Slam Perth Scene' (1968), *Go-Set*, 9 October: 6.
Victorian Legislative Assembly (1972), Victorian Parliamentary Debates, Legislative Assembly, vol. 309, 2 November: 1796.
Victorian Legislative Assembly (1973), Victorian Parliamentary Debates, Legislative Assembly, vol. 315, 15 November: 2157.
Victorian Legislative Assembly (1975), Victorian Parliamentary Debates, Legislative Assembly, vol. 322, 24 April: 5428.
Victorian Women's Trust (2016), *Equal Arts: A Discussion Paper*, Melbourne: Victorian Women's Trust.
VMDO (2020), *Music Consumer Insights*, Melbourne: Victorian Music Development Office.
Walker, C. (2000), *Buried Country*, Sydney: Pluto Press.
Walker, C. J., T. Hogan and P. Beilharz (2012), 'Rock "n" Labels: Tracking the Australian Recording Industry in "The Vinyl Age": Part Two: 1970–1995, and After', *Thesis Eleven*, 110 (1): 112–31.
Watson, A. (2008), 'Global Music City: Knowledge and Geographical Proximity in London's Recorded Music Industry', *Area*, 40 (1): 12–23
We're Livin' on Dog Food (2009), [Film], Dir. Richard Lowenstein, Australia: Ghost Pictures.
Whiteoak, J. (2007), 'Italo-Hispanic Popular Music in Melbourne before Multiculturalism', *Victorian Historical Journal*, 78 (2): 228–50.
Whiteoak, J. and A. Scott-Maxwell (2010), 'Cha-Cha-Cha to *Ciuff Ciuff*: Modernity, "Tradition" and the Italian-Australian Popular Music Scene of the 1960s', *Musicology Australia*, 32 (2): 301–18.
'Wild Cherries: Thoughts and Opinions' (1968), *Go-Set*, 3 April: 6.
Williams, K. (2010), 'Strings Attached in Live Music Fight', *The Age*, 15 February: 16.
Willingham, A. (2004), 'Immigrant Transformations: the Mediterranean Idiom', in P. Yule (ed), *Carlton: A History*, 475–83, Melbourne: MUP.
Wood, C. (1973), 'A Growing History of Australian Rock "n" Roll', *Go Set*, 10 February: 17.
Woods, C. (2020a), 'How Booking Maven Mary Mihelakos Became Melbourne Rock Royalty', *Playing Melbourne blog*, 19 October. Available online: https://www.audiofemme.com/ (accessed 11 February 2021).
Woods, C. (2020b), 'Cable Ties Foray into Gaming', *The Age*, 20 December. Available online: https://www.smh.com.au/culture/music/cable-ties-foray-into-gaming-20201220-p56p2f.html (accessed 22 February 2021).
World, S. (2017), Interview with Catherine Strong, 6 November.
Young, G. (2004), 'So Slide over Here': The Aesthetics of Masculinity in Late Twentieth-century Australian Pop', *Popular Music*, 23 (2): 173–93.
Young, G. (2008), Interview with Geoff King, 12 August.
Zukin, S. (1982), *Loft Living: Culture and Capital in Urban Change*, Baltimore and London: Johns Hopkins.

Index

3AK 73
3AW 68, 73
3CR 5, 73, 99
3DB 43, 90
3KND 85, 86, 155
3KZ 68, 73, 74, 94
3MBS 82
3PBS 5, 83, 85, 107
3RRR 5, 84, 85, 107, 134
3UZ 43, 73, 76, 90

AAV studio 102, 103, 111
AC/DC Lane 177
agent of change 11, 129–30, 184
Allen, Ian 41, 43, 93, 139, 174
APRA AMCOS 87, 104
Archie and Jughead's 99
Armstrong, Bill 76, 79, 90–2, 95, 103, 111, 118
Arthur, Malcolm 42, 92
ATV-0 (Channel 0) 52, 77, 78, 79, 96
Au Go Go record label 100
Austin, Texas 4, 13, 62, 130
Australian advertising content laws 103
Australian Music Vault 16, 174, 177, 179
Australian radio ban (1970) 96
Australian Research Council project
   archival work 15
   interviews 15
   methods 14, 20, 114
   themes 3

Bachelors from Prague 58
Bakehouse studio 108–9, 110
Bandstand (program) 72, 77, 118
Barber, Jim 95, 103
Beat magazine 85, 86
Beatles, the 34, 64
Bennett, Lou 150, 151, 153, 154, 155
Berlin 13

Bertie's discotheque 45, 46
Billboard 62, 104
Bill Hailey and the Comets 42
Birthday Party, the 99, 102
Blackboard Jungle (film) 65, 67
Bolte, Henry 45, 114
Boys Next Door, the 84, 101, 102
Bracken, George 72, 94
Brady, Mike 43, 92, 96
Bright, Bobby 92, 93
Browning, Michael 46, 97
Bundle, Robbie 150, 154, 155, 156, 157, 175

Cadd, Brian 91, 93
Cain, John 56, 169
Camilleri, Joe 22
Cave, Nick 83, 174
Catcher discotheque 46, 48
Ceberano, Kate 23, 62
Cersoli, Ugo 50
Chants R&B 46
Champion Hotel 55, 58, 166
Chelsea Set, the 46
Chester, Johnny 75, 76, 93, 94
Chrissy Amphlett Lane 159, 160, 177, 179
Ciro's nightclub 40
City of Melbourne 170, 176, 182, 185, 186
Cohen, Tony 101–2
Cold Chisel 34, 54, 64, 121
Corner Hotel 174, 176, 178
Corr, Chris 95, 103
Costa, Laila 146
Countdown (program) 72, 188
Crocker, Barry 70
creative city 9, 169
Crystal ballroom 55
cultural city 9
cultural heritage 6
cultural quarters 7
Cummings, Stephen 61, 62

Detroit 7
Daddy Cool 41, 54, 92
Dargie, Horrie 78, 79
Dingoes, the 54, 97, 98
Dirty Pool agency 60
Dixon, Rae 71, 72
Duncan, Wayne 41

Economist Intelligence Unit, 1
EON FM 77
ethnicities 2
Esplanade Hotel 61, 127, 173

Fable record label 97, 111
FairGo4Live Music 127, 129
Farnham, Johnny 92, 95, 177
Fast Forward 72, 84
Festival record label 72, 97, 98, 100, 110
Forrest, Sage 146
Frente! 62–3, 134–5

Gazzo, Jane 22, 131, 132, 133–4
Geddes, Graham 46–8, 64
gentrification 8, 183–4
Glass, Keith 99–100, 102
Goldsmith, Brian 59–60, 64
Go-Set magazine 81, 114, 115, 119–20, 140, 172
Go!! record label 96
Go!! Show (program) 72, 76, 77, 78, 79, 91
Gordon, Lee 42
Grant, Stuart 22, 166, 167
GTV-9 (Channel 9) 77, 78
Gudinski, Michael 6, 22, 60, 97, 98, 103, 110, 172

Hansen, Grant 81, 150, 152, 153, 154
Hardware nightclub 56, 59
Harbour agency 60
Happening (70/71/72) (program) 78
Hart, Angie 63, 134
Herald, The 67, 68, 69, 77
Hit Parade (program) 68, 70, 71
Hoadley's Battle of the Sounds 71
Horsfall, Bob 68, 73
Horwood, Heather 70, 74
HSV-7 (Channel 7) 52, 70, 71, 77

IFPI/Music Canada 11, 12
'Indie' record labels 6, 97, 98, 106, 107
Inflation nightclub 59–60, 168

Jitterbugging 40, 66
Jenkins, Jeff 62, 69, 131
Jo Jo Zep and the Falcons 22
Jones, Marcie 42, 71, 96, 139, 141

Kelly, Paul 101, 104, 114, 156
Kennedy, Caroline 133, 134, 143, 147
Kindellan, Grace 147, 148–9
Knight, Anthony 45, 48, 64
Kommotion (program) 78, 91
Koori Music Club 154, 155

La Greca, Joe 52
Lawrence, Jo 50, 77
Lee, Georgia 40, 92
live music 4, 5, 42
Liverpool 1, 7, 8
LISTEN collective 147–8
London 7
Lowenstein, Richard 29

Manchester 2, 7
Manuelle, Sam 51–3
Maas, Henry 41, 59, 64
Marcou, Helen 55, 108–9, 110, 125, 126, 148, 191
Master's Apprentices, the 91, 93, 95
Matthew Flinders Hotel 53–4
Maynard, Fiona Lee 144, 145
McLean, Quincy 55, 102, 104, 105, 108, 126
Melbourne
    1950s 17, 18
    1960s 19
    'baby boom' 24
    censorship 33, 34
    community music radio 82–86
    deindustrialization 28, 162–4, 182, 184
    discotheque scene 44–9
    economic restructuring 161–4, 182
    fashion 35, 36
    feminism 147, 162
    First Nations artists 149–57

Fitzroy scene 62–3
gender 2, 138–49
Immigration 18, 19, 20, 22, 23, 25, 27, 37
'indie' labels 99–107
inner suburbs 27, 28, 165–6
Italian ballroom scene 49–53, 188
juvenile delinquency 65–7
licensing laws 26, 27, 41, 43, 53, 54, 55, 59
Little Band scene 56
'Melbourne sound' 94, 111, 113
morality 31, 32, 68–9
music heritage 159–61, 170–176
music strategies 10, 170, 176
North Melbourne scene 107
'permissive city' 31
Postcode 3000 strategy 167
post-punk 29
punk 28, 55
recording studio changes 106–11
suburban 'beer barns' 55, 56, 58, 143, 175
teen radio 70–1
tourism 7, 11, 13, 65, 89, 160, 161, 163, 164, 165, 167, 168, 169, 171, 179
venue noise complaints 54, 64, 128–30
youth culture 65–9
Meldrum, Ian (Molly) 177, 178
Mihelakos, Mary 82, 83, 85
Milne, Bruce 71, 83, 84, 89, 99, 101, 120, 131, 132, 146
Missing Link record label 99–100
Models 102, 121–2
Monkey Grip (film) 29
Moomba festival 79, 92
Moore, Clare 106–7, 120–1, 145
Morris, Russell 80, 91
Mushroom record label 98, 102, 110, 175, 188
music city
 definitions 1, 7, 9, 14
 'global music city' 7
 intangible benefits 9
 reports 9
 UNESCO status 10
 and heritage 176–8
Myer Music Bowl 78, 79

Nashville 14
Nieuwenhuysen, John 56–8, 124
Night Cat nightclub 58
Night Mayor 12
Nimmervoll, Ed 81, 86
Now Sound: Melbourne's Listening (film) 8, 107, 137
Nucleus agency 60

O'Keefe, Johnny 50, 75, 76, 92
Olsen, Ollie 55
olympic games (1956) 17, 40, 41, 59
On the Beach (film) 17, 22
Oz rock 64, 141

Paine, Cameron 82
Palace Theatre 176–7
Paul Hester Walk 160, 177
Pepperell, David 99
Perring, Jon 127, 129, 131
Planet record label 92
Plastered Press (fanzine) 72, 83
Premier Artists agency 22, 60, 63
Phantoms, the 43
Planets, The 41, 43
Presley, Elvis 41, 64
Prince of Wales hotel 29, 60
Primitive Calculators, the 56, 104
Pulp (fanzine) 72, 99
Punters Club 61–2, 85, 123, 173–4
Push, the 15, 110–11, 145, 170, 172

Randell, Lynne 95, 139
Ramrods, the 41
Razor nightclub 56
Recording infrastructure 5, 106–11
Richmond Recorders studio 95, 101, 102, 103
Roach, Archie 150
Rofe, Stan 73, 75, 76, 94, 119
Rogers, Bob 74, 75
Rowe, Normie 80, 93
Rudd, Mike 46, 54, 119

San Remo ballroom 51
Savage, Roger 91, 95
Save Live Australian Music (SLAM) rally 9, 113, 125–7, 188

Sayers, John 91, 95
Schauble, Tony 79–80
Scheri, Chris 105, 142, 146
Schneider Sisters, the 90
Scott, Bon 160, 177
Schutt, Stefan 118
Sebastian's discotheque 45
'Second city' thesis 114–18, 182
Seekers, the 93
Sergio G and the Flippers 50–3
Sing Sing studio 103, 105, 110
Smart, Helen 122, 144
Smith, Broderick 46
Smith, Dennis 79
Sound Diplomacy 9, 11
Songlines Corporation 85
Sports, the 61, 104
Skyhooks 34, 55, 98
Stapleton, Wendy 103, 118, 141
Station hotel 54
Sweet Jayne 105, 142, 143, 145
Sydney-Melbourne rivalry 2, 5, 39, 49, 66, 74, 75, 92, 113, 116, 123, 181–2
Swallow's Parade (program) 70, 71
Swelter nightclub 56, 60

Tiddas 85, 153
Teenage Mailbag (program) 70, 71, 76
T.F. Much ballroom 45
Tote hotel 61, 127, 144, 166
Thorpe, Billy 81, 82
Triple J 115, 134

Thunderbirds, the 42, 94
Toxic Schock 143, 144
Tudor, Ron 72, 76, 93
Tweedie, Nick 130
Twilights, the 95

Underground nightclub 59
UNESCO 10
United Nations 9
UpTight (program) 72, 78
urban planning 4
urban regeneration 8

Valentines, the 115
Victorian Government
    Creative Victoria 111
    Live Music Accord 126–7
    'lockout laws' 124–5
    Melbourne music week 170
    'Music Works' strategy 16, 127
    pandemic funding relief 185
    Victorian Music Development Office 86, 87

Walker, Clinton 84, 99
W&G record label 70, 72, 74, 76, 79, 90, 93, 94
Wet Ones, the 142, 143, 145
World, Sue 142, 143, 147
We're Livin' on Dog Food (film) 29

Young, Johnny 80, 152

www.ingramcontent.com/pod-product-compliance
Lightning Source LLC
Chambersburg PA
CBHW062225300426
44115CB00012BA/2229